Springer Series in Cognitive Development

Series Editor
Charles J. Brainerd

Springer Series in Cognitive Development

Series Editor: Charles J. Brainerd

Children's Logical and Mathematical Cognition:
Progress in Cognitive Development Research
Charles J. Brainerd (Ed.)

Verbal Processes in Children:
Progress in Cognitive Development Research
Charles J. Brainerd/Michael Pressley (Eds.)

Children's Logical and Mathematical Cognition

Progress in Cognitive Development Research

Edited by
Charles J. Brainerd

Springer-Verlag
New York   Heidelberg   Berlin

Charles J. Brainerd
Department of Psychology
University of Western Ontario
London, Ontario
Canada N6A 5C2

Series Editor: Charles J. Brainerd

With 16 Figures

Library of Congress Cataloging in Publication Data
Children's logical and mathematical cognition.
(Springer series in cognitive development)
Includes bibliographical references and index.
Contents: Conservation–nonconservation /Curt Acredolo—
The acquisition and elaboration of the number word sequence /
Karen C. Fuson, John Richards, and Diane J. Briars—
Children's concepts of chance and probability /Harry W. Hoemann
and Bruce M. Ross—[etc.] 1. Mathematics—Study and teaching
(Elementary)—Addresses, essays, lectures. 2. Cognition in
children—Addresses, essays, lectures.
I. Brainerd, Charles J. II. Series.
QA135.5.C493   370.15′6   81-23264

Printed in the United States of America

9 8 7 6 5 4 3 2 1

ISBN 0-387-90635-5 Springer-Verlag New York Heidelberg Berlin
ISBN 3-540-90635-5 Springer-Verlag Berlin Heidelberg New York

Series Preface

For some time now, the study of cognitive development has been far and away the most active discipline within developmental psychology. Although there would be much disagreement as to the exact proportion of papers published in developmental journals that could be considered cognitive, 50% seems like a conservative estimate. Hence, a series of scholarly books to be devoted to work in cognitive development is especially appropriate at this time.

The *Springer Series in Cognitive Development* contains two basic types of books, namely, edited collections of original chapters by several authors, and original volumes written by one author or a small group of authors. The flagship for the Springer Series will be a serial publication of the "advances" type, carrying the subtitle *Progress in Cognitive Development Research*. Each volume in the *Progress* sequence will be strongly thematic, in that it will be limited to some well-defined domain of cognitive-developmental research (e.g., logical and mathematical development, semantic development). All *Progress* volumes will be edited collections. Editors of such collections, upon consultation with the Series Editor, may elect to have their books published either as contributions to the *Progress* sequence or as separate volumes. All books written by one author or a small group of authors will be published as separate volumes within the series.

A fairly broad definition of cognitive development is being used in the selection of books for this series. The classic topics of concept development, children's thinking and reasoning, the development of learning, language development, and memory development will, of course, be included. So, however, will newer areas such as social-cognitive development, educational applications, formal modeling, and philosophical implications of cognitive-developmental theory. Although it is anticipated that most books in the series will be empirical in orientation, theoretical and philosophical works are also welcome. With books of the latter sort, heterogeneity of theoretical perspective is encouraged, and no attempt will be made to foster some specific theoretical perspective at the expense of others (e.g., Piagetian versus behavioral or behavioral versus information processing).

                                                                    C. J. Brainerd

Preface

This is the first volume in a projected serial publication of the "advances" type that is to be concerned with the field of cognitive development, broadly defined. All volumes in this series will be published with the subtitle *Progress in Cognitive Development Research*. As this is the inaugural volume, some remarks about the guiding aims of the series are in order.

Like other "advances" publications, the principal goal is to present work that is on the growing tip of research in cognitive development and that meets the highest standards of our field. The format of individual volumes, however, will depart somewhat from the norm for "advances" series in psychology. A standard problem with most publications of this type is that only one or two contributions in any volume will be of interest to any given reader. The reason, of course, is that each volume, like individual issues of a technical journal, seeks to span the field as a whole. With the *Progress* series, however, no effort has been made to encompass cognitive-developmental research as a whole between the covers of single volumes. Instead, reasonable thematic structure has been imposed on each volume. For example, the theme of this book is children's logical and mathematical cognition. The next three books in the series will deal with verbal processes in children, children's learning, and new directions in cognitive-developmental theory, respectively. It is my hope that it will prove possible to identify themes that, on the one hand, will be sufficiently broad to be relevant to a significant proportion of the readership and that, on the other hand, will be sufficiently focused to interest any given reader in the contents of most of the contributions. To be sure, this will be a delicate balancing act that, in all probability, will not always succeed. I strongly encourage investigators who have themes to suggest to contact me about guest editing a *Progress* volume.

Another difficulty that commonly arises with "advances" series is that of being committed to a one-volume-per-year publication schedule, usually with strict page limits. This means that during certain years meritorious work has to be excluded on grounds of space constraints. To avoid this, the *Progress* series will be flexible with respect to the number of volumes published per year. There will be two this year (the present volume and *Verbal Processes in Children*) and two next year (*Recent Advances in Cognitive-Developmental Theory* and *Learning in Children*). Thereafter, however, the number of volumes published in any one year will depend only on the number of provocative themes.

A second departure in format in this series concerns the style of chapters in individual volumes. In most books of this type, especially those in the classic areas of experimental psychology, the prototype contribution is a chapter written by a prominent investigator in which results and conclusions from a cumulative program of research are discussed. There are, I think, two objections to imposing this familiar structure on an "advances" series in cognitive development. First, although the scientific study of cognitive development is a broad and active field, it is relatively new in comparison with areas such as psychophysics, memory, learning, animal behavior, and perception. Consequently, the numbers of laboratories and investigators engaged in large-scale, cumulative research (as opposed to isolated studies) are as yet modest. I doubt that these numbers are sufficient to support an "advances" series along the aforementioned lines, though I could certainly be mistaken in this. Second and more important, this structure quite obviously tends to preclude contributions by new investigators. This would be particularly unfortunate for a series in cognitive development, because at the moment the field seems to be blessed with many promising young researchers from whom we have much to learn. It is my hope that the work of such newer contributors will figure prominently in the pages of this series. In the case of the present volume, for example, there is a roughly equal division between chapters written by younger researchers and those by more senior workers. In *Verbal Processes in Children,* the slant toward younger contributors is even more apparent.

In place of the traditional distinguished-researcher-discusses-recent-work chapters, *Progress* volumes will normally aim for a mix of three types of contributions: (a) reports of new findings, (b) reviews of extant literatures, and (c) theoretical essays. Contributions in category (a), which are represented by the chapters by Siegel and Saxe in this volume, are intended to cover comprehensive programs of research dealing with problems whose significance is widely acknowledged. Here, the sorts of articles that are typically found in the *Journal of Experimental Psychology: General* are roughly what I have in mind. Contributions in category (b), which are represented by the chapter by Fuson, Richards, and Briars and that by Hoemann and Ross in this volume, are intended to be interpretative reviews that deal with some well-defined literature. Thus, *Psychological Bulletin* reviews come closer to the intent of category (b) than do the general literature overviews that one finds in, say, *Review of Child Development Research* or *Annual Review of Psychology*. Contributions in category (c), which are represented by the chapters by Acredolo and Brainerd in this volume, are intended to be serious attempts at integrative and explanatory theorizing, rather than speculative think pieces or critiques of the logical structure of some other theory. In other words, *Psychological Review* articles are nearer the mark than, say, *Behavioral and Brain Sciences* articles, or *Mind* articles, or *Human Development* articles.

Regarding the contents of this book, children's logical and mathematical cognition was selected as the theme for the first volume for reasons that are largely historical. It is this particular area of cognitive-developmental research that has been most closely connected to Piaget's theory, at least in the past. Since cognitive-developmental research owes its current prominence to the intensive interest in Piagetian theory that characterized the 1960s and early 1970s, it seems only fitting that the inaugural volume should deal with a topic on which Piaget's influence has been profound.

There are six chapters in all. Two of them focus on aspects of number development: Fuson, Richards, and Briars review the state of our knowledge of children's counting systems and report some new results from their laboratories. One of the most striking features of this chapter is that counting, which seems to be such a simple behavior to adults, turns out to have a remarkably complex structure. Saxe reports some recent findings from his ongoing studies of mathematical cognition among the Oksapmin tribes in Papua New Guinea. The Oksapmin have a unique numerical system based on body parts, and Saxe reports how this system is affected by contact with Western arithmetical ideas.

I should perhaps add that the fact that almost half the chapters are devoted to topics in number development is not accidental. At present, this seems to be the most active subdiscipline within the study of logical-mathematical development, and I would judge that at least half of the work that has appeared lately is somehow connected to number development. Since so much of the elementary school curriculum is devoted to transmitting basic numerical skills, the popularity of number-development research is hardly surprising.

The remaining chapters are by Acredolo, Hoemann and Ross, Siegel, and myself. In view of the enormous impact of conservation concepts on the study of logical-mathematical development, no volume devoted to this area can be considered complete without at least one chapter on conservation. Although conservation comes up in some of the other contributions, it is Acredolo's chapter that is principally concerned with these important concepts. Acredolo presents a new theory of the cognitive bases for conservation and summarizes the results of some previous experiments from which this theory evolved. In the chapter by Hoemann and Ross, the literature on children's probability concepts is reviewed. Since nearly all of the decisions that we make in everyday life are based on probabilistic information, probability concepts have long been extensively studied in the adult cognitive literature. Curiously, research on age changes in probability concepts has been much more sparse, with most of it concerned with testing one or another prediction from Piaget's theory. It is hoped that Hoemann and Ross' detailed, integrative review of the literature will awaken interest in what is potentially a very instructive research domain.

Siegel considers the perennial question of how children's linguistic competence interacts with the assessment of their logical-mathematical competence. She describes nonverbal assessment techniques for a variety of competences that have been productive with normal children and in assessing the logical-mathematical competence of children with linguistic disabilities. My own chapter is concerned with another perennial question, namely, children's learning of logical and mathematical concepts. I outline a general learning system for certain concepts that is based on a rule-sampling interpretation of a family of Markovian processes, and some relevant experiments are reported. The ability of this framework to deal with such thorny issues as learning–development interactions, transfer effects, and age changes in information-processing capacity is also analyzed.

C. J. Brainerd

Contents

List of Contributors

Curt Acredolo Department of Applied Behavioral Sciences, University of California, Davis, Davis, California 95616, U.S.A.

Charles J. Brainerd Department of Psychology, University of Western Ontario, London, Ontario, Canada N6A 5C2

Diane J. Briars Department of Psychology, Carnegie−Mellon University, Pittsburgh, Pennsylvania 15213, U.S.A.

Karen C. Fuson The School of Education, Northwestern University, Evanston, Illinois 60201, U.S.A.

Harry W. Hoemann Department of Psychology, Bowling Green State University, Bowling Green, Ohio 43403, U.S.A.

John Richards Division for Study and Research in Education, Massachusetts Institute of Technology, Cambridge, Massachusetts 02139, U.S.A.

Bruce M. Ross Department of Psychology, Catholic University of America, Washington, D.C. 20064, U.S.A.

Geoffrey B. Saxe Ph.D. Program in Education, The Graduate School and University Center of the City University of New York, New York, New York 10036, U.S.A.

Linda S. Siegel Department of Psychiatry, Faculty of Health Sciences, McMaster University, Hamilton, Ontario, Canada L8S 4J9

Children's Logical and Mathematical Cognition

1. Conservation—Nonconservation: Alternative Explanations

Curt Acredolo

Conservation and the Appreciation of an Identity Rule

As cognitively mature adults we know that a quantity remains constant across a transformation as long as there is no addition or subtraction of the specific quantity in question. That is, we appear to be aware of an identity rule: *In the absence of addition or subtraction quantity (amount) is maintained.* Furthermore, we appear to know that this rule is more than just one of many available cues for judging quantity. To the extent that the possibility of addition or subtraction can be monitored during a transformation, we know that the identity rule should take precedence over any other potential cue for judging the presence or absence of a change in quantity.

Piaget (1952; Piaget & Inhelder, 1974) observed that preschool children seem to think that quantities change across transformations, even in the absence of addition or subtraction. If this is true, then preschoolers obviously do not yet fully appreciate the identity rule. Thus was born the study of "conservation development," directed toward revealing precisely when and how the child does come to recognize that the absence of addition or subtraction is sufficient information for the assertion of quantitative invariance.

So defined, the study of conservation development hardly seems worthy of the tremendous amount of attention it has drawn over the last two decades. The pri-

I wish to thank Linda Acredolo, Anne Adams, Norman Anderson, R. Harter Kraft, Sheryl Flocchini, Jeannine Schmid, and Linda Siegel for commenting upon an earlier version of the chapter and offering encouragement. I particularly wish to thank Irwin W. Silverman for his detailed comments and suggestions.

mary reason for the popularity of this line of research rests with the pivotal status of the conservation-nonconservation event within Piaget's theory, and in particular with certain of Piaget's theoretical assertions concerning the development of this knowledge.

This chapter is organized around two central issues in the study of conservation development, one methodological and one theoretical. First is examined the question of whether Piaget's diagnostic procedures are overly conservative. The issue centers around the possibility that the use of Piaget's standard task results in a large number of false negatives—children who fail to give conservation judgments despite possessing an understanding of the identity rule. The second issue concerns Piaget's assertion that the identity rule emerges only in conjunction with the reversible operations of compensation and inversion. Evidence favoring the increasingly popular alternative position that the identity rule emerges prior to these logical operations will be summarized in the latter half of the chapter. These issues are actually related in that both involve the assertion that the identity rule emerges in development prior to the advent of consistent conservation in the standard task. They differ in orientation, however, in that the first blames the task procedures, while the second challenges Piaget's theoretical assumptions.

Before proceeding, I need to prepare the reader by clarifying certain terms and by briefly reviewing both Piaget's theory and the alternative model. I also need to comment briefly upon the precise nature of the standard assessment and its relationship to the identity rule.

Operational and Nonoperational Conservation

Readers familiar with Piaget's writings will recognize that the identity rule is equivalent to what Piaget calls quantitative identity. Henceforth, I shall use these two terms interchangeably.

Piaget theorizes that an emergence of quantitative identity coincides with the advent of consistent conservation and requires the prior development of the reversible operations of compensation and inversion. Piaget justifies this conclusion by noting that young children admit to the absence of addition or subtraction across a transformation and yet fail to conserve. He argues that the development of some additional knowledge must be required which then gives this observation a "power which it did not have before" (Piaget, 1976, p. 99). Quantitative identity

> can only take form in conjunction with other operations. . . . It is, then, the total system of grouping which is responsible for the formation of the conservations and not identity [alone]. Identity is but one element of the system, and an element which has been transformed by the system itself, rather than being the source of the system. (Piaget, 1976, p. 99)

It must be stressed that the above conclusion constitutes only an assumption on Piaget's part, one admittedly based upon a rational argument, but by no means the only argument available. It is particularly unfortunate that Piaget chose to presuppose the answer to what should have remained an empirical issue. But as Flavell (1963) noted, Piaget's model "has typically functioned as a theory *within* which to do research, rather than *from* which to do research" (p. 428). Piaget "examines the components of a given [logical] grouping and then tries, through a variety of experiments with children, to see if he can cull to the surface behavioral analogues or counterparts . . . of one or another of these components" (Flavell, 1963, p. 189). As a result, "Piaget often appears to force unwilling [or ambiguous] data into present theoretical molds. In accord with his own theory of mind, his interpretations of empirical phenomena show a great deal of assimilative activity, sometimes . . . at the expense of accommodations" (Flavell, 1963, p. 433). By taking a strong stand on the issue, Piaget directed attention away from the central epistomological question: How do children come to possess the identity rule?

Given his theoretical assumptions, Piaget was interested only in the development of what we may call *operational conservation*–consistent conservation supported by the logical operations, compensation and inversion. Conservation behavior in the absence of these operations is viewed as something less than true conservation–just conservation behavior, not conservation understanding–and Piaget and his colleagues have generally relegated such events to the status of *pseudoconservations*.

An alternative proposition, which will be discussed more thoroughly in the latter half of this chapter, states that a grasp of quantitative identity can emerge prior to compensation and inversion. A supportive network of logical operations is not actually required for children to begin recognizing the quantitative implications of an absence of addition or subtraction. Furthermore, it is hypothesized that children can acquire the identity rule at very young ages but still fail to use the rule in standard assessments because they do not yet recognize that the identity rule should always take precedence over other less reliable, but more immediate cues for judging quantity. Under this model, reliance on the identity rule and consistent conservation may simply await the increased reflectivity which accompanies general school readiness, and compensation and inversion can develop at some later time.

If one adopts this alternative proposition, then not all conservation behavior in the absence of compensation and inversion is immediately labeled pseudoconservation. A third possibility emerges. Interest in operational conservation is now supplemented by interest in what we may call *nonoperational conservation*–conservation based simply upon quantitative identity (the identity rule) in the absence of compensation and inversion.[1]

The differences between the two theories may be further clarified by noting the distinction between logical and natural necessities. The identity rule as understood by the adult is most certainly recognized as a natural necessity (Shultz, Dover, & Amsel, 1979; Strauss & Liberman, 1974; Shultz, Note 1) equivalent to what Carnap (1966) defines as "a universal empirical law," a regularity "observed at all times and all places without exception" (p. 3). Piaget suggests that, from its very first appearance, the identity rule takes on the additional status of a logical necessity as one component of a set of interrelated and interdependent logical-mathematical con-

---

[1] Elsewhere I refer to this as an identity theory of conservation (Acredolo, 1981; Acredolo & Acredolo, 1979, 1980).

structions (Piaget, 1971). In the alternative model, however, the identity rule may be grasped first as a natural necessity and only later as a logical necessity when compensation and inversion are added.

Nonconservation and the Overreliance on Perceptual Cues

According to Piaget (1952), if children are not aware of the identity rule, they cannot be said to understand quantity per se:

> Conservation is a necessary condition for all rational activity. . . . Whether it be a matter of continuous or discontinuous qualities, of quantitative relations perceived in the sensible universe, or of sets and numbers conceived by thought, whether it be a matter of the child's earliest contacts with number or of the most refined axiomatizations of any intuitive system, in each and every case the conservation of something is postulated as a necessary condition for any mathematical understanding. (pp. 3-4)

This argument is not disputed even by Piaget's strongest critics. For example, Bryant (1974) emphatically agrees, if a child "does not understand that a group of six objects remains a group of six objects unless something is added or taken away he does not understand what 'six' means" (p. 126). At issue, however, is whether nonconservation judgments in the standard procedure accurately indicate a complete lack of appreciation of this invariance.

In the standard conservation task, the identity rule is assessed by presenting children quantities (either continuous substances or discrete collections) undergoing so-called *perceptual transformations*—transformations involving changes in the immediately perceivable physical dimensions (e.g., changes in height, width, and depth, or changes in dispersal and density, respectively). If children fully appreciate the identity rule, they should view perceptual transformations as quantity irrelevant, given the absence of any obvious addition or subtraction. The great bulk of the research using the standard tasks strongly suggests, however, that preschool children believe that perceptual transformations do change quantity. Theoretically, they appear to adhere to what may be referred to as perceptual rules: *Quantities vary directly with one or more salient physical dimensions.*

Of course, in many situations the use of perceptual rules is not at all inappropriate. For example, if simply asked to judge which of two static quantities is larger, one is forced to rely on perceptual estimates by, for example, estimating relative water quantities on the basis of water levels or numerosities on the basis of item densities. Such rules may not be completely accurate, but in daily activities, they are not terribly inaccurate either. Furthermore, recent research on the development of such perceptual estimators is showing that with time they become increasingly sophisticated and accurate, moving from simple unidimensional to complex multidimensional rules (e.g., Anderson & Cuneo, 1978; Cuneo, 1980). In failing to conserve on the traditional task, the children's problem is not that they hold perceptual rules for judging relative quantities, but rather that they rely on these rules in situations where the identity rule should clearly take precedence.[2]

Thus, the standard conservation task does not actually measure the emergence of the identity rule itself; it measures only the decline in the overreliance upon perceptual rules. Whether these are actually reciprocal events is questionable.

In the following section, this issue will be ignored, at least initially, in order to explore the simpler problem of measurement error. The question is this: Are there aspects of the standard task that cause children to utilize perceptual judgments when in fact a reliance upon the identity rule is completely within their capacity? It will be noted that various alterations in the standard assessment procedure increase the incidence of conservation judgments. The standard procedure appears to be overly conservative. Eventually, however, we must return to the central question of whether or not these new conservation judgments indicate operational conservation.

Pseudononconservation

A conservation judgment in the standard task requires not only knowledge of the identity rule; it also requires a number of other skills, thereby introducing the possibility of measurement error. The following discussion focuses on the problem of pseudo*non*conservation–the strong likelihood that by using Piaget's standard conservation task a large number of children are misdiagnosed, being classified as nonconservers when in fact they do understand the identity rule. A similar argument has been presented by Brainerd (1973) concerning the use of Piaget's preferred judgment-plus-explanation criterion as opposed to a less stringent judgment-only criterion. The following discussion, however, goes one step further by suggesting that even with the judgment-only criterion use of the standard task results in the misidentification of a substantial proportion of children.

It is suggested that in the main the problem rests with Piaget's decision to use an *equivalence format* where, instead of asking the child specifically whether a

[2]It should also be noted that a reliance on perceptual cues will not invariably produce an incorrect response when judging the constancy of quantities across perceptual transformations. Perceptual transformations are not always quantity irrelevant. In certain situations perceptual transformations signify an imperceptible addition or subtraction of particular quantities and thus nonconservation. For example, shape transformations of a fixed two-dimensional area effect imperceptible variations (additions or subtractions) of perimeter. In this situation perimeter is not conserved. And alternatively, when perimeter is fixed it is area which is not conserved. These and similar special cases have provided researchers with the opportunity to demonstrate the strength of the identity rule among cognitively mature adults. The absence of an obvious addition or subtraction in these special situations leads most adults into making initial impulsive errors, judging there to be a conservation when in fact there is none (Lunzer, 1968; Pinard & Chase, 1977; Russell, 1976). Unlike children, adults think that all perceptual transformations are quantity irrelevant, and they require some reflection before they recognize the exceptions to this ancillary rule. In using the standard conservation task as an index of the point at which the identity rule consistently takes precedence over the perceptual rule, we would be quite content to find children making the same sort of errors as the adults described above.

single quantity is maintained across a transformation, as is done in the *identity format*, one instead asks whether an initial equivalence (or inequivalence) between two quantities is maintained across transformations of one or both. The possible methodological superiority of the identity format and other task variations is then discussed and an important issue is raised: Considering all the potential inaccuracies of the standard procedure, has it been shown "in a water-tight manner that the young child does not understand invariance" (Bryant, 1974, p. 128)? That is, are we certain that preschool children have no grasp of the identity rule whatsoever? Keep in mind that the intended purpose of the standard task is to index the emergence of an appreciation of the identity rule by monitoring the decline in a reliance on perceptual rules. The question at hand is whether the standard task succeeds in this purpose.

The Equivalence Format: A Source of Multiple Ills

First note that in Piaget's standard procedure the child is confronted with two quantities instead of just one. That is, rather than asking a child whether a single quantity remains constant across a transformation, the standard procedure involves asking the child to judge whether an initial equivalence (or inequivalence) of two quantities remains constant across a transformation. It is assumed that a two-quantity, equivalence-format task indexes the same knowledge as a one-quantity, identity-format task, but over the past 20 years of research and thought, it has often been noted that the two-quantity task actually requires a number of additional competencies not required in the one-quantity task.

Elkind (1966, 1967) was the first to suggest that conservation in the identity format emerges prior to conservation in the standard equivalence format, and that the former offers a purer index of conservation. While not all researchers have been able to detect a significant difference in the incidence of conservation across the two formats, the direction of difference is quite consistent (see the reviews by Brainerd & Hooper, 1975, 1978; and S. A. Miller, 1978; and the reports by Cowan, 1979; and Shultz, Dover, & Amsel, 1979), and it now seems certain that in at least some domains, there exists a period during which a conservation judgment is more likely in the identity format than in the equivalence format. This is commonly referred to as the *identity-equivalence décalage*.

Why did Piaget select the equivalence format instead of the simpler identity format in the first place? The equivalence format has the advantage of presenting the child with concrete illusions which are absent in the identity format, and Piaget (1952) believed that conservation should be assessed under strong misleading perceptual cues in order to guard against *pseudoconservation*—conservation responses based upon simple perceptual rules coupled with a failure to remember (or anticipate) the change in physical dimensions (Elkind, 1967; Piaget, 1967, 1968). Thus, a child who judges water quantities by water levels might give a conservation response following the transformation in the identity format simply as a result of forgetting the water level prior to pouring. However, as Elkind (1967) notes, such an event can be made extremely unlikely by using large transformations and verbal and physical reminders, and even if it does occur, it may be easily detected through multiple trials and counterarguments, and so the possibility of a small number of false positives is not in itself sufficient reason to abandon the identity format. Furthermore, non-Genevan researchers have expressed concern about the incidence of false negatives as well as false positives, and it now seems likely that the equivalence format reduces false positives only at a very high cost in false negatives.

Elkind suggested that the cause of the identity-equivalence *décalage* could be attributed directly to the need for a transitive inference in the equivalence format and the absence of such a need in the identity format. Given initial quantities P and Q, with P equal to Q, and the perceptual transformation of Q to Q', the child may appreciate the identity rule and recognize that quantity Q must equal quantity Q', and thus have sufficient knowledge to pass a task in the identity format, but in order to pass the task in the standard equivalence format, the child must also be able to remember that P equals Q, and that Q equals Q', and be able to combine these facts through a transitive inference to deduce that quantity P equals quantity Q'. Thus, rather than indicating an absence of the identity rule, failure in the equivalence format may reflect memory limitations, or as Elkind suggested, an inability to perform transitive inferences.

It now appears unlikely that an inability to make inferences accounts for the *décalage* since Bryant and Trabasso (1971) and others (see the review by Thayer & Collyer, 1978) have demonstrated that, barring memory difficulties, most young children are capable of such inferences, though debate on this issue is continuing (e.g., Breslow, 1981; Perner, Steiner, & Staehelin, 1981). Memory limitations might be responsible, but existing memory research suggests that this is also an unlikely explanation (Bryant, 1974). What, then, might explain the observed *décalage*? As discussed in the next section, the equivalence format may increase the incidence of semantic misunderstandings. Alternatively, as discussed in a later section, nonconservation in the equivalence format may result from a child's inability to judge the initial relationship confidently. That is, a child may recognize that Q must equal Q' but be uncertain about the asserted initial equivalence of P and Q, and following the transformation, the child may decide that actually P is not equal to Q and therefore deduce, by a logical inference, that neither can P equal Q'.

The multiple problems with the standard equivalence format casts a shadow over our understanding of the conservation-nonconservation phenomenon. The more we explore such variations on the standard procedure, the more we seem to sense that somewhere along the line we may have taken the wrong path.

Understanding the Question and the Importance of Context

Many writers have raised the possibility that nonconservation judgments often, if not always, imply a misunderstanding of the questions rather than an inappreciation of the identity rule (e.g., Braine & Shanks, 1965a, 1965b; Griffiths, Shantz, & Sigel, 1967; Hood, 1962; Lumsden & Poteat, 1968; Maratsos, 1974; Rothenberg, 1969; Siegel, 1978). I shall only briefly review the problem, as it is also discussed by Linda Siegel in Chapter 4 of this volume (see also Siegel, 1978).

The fact that young children have a poor understanding of relational terms such as *more, less*, and *the same*, and quantity terms such as *number, amount*, and *length* has been well established. For example, a number of researchers have documented the slow development of the relational term *less* as opposed to the early development of the term *more* (e.g., Clark, 1970; Donaldson & Balfour, 1968; Donaldson & Wales, 1970; Palermo, 1973, 1974; Weiner, 1974). At younger ages and in particular contexts children appear to equate the two terms. Also Griffiths, Shantz, and Sigel (1967) report evidence suggesting that children correctly interpret *the same* even less often than *less*. Children are reluctant to apply *the same* to two equal quantities. They seem to feel that it can apply only when the two quantities are the same in all (or almost all) respects, as the two quantities are prior to but not after the transformation in the standard conservation of equality task. Smedslund (1966) reported instances in which, without any transformation at all, children changed their initial judgment that two small collections possessed *the same* number of items, and others have reported the frequency with which even 5- and 6-year-old children prefer the phrase, "Both have more," when confronted with an equality. Children seem to equate *more* with *many* or *much* (Donaldson & Wales, 1970; Weiner, 1974), and thus, it is possible in their eyes for two equal quantities to each have more.

Rothenberg (1969) expressed particular concern with the observation that when confronted with two collections of equal numerosity, young children often answer "Yes" to both of the following questions: "Are there the same number in each?" "Does one have more?" This logical inconsistency may reflect just that, a logical inconsistency, or it may reflect an interpretation of *the same* and *more* that differs from that intended by the adult. For example, young children may interpret *the same* simply to mean "looks the same" (Braine & Shanks, 1965a, 1965b; Clark, 1970), and they may interpret *more* as referring to the space occupied (Hood, 1962). As a result it is quite easy to see how, following the transformation in the standard number task, the young child might argue that the two collections are "the same" (in general appearance) but one collection has "more" (spread). The child is not actually attending to number in either case.

Similar concerns have been expressed about the use of certain quantitative terms. As Maratsos (1974) notes, "preschool children tend . . . to define quantitative concepts and words along one dimension" (p. 367). Research on the word *bigger*, for example, has shown that children persist in interpreting this term as referring to height (e.g., Hulsebus, 1969; Lumsden & Kling, 1969; Lumsden & Poteat, 1968; Maratsos, 1973, 1974; Poteat & Hulsebus, 1968; Phye & Tenbrink, 1972). A conservation of area, mass, or liquid task in which children are asked, "Are they just as big, or is one bigger?," might thus produce a large number of false negatives. In line with this hypothesis, Lumsden and Kling (1969) have demonstrated that pretraining on the correct interpretation of the term *bigger* results in an increase in the incidence of area conservation among older children.

Other investigations of the effect of verbal pretraining on the frequency of conservation have not always been successful (e.g., Inhelder, Sinclair, & Bovet, 1974), but simply training children on a particular meaning of a word may be insufficient to prevent misunderstandings. A child may come to understand a term correctly in one context, but still misinterpret it in another. *More*, for example, may be used to indicate either an occurrence (addition) or a static relationship (Weiner, 1974), and the term may be used in reference to any one of several available quantitative dimensions, such as number, length, or height. The verbal and nonverbal context helps specify which meaning is intended, but young children are particularly dependent on nonverbal context (Bates, 1976), and so they may be easily confused when the nonverbal context is at odds with the verbal content. Recent research has suggested that the contextual features of the standard conservation task create a situation particularly conducive to misunderstandings of this sort (McGarrigle & Donaldson, 1975; Rose & Blank, 1974; Silverman, 1979).

McGarrigle and Donaldson (1975), for example, focused their investigation upon the "contextual information" imparted in the adult's deliberate manipulation of physical dimensions in the standard conservation task and the possibility that this action induces children to interpret the standard question as referring to alterations in the physical dimensions. They note that in most adult-child communications, nonverbal behaviors play a large role in guiding the child's interpretation, but the standard task disassociates the verbal and nonverbal components of the communication and thus creates ambiguity. In the number task, "it is as if the experimenter refers behaviorally to length although he continues to talk about number" (McGarrigle & Donaldson, 1975, p. 343). And thus, "if would not be surprising if he [the child] ignored normal word-referent relationships and interpreted the question on the basis of the experimenter's intentions as evidenced in his behavior" (p. 343).

McGarrigle and Donaldson suggested that the conservation question can be disambiguated by having the transformation occur as if by accident or by a third party. Adults may then ask about the maintenance of quantity without suggesting that they are referring to the physical dimensions. Using number and length tasks in the equivalence format, McGarrigle and Donaldson demonstrated that conservation judgments were much more likely when the transformation was performed by a third party, an errant and mischievous teddy bear. They conclude that "traditional procedures seriously underestimate the child's knowledge" (McGarrigle and Donaldson, 1975, p. 348). If "the length of a row changes, but without the experimenter appearing to have intended it, the child has no conflicting behavioral evidence relevant to his interpretation of the questions, and so he can correctly answer the experimenter's question on the basis of number" (p. 349). McGarrigle and Donaldson's findings have been validated recently in both an exact and a modified replication by Dockrell, Campbell, and Neilson (1980).

In the same vein, Rose and Blank (1974) were concerned with the possibility that asking a question both immediately before and immediately after the transformation, the standard procedure in the equivalence format, might suggest to the child that a new judgment is expected. In everyday discourse we are seldom asked a question that we have just answered. When such an event occurs, it implies that either our first answer was incorrect or some event has occurred that might necessitate a change in response. The young child might recognize the maintenance of the quantity across the perceptual transformation, and although the standard conservation question explicitly refers to this quantity, its unexpected repetition might seem sufficiently strange to suggest to the child that the adult expects a change in response and thus really means to refer to the changing dimensions and not the unchanging quantity. It is as if the repetition of the question disambiguates the adult's question, but in the wrong direction.

Using the number task in the equivalence format with a deliberate transformation, Rose and Blank (1974) compared the frequency of conservation when the standard question was asked just once, following the transformation, rather than both before and after the transformation. The frequency of conservation judgments rose substantially in the after-only variant. They conclude:

> when the child has just declared the rows equal, he interprets the request for a second judgment as a signal to change his response. When he is not in this predicament (by having to judge the arrays once), he is more likely to respond to what is supposed to be the central demand of the task, namely, the evaluation of number. (Rose & Blank, 1974, pp. 500-501).

Although Miller (1977) was unable to replicate this finding, Silverman (1979) has replicated it, and he addresses the relationship between the Rose and Blank paradigm and that offered by McGarrigle and Donaldson. While McGarrigle and Donaldson questioned their children both before and after the transformation, the use of an accidental transformation makes the repeated question seem appropriate. The context does not suggest a change in the interpretation of the question. In fact, the context strongly suggests a continued interpretation of the standard question as referring to quantity. Thus, the use of either nondeliberate transformations or after-only questioning would seem a necessary component of any attempt to assess accurately knowledge of the identity rule.

The research discussed in this section suggests that semantic confusions are a major source of false negatives in the assessment of the identity rule. It is still unclear to what degree this will require readjustments of Piaget's model, but it is apparent that semantic confusions alone cannot completely account for nonconservation. A variety of techniques have been found for reducing the disruptive role of language comprehension in assessing conservation, and nonconservation is still observed. Nonverbal assessments generally result in only small to moderate increments in the number of children diagnosed as conservers (e.g., Miller, 1977; Silverman & Schneider, 1968; Wheldall & Poborca, 1980; see the review of nonverbal methods provided by Miller, 1976b), though it must still be recognized that nonverbal methods (and other procedures for reducing the incidence of semantic confusions) may contain still other sources of potential measurement error (Siegel, 1978). Accurate assessments of the identity rule will require the control of these other sources of error as well.

Because of contextual features, the conservation task in the equivalence format would seem to be more likely to evoke misunderstanding than the same task in the identity format. The necessity of drawing attention to the perceptual cues as a means of establishing the initial equivalence (or inequivalence) and the need for before-and-after questioning may increase the number of children who interpret the questions as referring to the perceptual cues instead of to the quantities. Since both formats, however, usually involve deliberate rather than accidental transformations, misunderstandings induced by contextual features may interfere as well with accurate assessments using the identity format, though not necessarily to the same degree.

S. A. Miller (1977) attempted to test the hypothesis that the lower incidence of conservation in the equivalence format could be attributed to the presence of before-and-after questioning. He intended to compare the incidence of conservation in the identity format with the incidence in two forms of the equivalence format: one with the usual before-and-after questioning and a second with after-only questioning. Unfortunately he failed to produce the *décalage* and so could not address the question of causality. However, Cowan (1979) recently repeated Miller's experiment, this time producing the *décalage*, and found that after-only questioning is not sufficient to equate the equivalence and identity formats.

The Initial Equivalence: Confident Judgment or Best Estimate?

The standard conservation task begins with an attempt to establish in the child's mind that there is an equivalence between two quantities. With two sets of equal numerosity the items are arranged in parallel rows of equal length and item density, and thus the items are placed in a perceivable one-to-one correspondence. Similarly, with liquid and other continuous substances, the physical shapes of the two equal quantities, their height, width, and depth, are equated. Thus, at the beginning of the task, the equivalence of the perceptual features is impressed upon the children in the hope that this will convince them that the quantities are also equivalent. To adults this is sufficient information, but it is only assumed that it is also sufficient for young children. As further insurance, the children are also encouraged to participate in the construction of the equivalence and to express their confidence in the equivalence, but the sufficiency of these operations may still be questioned.

Gelman (1972; Gelman & Gallistel, 1978) and Bryant (1972, 1974) suggest that preschool children do not grasp the quantitative implications of perceptual equivalences, and as a result, these children regard the standard task as calling for a series of estimations. In the opinion of these researchers, nonconservation merely signifies a revision in the child's initial judgment rather than an inappreciation of the identity rule.[3]

Gelman and Gallistel (1978) argue that the ability to make confident judgments of numerical equivalence based on one-to-one correspondence is a late acquisition in the child's developing sense of quantity. This is virtually a complete reversal of Piaget's model. Whereas Piaget holds that young children grasp the implications of one-to-one correspondences but lack the identity rule, Gelman and others argue that young children grasp the identity rule but lack instead the capacity to appreciate the implications of one-to-one correspondence. As Bryant (1972) notes, "this explanation [of the nonconservation response] seems as cogent as Piaget's" (p. 80).

Although there is as yet no direct evidence supporting this line of reasoning over

---

[3] Although these authors have addressed this problem only in reference to the number task, I have taken the liberty of presenting a broader view.

Piaget's, there is indirect evidence. Smedslund (1966) provides some support for this interpretation in noting the unwillingness of children to agree that two sets are equal in number despite constructing the sets themselves:

> The many errors on the first repeated standard question [where, prior to any transformation, the children were asked to assert the existence of a numerical equivalence they had helped to create] represents a puzzling and methodologically important finding. Forty-four percent of the kindergarten children and 21 percent of the first graders failed to give a judgment of "equal" immediately after having selected the two collections as being equal and after having heard the experimenter emphatically affirm the equality. Even after having been corrected, a considerable number of children continued to make errors. . . . Only after a second correction did nearly all the children accept the idea of equality. However, their responses clearly revealed the degree to which the notion was foreign to them in this type of situation. (p. 151)
>
> The . . . difficulty of the equal category in two-object situations mean that many . . . findings on conservation must be considered highly ambiguous. Failure on a conservation task may simply mean that the subject has not understood the initial equality of the two objects or collections. (p. 152)

Bryant (1974) also points to the fact that conservation occurs more frequently in the identity format, and since the identity format eliminates the problem of judging an initial equivalence, this may be interpreted as proof that reestimations contribute to the frequency of nonconservation in the equivalence format. He also notes that dramatic increments in the frequency of conservation have resulted when researchers have trained children to ignore misleading perceptual cues and attend instead to one-to-one correspondences (Bryant, 1972, Experiment 3) or to actual quantity (Gelman, 1969).

A more direct test of the hypothesis is certainly needed and may now be available. Gelman and Gallistel (1978) have recently provided evidence that even very young children (3-year-olds) can make confident judgments of numerical equivalence (or inequivalence) by counting. Children's confidence in their own counting, however, seems to mirror the limits of their actual counting ability. Children may be able to count to 20 or 30, but a close assessment of their repeated counting behavior may show that they begin to make errors (e.g., coordination or partitioning) at around seven or eight in the counting sequence. Gelman and Gallistel find that children stop using the cardinal principle (i.e., the last tag equals the numerosity of the set) when set sizes become large enough that they cause counting errors. They suggest that children stop using the cardinal principle when they become uncertain about their own counting. If Gelman and Gallistel are correct, we should be able to use counting behavior as an index of when children would have confidence in an initial numerical equality. If nonconservation in the standard number task often represents reestimations based on a lack of confidence in the initial judgment, we should find children conserving number when the initial equality is established by counting (as opposed to perceptually) and when the number of items in the sets are within the child's range of confident counting (as opposed to outside that range), even though counting is not allowed following the transformation. While it is true that this hypothesis predicts conservation with small set sizes and nonconservation with large set sizes, a phenomenon which has already been observed (e.g., Gelman, 1972; Winer, 1974, 1975; Zimilies, 1966), it assumes that confidence in the initial equivalence is the crucial variable. The presence or absence of confidence should prove a stronger predictor than set size, and it should remain strong even after controlling (methodologically or statistically) for the influence of set size.

In Search of Accuracy

Given the foregoing arguments, one must wonder, as does Bryant (1974), whether Piaget was correct in asserting that up until the middle years, children are "not prepared to believe that a given quantity . . . remains the same irrespective of changes in shape" (Piaget, 1952, p. 8). It seems that a number of questions once thought answered have not been: At what ages do children clearly exhibit a consistent overreliance on perceptual cues in situations where the identity rule should take precedence? Is such a period of true nonconservation found in all children? To what extent is true nonconservation specific to the type or sizes of the quantities involved?

It is obvious that in assessing the appreciation of the identity rule we need to make greater use of the identity format (including, of course, procedures to guard against pseudoconservation), thus eliminating the potential for errors induced by memory limitations, an inability to carry out transitive inferences, or an inability to grasp the quantitative implications of perceptual correspondences. While it is true that a high incidence of nonconservation is generally still observed with the identity format, semantic confusions may be responsible, and so these sources of error also need to be controlled.

A recent study by Pennington, Wallach, and Wallach (1980) is a good example of the sort of assessments which should be done more often. They presented 130 disadvantaged third graders with a conservation of numerical equivalence task (Piaget's standard procedure) and a comparable task in the identity format. Out of 45 standard nonconservers, only 19 failed the task in the identity format, an example of the identity-equivalence *décalage*. Then, in an attempt to reduce the incidence of pseudononconservation attributable to semantic confusions, the identity task was repeated using the actual cardinal number when questioning the child ("Are there still 13?") rather than the standard verbal formula ("Are there the same number as before?"). The incidence of nonconservation now dropped to just eight.[4] That these few children were still misunderstanding the task was suggested by the fact that they still failed to conserve when the task was repeated with a mere displacement and no change in perceptual cues.

Given studies such as this, one cannot help but wonder if preschool nonconservation might disappear entirely if all the problems with the standard procedure

---

[4]One may argue that these additional conservers were not true conservers since they may have been capable to recognizing the invariance of cardinal number but not quantity. On the other hand, we must admit that the procedure may also operate by disambiguating the task and consequently revealing true conservation. Further research is needed to determine to what extent these counteracting events occur.

were corrected simultaneously—a minimally verbal task in the identity format with a nondeliberate transformation. Of course, we must be concerned with the possibility that such procedures yield something other than operational conservation. This supposition reintroduces the notion that children may understand the identity rule prior to grasping compensation and inversion (and appreciating the rule as a logical necessity), and that they may conserve on the basis of the identity rule in some situations while still overrelying on perceptual rules in other situations.

Nonoperational Conservation

As noted earlier, in Piaget's model, the young child's capacity to recognize the absence of addition or subtraction is given little importance. Preschool children readily admit the absence of addition or subtraction across perceptual transformations and yet most do not conserve, and thus Piaget (1952; Wallach, 1969) felt that young children must be incapable of sensing the natural affordance of these observations. He hypothesized that compensation and inversion must be added before children can grasp the logical implications of the absence of addition or subtraction. Furthermore, since compensation, inversion, and quantitative identity could comprise a set of interdependent logical axioms, Piaget supposed that the identity rule emerges as a logical necessity with the onset of consistent conservation. But is the identity rule completely absent before the emergence of the logical operations, and consistent conservation, and is conservation in the standard task really based upon the recognition of a logical necessity? Many individuals have now challenged Piaget on these primary assumptions (e.g., Acredolo, 1981; Acredolo & Acredolo, 1979, 1980; Anderson & Cuneo, 1978; Brainerd, 1977; Bruner, 1966; Bryant, 1972, 1974; Flavell, 1963; Gelman, 1969, 1972; Gelman & Gallistel, 1978; Gibson, 1969; Hamel, 1971; Hamel, Van der Veer, & Westerhof, 1972; Klahr & Wallace, 1976; Mehler & Bever, 1967; P. H. Miller & Heldmeyer, 1975; Pennington, Wallach, & Wallach, 1980; Shultz, Dover, & Amsel, 1979; Siegler, 1981), and as early as 1963, Flavell foresaw the emergence of these alternative views:

> It is our judgment that Piaget's bent toward mathematics and logic, towards systemization, towards symmetry and order has led him to see more coherence and structure in the child's intellectual actions than really are there. . . . What we are suggesting is that an accurate picture of intellectual life in this period would probably show a somewhat lower order of organizations, a somewhat looser clustering of operations, in short, a somewhat less strong and less neat system than Piaget's grouping theory postulates. (Flavell, 1963, p. 438)

As emphasized earlier, a nonconservation response indicates only that the child is overrelying on perceptual rules. It does not necessarily mean that the child is completely unaware of the identity rule altogether, and many individuals have expressed the opinion that children possess a "sense" of quantitative invariance long before the emergence of consistent conservation. For example, Pennington,

Wallach, and Wallach (1980) argue that "the young child seems to have a partial and not well integrated concept of number [invariance], and ... this concept functions effectively as an implicit principle long before it is articulated as a clear and consistent rule" (p. 242). Similarly, Anderson and Cuneo (1978) discuss the existence of a "conservation tendency," and P. H. Miller and Heldmeyer (1975) argue that "many kindergarteners appear to hold two conflicting beliefs–a belief in nonconservation and a belief in conservation ... [and] which is expressed depends on the amount or type of perceptual information in the testing situation" (p. 591).

On reflection it seems entirely possible that young children could come to appreciate the implications of an absence of addition or subtraction prior to the acquisition of compensation and inversion and that they could possess an understanding of the identity rule for a considerable period of time prior to finally grasping the rule as preeminent. The identity rule may be present and quite functional in promoting the development of number and quantity concepts, and yet in certain situations the young child may inexplicably neglect to utilize this knowledge.[5]

In the first half of this chapter, I discussed the identity rule as Piaget does, as if it were essentially an all-or-none acquisition. Thus, the issue so far has been whether or not the standard conservation task accurately measures the capacity for consistent conservation. If the model presented above is accurate, however, then our research has been misdirected in focusing so completely on the emergence of consistent conservation. As Piaget argues, the emergence of an understanding of the identity rule surely signifies the establishment of a vital foundation in the child's developing conceptions of number and quantity. Piaget supposed, however, that the identity rule first emerged only with the advent of consistent conservation. If it emerges earlier, then the advent of consistent conservation may simply mark the total elimination of an overreliance of perceptual rules with little or no fundamental change in the understanding of the identity rule itself. In fact, the relative ease of conservation "extinction" (e.g., see reviews by S. A. Miller, 1976a, and Hall and Kaye, 1978; and the report by Shultz, Dovel, & Amsel, 1979) suggests that even consistent conservation on the standard task is not based upon the recognition of a logical necessity. Thus, the issue of whether or not some feeling for the identity rule is present prior to the grasp of compensation and inversion and prior to the advent of consistent conservation is quite important.

Demonstrations of an Early Understanding of the Identity Rule

Bruner (1966) was the first to call attention to the fact that a large proportion of nonconserving children anticipate conservation when asked simply to imagine the transformations. This now common observation (e.g., Acredolo & Acredolo, 1979, 1980; Leahy, 1977; P. H. Miller & Heldmeyer, 1975; Piaget & Inhelder, 1969, 1971) suggests that young children possess a capacity to conserve well before

---

[5] Each of us, after all, is prone toward impulsive errors and toward the use of "shortcut" strategies. This is often seen in the case of formal operational tasks, where adults behave like concrete operational or even preoperational children despite obviously knowing better (Flavell, 1977).

the emergence of consistent conservation in the standard task. Bruner argued that the standard task encourages an overreliance on perceptual rules and hides the fact that the child also possesses a sense of quantitative invariance. Given Bruner's observations, we may conclude that knowledge of the identity rule will appear when one protects the child from disruptive illusions.

Piaget (1967, 1968, 1976), however, challenged this interpretation of the anticipation phenomenon, suggesting that it actually constitutes an instance of pseudoconservation. He argued that nonconserving children anticipate conservation only because they fail to anticipate a change in the physical dimensions. That is, he held that their anticipations of conservation actually represent a continued reliance on perceptual rules. Since children fail to anticipate a change in perceptual cues, which they normally use for estimating quantity, the perceptual rules themselves dictate a conservation response.[6]

Piaget and Inhelder (1969, 1971) provided "proof" of his explanation by citing a study by Piaget and Taponier in which it was demonstrated that the only nonconserving children who will anticipate conservation are those who fail to anticipate a change in the salient physical dimensions. This study has often been questioned, however, since only a sparse and confusing account of the procedures and results is given. In addition, it now appears that Piaget and Taponier's findings are not replicable. It has recently been found that many nonconserving children who anticipate liquid, number, area, and length conservation also anticipate a change in the salient perceptual cues (Acredolo & Acredolo, 1979, 1980). In fact, it was found that many children anticipated conservation immediately after they had anticipated changes in the salient dimensions.

In order to explain these observations within Piaget's theory, it is necessary to assume that the children were transitional conservers, capable of applying the logical operations to small transformations only, in this case, imagined. While such a post hoc explanation does regain the integrity of Piaget's theory, it is neither parsimonious nor particularly satisfying, and it seems a good example of Flavell's (1963) notion of "unwilling data."

Further disproof of Piaget's pseudoconservation explanation of the anticipation phenomenon, is provided by P. H. Miller and Heldmeyer's (1975) observation that a high proportion of anticipation of conservation judgments are followed by logical explanations of the identity type—appeals to the initial equality and to the absence of addition or subtraction: "If logical explanations reflect operations, then these

---

[6]The following statements by Piaget and Inhelder (1971) further clarify Piaget's interpretation of the anticipation of conservation phenomenon, in this case, within the liquid task:

The youngest subjects expect some kind of generalized conservation or pseudoconservation that involves levels. They abandon this only when they actually see the liquids being poured . . ., since they can then observe, contrary to expectations, the levels are different. (p. 260)
. . . He starts off by postulating the "persistency" of the rest, of the quantity, that is, and of the level (height), the latter being his gauge for the former. Thus it is only when the liquid is visibly transferred . . . that the subject feels constrained to accept non-conservation of the quantity, since he can no longer believe in the persistence of the level, and since he uses the latter to gauge the former and is incapable of dissociating them. (p. 262)

children possessed the underlying cognitive operations normally attributed only to 'true conservers'" (p. 591).

Bryant (1972) reports a second way to demonstrate the presence of the identity rule and conservation among otherwise nonconserving children, this time with visible transformations and only a very slight modification of the standard Piagetian task. In his demonstration, Bryant used a transformation that results in a quantity-ambiguous static display where undimensional perceptual rules are of no utility. Unequal collections of items were displayed such as those shown in Figure 1.1. Three- to 6-year-old children were first presented these static arrays and asked to judge (without counting) which row had more. In display A of Fig. 1.1, attention to one-to-one correspondence generates a correct response. In display B, there is no one-to-one correspondence, and so the child is left with estimates based on a perceptual cue such as length, which generates the incorrect response (or density, which generates the correct response). Finally, in display C neither one-to-one correspondence nor length (or density) offer cues to relative quantity. Bryant established that judgments were random on C, poorer than chance on B (number judgments based on density are rare), and better than chance on A.

He then used these same displays in a conservation of inequality task (before and after questioning in the equivalence format), transforming A to B or C, and B to A or C. When A was transformed to B, or vice versa, the children displayed what is typically interpreted as a nonconservation response. They switched which row they thought had more. When either A or B was transformed to C, however, the children persevered in their initial judgment. If as Piaget argues, children equate number with length, we might expect an abandonment of their initial decisions and a tendency toward more random responding. This was not the case. The children could transfer information about relative numerosities across the transformation

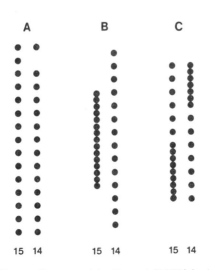

Fig. 1.1 Displays similar to those used by Bryant (1972) in demonstrating an early awareness of the identity rule.

when the resulting display did not suggest a change in their initial judgment. These results again suggest that children can and do use the identity rule and thereby deduce that, since nothing is added or taken away, the initial judgment remains the best guess.

Again, the pseudoconservation argument does not work here. The children were directly confronted with the changing perceptual cues, and yet they persisted in their initial judgments. It must be noted, however, that Katz and Beilin (1976) were unable to replicate Bryant, and Starkey (1981) has recently demonstrated that a subtle procedural factor may have accounted for Bryant's observations.

The Effects of Training Children to Ignore Perceptual Cues

A major implication of the alternative model is that conservation based upon an understanding of the identity rule will emerge spontaneously simply by eliminating the overreliance on perceptual rules. There are several successful conservation training studies that are particularly relevant to this hypothesis (Bryant, 1972; Gelman, 1969; Hamel & Riksen, 1973; Smedslund, 1961; Winer, 1968). I briefly consider two of them.

Gelman (1969) used an oddity learning format to persuade children to judge relative quantities in static displays on the basis of real quantity cues instead of merely "estimating" quantities on the basis of misleading perceptual cues. In short, she trained children to ignore length and density when judging relative numerosities, and to ignore left-right end point misalignments when judging relative lengths. Using a pretest-posttest design, the incidence of number and length conservation rose dramatically, and the effects of training even generalized to mass and liquid conservation. Gelman (1969) concluded that "the five-year-old child apparently does have to learn to respond consistently to quantity and not be distracted by irrelevant cues, but does not have to learn, *de novo*, to define quantity and invariance. . . . These responses are present in a child's repertoire, but are dominated by strategies under the control of irrelevant stimuli" (p. 185).

Like Gelman, Bryant (1974) also suggested that young children understand the identity rule but, nevertheless, often adhere to perceptual rules and are thus caught in a conflict between the two. Referring to number judgments, Bryant states, "It seems that children have two rules. . . . One rule is that number is invariant unless something is added or taken away. The other is that if two different rows have different lengths, the longer one is usually the more numerous" (p. 152). Bryant (1974) argued that Gelman's study "certainly suggests that the young child's difficulty with the conservation task is not a difficulty in understanding invariance but in knowing which of two judgments is the better one" (p. 142).

Bryant (1972) provided a successful variation in Gelman's procedure. He also trained children to distrust unreliable perceptual cues and to rely instead on more reliable quantity cues, in this case the information imparted by one-to-one correspondence. Bryant's initial displays were similar to those shown in the left-hand columns of Fig. 1.2. The diagrams to the right show the results of progressive transformations. In each case, the children were required to indicate which row had

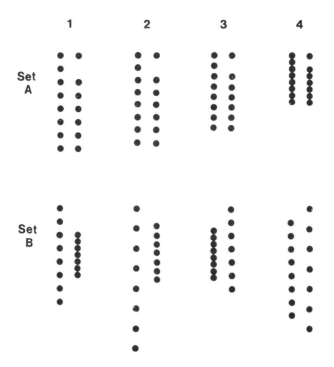

Fig. 1.2 Displays similar to those used by Bryant (1972) in training children to ignore perceptual cues.

more items. With this procedure, Bryant could demonstrate to the children that judgments based on undimensional perceptual rules (e.g., length) result in switching judgments back and forth between the two rows, while judgments based one one-to-one correspondence yield consistent judgments. Following training the children were exposed to a standard conservation of inequality task.

As in Gelman's study, the incidence of conservation rose, but Bryant makes an additional point. If children have no understanding of the identity rule at all, why should their inconsistent judgments based on length have caused them to abandon this perceptual cue? As Bryant (1974) surmises, "the effects shows that the child is not swamped by perceptual cues. He realizes that the number has not changed and is perturbed at having to change his mind so often" (p. 146). Hence, these results demonstrate in still another fashion that young conserving children must be aware of the identity rule.

Conservation and Compensation

Given the foregoing studies, we must consider the possibility that, for some children, an awareness of the conflict between the identity and perceptual rules may be solely responsible for the eventual abandonment of incorrect perceptual rules. Consistent conservation may emerge prior to the grasp of compensation

(Acredolo, 1981; Acredolo & Acredolo, 1979). A large number of studies have now focused specifically on the relationship between conservation and compensation (e.g., Acredolo & Acredolo, 1979, 1980; Anderson & Cuneo, 1978; Brainerd, 1977; Curcio, Kattef, Levine, & Robbins, 1972; Gelman & Weinberg, 1972; Goodnow, 1973; Larsen & Flavell, 1970; Lee, 1971; Piaget & Inhelder, 1969; Sheppard, 1974; Siegler, 1981), and despite the fact that some researchers have neglected to maintain a strict distinction between empirical covariation and logical compensation (Acredolo, 1981), the overall picture is that the identity rule can emerge prior to compensation. I shall not dwell long on this research as two recent reviews on the relationship between conservation and compensation are available (Acredolo, 1981; Silverman & Rose, in press).

A major problem in this line of investigation is the lack of an adequate test of compensation. Tasks that call upon the child to anticipate a change in one dimension (e.g., water height) given a specific change in another dimension (e.g., column width) over the course of a specific anticipated perceptual transformation (pouring) measure knowledge of covariation, not compensation (Acredolo, 1981). However, if children fail to anticipate any change in the dimension at all—that is, if they lack knowledge of covariation—then clearly they do not understand compensation either. Thus, a covariation task may be used to infer the absence of compensation knowledge. The question is, Do any children pass a conservation task despite failing a covariation task?

One line of evidence comes from the previously discussed research on the anticipation of conservation phenomenon. If we assume that conservation in the standard task indicates the presence of compensation whereas nonconservation indicates the absence of compensation, then the observation of a large proportion of nonconserving children anticipating conservation despite passing a covariation task (i.e., anticipation that can not be attributed to pseudoconservation) indicates conservation by identity preceding compensation. These premises are questionable, however, as one may argue that compensation (like the identity rule) may also emerge prior to consistent conservation.

Stronger evidence that the identity rule develops before compensation comes from observations by both Acredolo and Acredolo (1979) and Piaget and Inhelder (1969). They observed that a small percentage of conserving children fail a simple covariation task, 9% and 11%, respectively, when using the equivalence format. Even Piaget refers to this as an instance of conservation by identity (Piaget & Inhelder, 1969, 1971), though he chose to ignore the theoretical implications of the observation. When Acredolo and Acredolo assessed conservation using the identity format (judgment-plus-explanation scoring, with counterarguments), the number of children conserving without compensation rose to 37%. Silverman and Rose (in press) note that similar observations have been made by Brainerd (1977), Curcio, Kattef, Levine, and Robbins (1972), Gelman and Weinberg (1972), Leahey (1977), and Lee (1971).[7]

Another line of evidence suggesting that the identity rule emerges prior to com-

---

[7]Acredolo and Acredolo (1979) provide additional data indicating that conservation in the absence of covariation may be somewhat less stable than conservation accompanied by covari-

pensation comes from recent work on the development of perceptual rules—rules for using one or more physical dimensions of a quantity to estimate the relative or absolute size of that quantity. Obviously, if children understand compensation, they should attend to more than just one dimension when estimating relative quantities, but Anderson and Cuneo (1978) observed that 20% of their liquid-conserving 5-year-old children still estimated relative quantities solely by water levels. Furthermore, Silverman and Briga (Note 2) report that successful conservation training has no concomitant influence on the selection of perceptual rules.

The Presence of Counting and Math Skills Among Nonconservers

If the advent of consistent conservation marks the emergence of the identity rule, then number nonconserving children should display only imitative counting and math skills. Evidence of any real conceptual understanding of number should be absent. Recent research, though still quite tentative, is beginning to show, however, that young children possess a fairly extensive understanding of number despite lacking the ability to consistently conserve on the standard task.

For example, Pennington, Wallach, and Wallach (1980) note that among 8- to 10-year-old disadvantaged children, the nonconservers possessed computational skills (addition, subtraction, multiplication) that were quite comparable to those of the conserving children. Furthermore, Gelman and Gallistel (1978) provide evidence that, by age 3, the average child has a grasp of many basic counting and numerical reasoning principles. Whether this represents conceptual knowledge or something less is still debatable, but the research gathered so far suggests it may

> ... be an error to assume that a child must be able to [consistently] conserve if he is to be able to learn arithmetic with understanding. ... If children deny invariance only under special conditions ... then—contrary to the usual expectations—nonconservers may have little difficulty understanding and using counting and arithmetic. (Pennington, Wallach, & Wallach, 1980, pp. 234-235)

Conclusions

In the first half of this chapter, a number of variations in Piaget's standard conservation procedure were discussed. Use of these variations results in an increase in the incidence of conservation judgments among preschool children. However, do the recommended task variations (e.g., minimally verbal tasks using the identity format with nondeliberate transformations) increase the detection of operational conservation, or are we seeing merely further evidence of the existence of nonoperational conservation?

Recall that Piaget was interested only in operational conservation, and while he seems to have recognized the possibility of nonoperational conservation occurring

---

ation, an observation which merges well with research on conservation extinction. As S. A. Miller (1973) has suggested, the appreciation of conservation as a logical necessity resistant to counterargument may come late in development.

at least occasionally (Piaget & Inhelder, 1969, 1971), he did not wish to view it as true conservation. This is all well and good. The emergence of compensation and inversion should be charted. What the research suggests, however, is that nonoperational conservation is more pervasive than Piaget seems to have suspected. Whether or not one is willing to consider this an instance of true conservation or an instance of false positive really depends entirely upon how one wishes to define conservation. The issue is relatively unimportant, however, since our primary aim ought to be to measure both the presence of the identity rule and its full appreciation as a logical necessity. How we chose to use the term "conservation" is merely a matter of convention.

Regardless, the point is this: The standard assessment procedure may not be up to the task of measuring either operational or nonoperational conservation accurately, and many researchers, including Piaget, may have frequently mistaken nonoperational for operational conservation. The use of a judgment-plus-explanation criterion may help in detecting true operational conservation, but as noted by Acredolo (1981), the presence of what we normally think of as "compensation" and "inversion" explanations is not conclusive proof that these logical operations are actually present in the child's thinking.

Thus, we see that the standard task may be too liberal in the assessment of operational conservation but too conservative in the assessment of nonoperational conservation. On the one hand, the identity rule may emerge in the child's knowledge at a much younger age than indicated by the advent of consistent conservation in the standard task, while on the other, the logical operations of compensation and inversion may emerge considerably later.

The review of the research suggests that there are actually multiple routes to an adult comprehension of quantitative invariance, and which route is most frequently taken is still to be discovered. Four possible routes are reviewed in Table 1.1. Three milestones in observable task behavior are considered: (1) the transition from consistent nonconservation (an overreliance on perceptual rules) to partial conservation —that is, conservation in only some variations of the task (e.g., in a nonverbal task but not in the verbal variation, in the identity format but not in the equivalence format, or when the transformations are imagined but not when they are actually seen); (2) the transition from partial conservation to consistent conservation (conservation in all task variations); and (3) the transition from consistent conservation to consistent conservation with resistance to extinction.

The first alternative in Table 1.1 represents the Piagetian model. All conservation behavior, including partial conservation, is attributed to the child's grasp of compensation and inversion as well as quantitative identity. In this model, the second and third transitions are difficult to explain. In the second alternative, a slight alteration of Piaget's formulation, partial conservation emerges as a result of an early grasp of the identity rule, but consistent conservation awaits the development of compensation and inversion. Only the last transition remains a mystery. In the third alternative, both partial conservation and the development of consistent conservation are nonoperational. The transition from partial to consistent conservation is attributed to the recognition of the identity rule as preeminent among available

Table 1.1 Alternative Pathways in the Development of an Understanding of Quantitative Invariance[a]

Models	Consistent nonconservation (or pseudoconservation) in task variations	Progressive developments in observable behavior		Resistance to extinction
		Transitional conservation (i.e., conservation in only some task variations)	Consistent conservation in all task variations	
I	Perceptual boundness	Partial grasp of the logical grouping (i.e., operational conservation)	Full grasp of the logical grouping (i.e., operational conservation)	?
II	Perceptual boundness	Partial grasp of the identity rule (i.e., nonoperational conservation)	Full grasp of the logical grouping (i.e., operational conservation)	?
III	Perceptual boundness	Partial grasp of the identity rule (i.e., nonoperational conservation)	Full grasp of the identity rule as preeminent (i.e., nonoperational conservation)	Full grasp of the logical grouping (i.e., operational conservation)
IV	Perceptual boundness	Partial grasp of the identity rule (i.e., nonoperational conservation)	Full grasp of the identity rule as preeminent (i.e., nonoperational conservation)	?

[a] Adapted from Acredolo and Acredolo (Note 3).

cues for judging quantities. Resistance to extinction awaits the development of operational conservation. Finally, in the fourth alternative, a nonoperational grasp of quantitative invariance supports partial conservation, consistent conservation, and resistance to extinction. In this case, the third transition again remains to be explained.

Obviously, the third alternative is most attractive since explanations exist for all three transitions, but the specification of additional milestones would undoubtedly complicate the picture. The point of this exercise, however, is merely to demonstrate the increased complexity of charting conservation development once we accept the possibility of nonoperational as well as operational conservation.

Future Research: The Development of the Identity Rule

Given the foregoing conclusion that a grasp of the identity rule can develop early in life and even support, on its own, consistent conservation, we need to begin charting the slow growth of the identity rule from first emergence to ultimate status as an abstract principle. So far, we have relatively little research aimed directly at revealing the nature of the identity rule across its full range of development, but in closing, I shall discuss just a few of the opinions now emerging.

The first task is to account for an early emergence of the identity rule. One way is by appealing to James Gibson's (1979) notion of affordances and to Eleanor Gibson's (1969) theory of perceptual learning. The Gibsons would argue that the observation of an absence of addition or subtraction naturally signifies an invariance in quantity just as the slow occlusion of an object by an edge naturally signifies its continued existence behind something else. Under the theory of perceptual learning, these "meanings" do not have to be empirically confirmed. They spring spontaneously from the perceptions. The affordances are in the information provided at the eye, and no further (constructive) effort is demanded of the individual other than in attending to what is there and recognizing it as relevant. In this case, experience is the crucial variable. Our perceptions carry a great deal of information, and we generally require repeated exposures before we begin recognizing which bit of information is important and which is not. Thus, the very young child may take more notice of what a substance is and much less in how much is present. Children would not be expected to show any concern about amounts until that age at which they gain some ability to affect amounts. Even so, children may take some time before they begin recognizing the relevance of an absence of addition or subtraction during quantity transformations.

An alternative argument is that children first learn the identity rule empirically through their experience with small numbers, a theory favored by Gelman and Gallistel (1978), Klahr and Wallace (1976), Siegler (1981), and Winer (1974), to name a few. Ignoring the debate over whether subitizing precedes or follows quantification by counting, the possibility exists that by repeatedly counting-subitizing small collections over the course of perceptual transformations, children learn directly that the cardinal number remains constant as long as there is no addition or subtraction. Klahr amd Wallace (1976) note that "there is ample opportunity for children to employ Qs [subitizing] to detect the consistent effects of addition, subtraction, and perceptual transformations on small quantities of discrete items such as the other members of his family, toys, shoes, cutlery, and so on" (p. 115), and Siegler (1981) suggests that "counting and pairing may be thought of as providing outside referents for verifying whether conservation does or does not obtain in any particular situation" (p. 54).

Evidence against this notion that children *must* learn the identity rule empirically through their early experience with small numbers comes from a recent observation by Woodruff, Premack, and Kennel (1978) working with Sarah, the illustrious language-trained chimpanzee. They observed that Sarah was quite capable of conserving liquid and mass but not number. Apparently Sarah acquired the notion of liquid and mass invariance without having to learn the identity rule through empirical confirmation by counting. Their results suggest that perceptual learning may be sufficient to account for the early emergence of the identity rule, but nevertheless, the course of conservation development may be modified, augmented, and hastened in children by their ability to empirically verify the identity rule through counting and subitizing small collections.

A number of researchers have suggested that, in point of fact, the identity rule does first emerge as a reasoning principle applicable only to small, specifiable numerosities. For example, Gelman and Gallistel (1978) "take the position that initially the young child reasons about number only when he can obtain a specific consistent numerical representation of a collection" (p. 229). Initially "his reasoning principles do not tell him how transformations affect relations; they tell him how transformations affect numerosity" (p. 232). That is, initially the identity rule may take a restricted form: In the absence of addition or subtraction, cardinal number remains constant. Thus, the child may recognize that perceptual transformations leave the cardinal tag unchanged and yet still insist that the amount has changed, as in the common observation of children who insist that lengthening a line of six chips still results in *six* chips and yet at the same time more than there were before.[8]

In line with this hypothesis, many researchers have confirmed that young children will exhibit knowledge of quantitative invariance when it comes to very small collections though not with the more commonly used large collections (Gelman, 1972; Gelman & Tucker, 1975; P. H. Miller & Heller, 1976; Siegler, 1981; Silverman, Rose, & Phillis, 1979; Winer, 1974, 1975; Zimilies, 1966). However, a recent study by Silverman and Briga (1981) suggests that these observations may not signify even a partial understanding of the identity rule. They demonstrated that young children can conserve small collections only if they are allowed to recount (or subitize) the sets after the transformation. That is, young children seemed capable of recognizing the invariance of number across perceptual transformations only when it could be directly confirmed that the cardinal tags had

---

[8] See Footnote 4.

remained constant. Thus, the conservation of small numbers may not be based on the appreciation of the absence of addition or subtraction at all.

Similarly, the results of Gelman's "magic" paradigm may be questioned (Gelman, 1972; Gelman & Tucker, 1975; Silverman, Rose, & Phillis, 1979). In this paradigm, children are first trained across a sequence of trials to recognize which of two small, unequal collections is "the winner," and then they are confronted with unexpected, surreptitious transformations involving either an addition/subtraction, a perceptual transformation, or a substitution. Between trials the individual collections are covered and then shuffled as in a shell game. Surprise following the transformation is the main dependent variable. The data from these studies indicate that children choose to define "the winner" in terms of number rather in terms of perceptual cues, and further that they are surprised when confronted with an unexpected addition or subtraction but relatively unconcerned when confronted with perceptual transformations. Gelman and Gallistel (1978) hold that these results indicate that 3-year-old children already "recognize the existence of a large class of transformations (manipulations) that can be performed on a set without altering the numerosity of the set" (p. 168). However, in light of Silverman and Briga's observations, one may argue that the lack of surprise by children when faced with the perceptual transformations results only from the fact that they continue to obtain the same count they had in past trials and not from a specific appreciation of the absence of addition or subtraction per se. Obviously, however, much more research on this phenomenon is needed before we can be certain what it signifies.

Regardless of whether or not 3-year-olds' conservation of small numbers represents knowledge of the identity rule, it is still commonly anticipated that the identity rule first emerges in reference to small, specifiable numerosities. It is expected that once the identity rule is mastered in one domain, it is then simply generalized to others, to larger collections and then to various continuous quantities (e.g., Siegler, 1981). As Anderson and Cuneo (1978) suggest, "once this concept has reached some level of development, especially once it can be verbalized, then it can function as an independent idea. As such it may aid in its own further development" (p. 370).

All the while, the child may be led into overrelying on perceptual cues in certain situations despite knowledge of the identity rule. The problem, however, is not in the lack of competence, but in a failure in performance. It is not that the child lacks the reasoning principles but rather "the problem is that the child fails to *use* his reasoning principles. What we need is an explanation of why he does not apply his principles" (Gelman & Gallistel, 1978, p. 229).

An awareness of compensation may play no role in the initial recognition of the identity rule, and, in fact, compensation may be an eventual consequence rather than a cause of the child's initial grasp of the rule (cf. Acredolo, 1981; Acredolo & Acredolo, 1979; Anderson & Cuneo, 1978; Silverman & Rose, in press). As noted in an earlier article on liquid conservation (Acredolo & Acredolo, 1979), a child who begins occasionally conserving liquid solely on the basis of the identity rule would still be "motivated to explain the illusions associated with the water levels, and this requires the development of compensation" (p. 533). In turn, the eventual grasp of compensation may add still greater legitimacy to the identity rule and hasten its generalization to other quantities.

Reference Notes

1. Shultz, T. R. *Concepts of natural and logical necessity*. Paper presented at the biennial meeting of the Society for Research in Child Development, April 1981.
2. Silverman, I. W., & Briga, J. *Does conservation training provoke the child to discover new rules for judging quantity*. Paper presented at the biennial meeting of the Society for Research in Child Development, April 1981.
3. Acredolo, C., & Acredolo, L. P. *Equilibration and conservation*. Paper presented at the meeting of the Piaget Society, May 1980.

References

Acredolo, C. The acquisition of conservation: A clarification of Piagetian terminology, some recent findings, and an alternative formulation. *Human Development,* 1981, *24*, 120-137.

Acredolo, C., & Acredolo, L. P. Identity, compensation, and conservation. *Child Development*, 1979, *50*, 524-535.

Acredolo, C., & Acredolo, L. P. The anticipation of conservation phenomenon: Conservation or pseudoconservation. *Child Development*, 1980, *51*, 667-675.

Anderson, N. H., & Cuneo, D. O. The height + width rule in children's judgment of quantity. *Journal of Experimental Psychology: General*, 1978, *107*, 335-378.

Bates, E. *Language and context.* New York: Academic Press, 1976.

Braine, M. D. S., & Shanks, B. L. The conservation of a shape property and a proposal about the origin of conservations. *Canadian Journal of Psychology*, 1965, *19*, 197-207. (a)

Braine, M. D. S., & Shanks, B. L. The development of conservation of size. *Journal of Verbal Learning and Verbal Behavior,* 1965, *4*, 227-242. (b)

Brainerd, C. J. Judgments and explanations as criteria for the presence of cognitive structures. *Psychological Bulletin*, 1973, *79*, 172-179.

Brainerd, C. J. Feedback, rule knowledge, and conservation learning. *Child Development*, 1977, *48*, 404-411.

Brainerd, C. J., & Hooper, F. H. A methodological analysis of developmental studies of identity conservation and equivalence conservation. *Psychological Bulletin*, 1975, *82*, 725-737.

Brainerd, C. J., & Hooper, F. H. More on the identity-equivalence sequences: An update and some replies to Miller. *Psychological Bulletin*, 1978, *85*, 70-75.

Breslow, L. Reevaluation of the literature on the development of transitive inferences. *Psychological Bulletin*, 1981, *89*, 325-351.

Bruner, J. S. On the conservation of liquids. In J. S. Bruner, R. R. Olver, P. M.

Greenfield, et al. (Eds.), *Studies in cognitive growth.* New York: Wiley, 1966.

Bryant, P. E. The understanding of invariance by very young children. *Canadian Journal of Psychology*, 1972, *26*, 78-96.

Bryant, P. E. *Perception and understanding in young children: An experimental approach.* New York: Basic Books, 1974.

Bryant, P. E., & Trabasso, T. Transitive inferences and memory in young children. *Nature*, 1971, *232*, 456-458.

Carnap, R. *Philosophical foundations of physics.* New York: Basic Books, 1966.

Clark, H. The primitive nature of children's relational concepts. In J. R. Hayes (Ed.), *Cognition and the development of language.* New York: Wiley, 1970.

Cowan, R. A reappraisal of the relation between performance of quantitative identity and quantitative equivalence conservation tasks. *Journal of Experimental Child Psychology*, 1979, *28*, 68-80.

Cuneo, D. O. A general strategy for quantity judgments: The height + width rule. *Child Development*, 1980, *51*, 299-301.

Curcio, F., Kattef, E., Levine, D., & Robbins, O. Compensation and susceptibility to conservation training. *Developmental Psychology*, 1972, *7*, 259-265.

Dockrell, J., Campbell, R., & Neilson, I. Conservation accidents revisited. *International Journal of Behavioral Development*, 1980, *3*, 423-439.

Donaldson, M., & Balfour, G. Less is more. *British Journal of Psychology*, 1968, *59*, 461-471.

Donaldson, M., & Wales, R. On the acquisition of some relational terms. In J. R. Hayes (Ed.), *Cognition and the development of language.* New York: Wiley, 1970.

Elkind, D. Conservation across illusory transformations in young children. *Acta Psychologia*, 1966, *25*, 389-400.

Elkind, D. Piaget's conservation problems. *Child Development*, 1967, *38*, 15-27.

Flavell, J. H. *The developmental psychology of Jean Piaget.* New York: Van Nostrand-Reinhold, 1963.

Flavell, J. H. *Cognitive development.* Englewood Cliffs, New Jersey: Prentice-Hall, 1977.

Gelman, R. Conservation acquisition: A problem of learning to attend to relevant attributes. *Journal of Experimental Child Psychology*, 1969, *7*, 167-186.

Gelman, R. Logical capacity of very young children: Number variance rules. *Child Development*, 1972, *43*, 75-90.

Gelman, R., & Gallistel, C. R. *The child's understanding of number.* Cambridge, Massachusetts: Harvard University Press, 1978.

Gelman, R., & Tucker, M. R. Further investigations of the young child's conception of number. *Child Development*, 1975, *46*, 167-175.

Gelman, R., & Weinberg, D. H. The relationship between liquid conservation and compensation. *Child Development*, 1972, *43*, 371-383.

Gibson, E. J. *Principles of perceptual learning and development.* New York: Appleton-Century-Crofts, 1969.

Gibson, J. J. *The ecological approach to visual perception.* Boston, Massachusetts: Houghton Mifflin, 1979.

Goodnow, J. J. Compensation arguments on conservation tasks. *Developmental Psychology*, 1973, *8*, 140.

Griffiths, J. A., Shantz, C. A., & Sigel, I. A methodological problem in conservation studies: The use of relational terms. *Child Development*, 1967, *38*, 841-848.

Hall, V. C., & Kaye, D. B. The necessity of logical necessity in Piaget's theory. In

L. S. Siegel & C. J. Brainerd (Eds.), *Alternatives to Piaget: Critical essays on the theory.* New York: Academic Press, 1978.

Hamel, B. R. On the conservation of liquids. *Human Development*, 1971, *14*, 39-46.

Hamel, B. R., & Riksen, B. O. M. Identity, reversibility, verbal rule instruction and conservation. *Developmental Psychology*, 1973, *3*, 66-72.

Hamel, B. R., Van der Veer, M. A. A., & Westerhof, R. Identity, language-activation training and conservation. *British Journal of Educational Psychology*, 1972, *42*, 186-191.

Hood, H. B. An experimental study of Piaget's theory of the development of number in children. *British Journal of Psychology*, 1962, *53*, 273-286.

Hulsebus, R. C. An interaction between vertical dimension and age in children's judgment of size. *Perceptual and Motor Skills*, 1969, *28*, 841-842.

Inhelder, B., Bovet, M., Sinclair, H., & Smock, C. D. On cognitive development. *American Psychologist*, 1966, *21*, 160-164.

Inhelder, B., Sinclair, H., & Bovet, M. *Learning and development of cognition.* Cambridge, Massachusetts: Harvard University Press, 1974.

Katz, H., & Beilin, H. A test of Bryant's claims concerning the young child's understanding of quantitative invariance. *Child Development*, 1976, *47*, 877-880.

Klahr, D., & Wallace, J. G. *Cognitive development: An information-processing view.* Hillsdale, New Jersey: Lawrence Erlbaum Assoc., 1976.

Larsen, G. Y., & Flavell, J. H. Verbal factors in compensation performance and the relationship between conservation and compensation. *Child Development*, 1970, *41*, 965-977.

Leahey, T. H. The development of conservation abilities: An intertask analysis of continuous quantity. *Merrill-Palmer Quarterly of Behavior and Development*, 1977, *23*, 215-225.

Lee, L. C. The concomitant development of cognitive and moral modes of thought: A test of selected deductions from Piaget's theory. *Genetic Psychology Monographs*, 1971, *83*, 93-146.

Lumsden, E. A., & Kling, J. K. The relevance of an adequate concept of "bigger" for investigations of size conservation: A methodological critique. *Journal of Experimental Child Psychology*, 1969, *8*, 82-91.

Lumsden, E. A., & Poteat, B. W. S. The salience of the vertical dimension in the concept of "bigger" in five- and six-year-olds. *Journal of Verbal Learning and Verbal Behavior*, 1968, *7*, 404-408.

Lunzer, E. A. Formal reasoning. In E. A. Lunzer & J. F. Morris (Eds.), *Development in human learning.* New York: American Elsevier, 1968.

Maratsos, M. P. Decrease in preschool children's understanding of the word *big*. *Child Development*, 1973, *4*, 747-752.

Maratsos, M. P. When is a high thing the big one. *Developmental Psychology*, 1974, *10*, 367-375.

McGarrigle, J., & Donaldson, M. Conservation accidents. *Cognition*, 1975, *3*, 341-350.

Mehler, J., & Bever, T. C. Cognitive capacity of very young children. *Science*, 1967, *158*, 141-142.

Miller, P. H., & Heldmeyer, K. H. Perceptual information in conservation: Effects of screening. *Child Development*, 1975, *46*, 588-592.

Miller, P. H., & Heller, K. Facilitation of attention to number and conservation of number. *Journal of Experimental Child Psychology*, 1976, *22*, 454-467.

Miller, S. A. Contradiction, surprise, and cognitive change: The effects of discon-
    firmation of belief on conservers and nonconservers. *Journal of Experimental
    Child Psychology*, 1973, *15*, 47-62.
Miller, S. A. Extinction of Piagetian concepts: An updating. *Merrill-Palmer Quarter-
    ly of Behavior and Development*, 1976, *22*, 257-281. (a)
Miller, S. A. Nonverbal assessment of Piagetian concepts. *Psychological Bulletin*,
    1976, *83*, 405-430. (b)
Miller, S. A. A disconfirmation of the quantitative identity-quantitative equiva-
    lence sequence. *Journal of Experimental Child Psychology*, 1977, *24*, 180-189.
Miller, S. A. Identity conservation and equivalence conservation: A critique of
    Brainerd and Hooper's analysis. *Psychological Bulletin*, 1978, *85*, 58-69.
Palermo, D. S. More about less: A study of language comprehension. *Journal of
    Verbal Learning and Verbal Behavior*, 1973, *12*, 211-221.
Palermo, D. S. Still more about the comprehension of 'less.' *Developmental Psy-
    chology*, 1974, *10*, 827-829.
Pennington, B. F., Wallach, L., & Wallach, M. A. Nonconservers' use and under-
    standing of number and arithmetic. *Genetic Psychology Monographs*, 1980, *101*,
    231-243.
Perner, J., Steiner, G., & Staehelin, C. Mental representation of length and weight
    series and transitive inferences in young children. *Journal of Experimental Child
    Psychology*, 1981, *31*, 177-192.
Phye, G., & Tenbrick, T. Stimulus position and functional direction: Confounds in
    the concept of "bigger" in 5- and 6-year-olds. *Psychonomic Science*, 1972, *29*,
    357-359.
Piaget, J. *The child's conception of number.* New York: Humanities Press, 1952.
Piaget, J. Cognitions and conservations: Two views. *Contemporary Psychology*,
    1967, *12*, 532-533.
Piaget, J. Quantification, conservation, and nativism. *Science*, 1968, *162*, 976-979.
Piaget, J. *Biology and knowledge.* Chicago: University of Chicago Press, 1971.
Piaget, J. Identity and conservation. In B. Inhelder & H. H. Chipman (Eds.), *Piaget
    and his school.* New York: Springer-Verlag, 1976.
Piaget, J., & Inhelder, B. Images and thought: The role of images in the preparation
    and function of operations. In P. Fraisse & J. Piaget (Eds.), *Experimental psy-
    chology: Its scope and method, Vol. 7: Intelligence.* New York: Basic Books,
    1969.
Piaget, J., & Inhelder, B. *Mental imagery in the child.* New York: Basic Books, 1971.
Piaget, J., & Inhelder, B. *The child's construction of quantities: Conservation and
    atomism.* London: Routledge and Kegan Paul, 1974.
Pinard, A., & Chase, G. Pseudoconservation of volume and surface area of a solid
    object. *Child Development*, 1977, *48*, 1559-1566.
Poteat, B. W. S., & Hulsebus, R. C. A vertical dimension: A significant cue in the
    preschool child's concept of "bigger." *Psychonomic Science*, 1968, *12*, 369-370.
Rose, S. A., & Blank, M. The potency of context in children's cognition: An illus-
    tration through conservation. *Child Development*, 1974, *45*, 499-502.
Rothenberg, B. A. Conservation of number among four- and five-year-old children:
    Some methodological considerations. *Child Development*, 1969, *40*, 383-406.
Russell, J. Nonconservation of area: Do children succeed where adults fail. *Devel-
    opmental Psychology*, 1976, *12*, 367-368.
Shultz, T. R., Dover, A., & Amsel, E. The logical and empirical bases of conser-
    vation judgments. *Cognition*, 1979, *7*, 99-123.

Sheppard, J. L. Compensation and combinational systems in the acquisition and generalization of conservation. *Child Development*, 1974, *45*, 717-730.

Siegel, L. S. The relationship of language and thought in the preoperational child: A reconsideration of nonverbal alternatives to Piagetian tasks. In L. S. Siegel & C. J. Brainerd (Eds.), *Alternatives to Piaget: Critical essays on the theory*. New York: Academic Press, 1978.

Siegler, R. S. Developmental sequences within and between concepts. *Monographs of the Society for Research in Child Development*, 1981. *46* (Whole No. 189).

Silverman, I., & Schneider, D. S. A study of the development of conservation by a nonverbal method. *Journal of Genetic Psychology*, 1968, *112*, 287-291.

Silverman, I. W. Context and number conservation. *Child Study Journal*, 1979, *9*, 205-212.

Silverman, I. W., & Briga, J. By what process do young children solve small number conservation problems. *Journal of Experimental Child Psychology*, 1981, *32*, 115-126.

Silverman, I. W., & Rose, A. P. Compensation and conservation. *Psychological Bulletin*, in press.

Silverman, I. W., Rose, A. P., & Phillis, D. E. The "magic" paradigm revisited. *Journal of Experimental Child Psychology*, 1979, *28*, 30-42.

Smedslund, J. The acquisition of conservation of substance and weight in children: V. Practice in conflict situations without external reinforcement. *Scandanavian Journal of Psychology*, 1961, *2*, 156-160.

Smedslund, J. Microanalysis of concrete reasoning: I, II, III. *Scandanavian Journal of Psychology*, 1966, *7*, 145-167.

Starkey, P. Young children's performance in number conservation tasks: Evidence for a hierarchy of strategies. *Journal of Genetic Psychology*, 1981, *138*, 103-110.

Strauss, S., & Liberman, D. The empirical violation of conservation laws and its relation to structural change. *Journal of Experimental Child Psychology*, 1974, *18*, 464-479.

Thayer, E. S., & Collyer, C. E. The development of transitive inference: A review of recent approaches. *Psychological Bulletin*, 1978, *85*, 1327-1343.

Wallach, L. On the bases of conservation. In D. Elkind & J. H. Flavell (Eds.), *Studies in cognitive development: Essays in honor of Jean Piaget*. New York: Oxford University Press, 1969.

Weiner, S. L. On the development of *more* and *less*. *Journal of Experimental Child Psychology*, 1974, *17*, 271-287.

Wheldall, K., & Poborca, B. Conservation without conversation? An alternative, non-verbal paradigm for assessing conservation of liquid quantity. *British Journal of Psychology*, 1980, *71*, 117-134.

Winer, G. A. Induced set and acquisition of number conservation. *Child Development*, 1968, *39*, 195-205.

Winer, G. A. Conservation of different quantities among preschool children. *Child Development*, 1974, *45*, 839-842.

Winer, G. A. Analysis of the relation between conservation of large and small quantities. *Psychological Reports*, 1975, *36*, 379-382.

Woodruff, G., Premack, D., & Kennel, K. Conservation of liquid and solid quantity by the chimpanzee. *Science*, 1978, *202*, 991-994.

Zimilies, H. The development of conservation and differentiation of number. *Monographs of the Society for Research in Child Development*, 1966, *31* (6, Serial No. 180).

2. The Acquisition and Elaboration of the Number Word Sequence

Karen C. Fuson, John Richards, and Diane J. Briars

In this chapter we describe children's acquisition and elaboration of the sequence of counting words from its beginnings around age two up to its general extension to the base ten system notions beyond one hundred (around age eight). This development occurs, in our view, in two distinct, though overlapping, phases: an initial acquisition phase of learning the conventional sequence of number words and an elaboration phase, during which this sequence is decomposed into separate words and relations upon these pieces and words are established. During acquisition, the sequence begins to be used for counting objects. Near the end of the elaborative phase, the words in the sequence themselves become items which are counted for arithmetic and relational purposes.

Learning the ordered sequence of counting words up to twenty is essentially a serial recall task: The words in the sequence must be recalled and they must be pro-

Thanks to James W. Hall, Walter Secada, and Leslie Steffe for helpful comments on an earlier draft of this paper, to Lloyd Kohler for endless hours of painstaking coding and data reduction, and to the many undergraduates who so patiently and enthusiastically worked on the data collection or analysis: Kathy Amoroso, Holly Arnowitz, Patty Bloom, Steve Cieslewicz, Chris Daley, Del Flaherty, Steven Meyers, Joanne Murabito, Sharon Nussbaum, Krista Peterson, Debbie Rubins, Arlene Siavelis, Karen Simon, and Toya Wyatt. Special thanks to Betty Weeks, Leona Barth, and Dee Mihevec for arranging and coordinating our data gathering efforts and to the teachers at the National College of Education Demonstration School, the Walt Disney Magnet School, and the School for Little Children for their very considerable help. Thanks to Jolene Hocott and Mary Ann Hinkle for allowing us to use their students in several studies. This material is based upon work supported by the National Science Foundation and the National Institute of Education under Grant No. SED 78-22048 and Grant No. SED 78-17365. Any opinions, findings, and conclusions or recommendations expressed in this publication are those of the authors and do not necessarily reflect the views of the National Science Foundation or the National Institute of Education.

duced in the correct order. "Learning" and "test" trials (e.g., "Show Grandma how you can count, dear") are presented in a haphazard fashion over a period of as much as 3 years. The acquisition of the sequence from twenty to one hundred is also a serial recall task, but one of a list with a repeating pattern. In the acquisition phase, the sequence functions as a single, connected, serial whole from which interior words cannot be produced independently. In the elaboration phase, the links between individual words become strengthened, and contiguous words (with their connecting link) can be separated and produced apart from the total sequence. Each word in the sequence then can serve as the stimulus for the recall of the next word— each word is a "bead" connected only to the immediately preceding and immediately following words. Therefore, in naturally occurring serial lists such as the number word sequence, the latter elaborative phase has the structure of an associative chain, but the former acquisition phase does not. Evidence supporting this view will be discussed in the "Elaboration of the Sequence" section of this chapter.

Several years are required for the acquisition and elaboration of the sequence of number words. Consequently, different parts of the sequence may be in different phases of development at the same time. For example, relations may be established between words at the beginning of the sequence at the same time that the child is acquiring words later in the sequence. Thus, statements in this chapter about particular phases or levels of development refer to some portion of the sequence rather than to the whole sequence. Typically, the most advanced development is at the beginning of the sequence, with progressively less advanced development toward the end.

Young children hear number words in a variety of contexts. The number words vary in meaning according to the contexts in which they are used, and early in their learning of these words, children build up separate, context-specific areas of meaning. As children age, these areas begin to connect. Fuson and Hall (in press) have reviewed the literature on some of these meanings and uses, namely, sequence meanings (arising from the number words in their conventional sequence), counting meanings (arising from the use of the conventional sequence in counting entities), cardinal meanings (arising from the use of a number word to refer to the numerosity of some group of entities), ordinal meanings (arising from the use of a number word to refer to the relative position of some entity), measure meanings (arising from the use of a number word to refer to the numerosity of the units in some quantity), and quasi- or nonnumerical meanings (e.g., street addresses and telephone numbers). In this chapter we outline the development of meanings for sequence words and, where appropriate, relate this development to other meanings and uses of number words. We use the terms above (sequence, counting, cardinal, ordinal, and measure number words) to refer to the use of a number word in the specified context (e.g., a number word used in a cardinal context we term a cardinal number word). The details of the meaning of any such use depend upon the meaning the user and the listener construct. By the use of these terms we do not impute to a child an adult or mature understanding of sequence, counting, cardinal, ordinal, or measure numbers. Rather, we use these terms to emphasize the different contexts in which number words are used.

The developmental sequence presented in this chapter has resulted from successive interactions between empirical and conceptual analyses. The empirical work has ranged from pilot work with a few subjects to full-scale studies. Much of this work is preliminary. We fully expect that the levels of development that we describe now will be modified in various ways both by ourselves and by others as additional data are generated.

Acquisition of the Sequence

Distinction between Sequence and Nonsequence Words

Children seem to learn very early the distinction between counting words and noncounting words, and the words they produce in counting contexts (e.g., when asked to "count" or to "count these blocks") are confined almost entirely to counting words. In our counting experiments with 3-, 4-, and 5-year-old, subjects have never used anything but counting words. With over 30 middle class 2-year-olds, two children have used letters from the alphabet (mixed in with number words) on one trial each. Gelman and Callistel (1978) also reported very infrequent use of noncounting words by 2- to 5-year-olds. The noncounting examples given by them were two 2-year-olds who used the alphabet on some trials. Thus, the identification of counting words and counting contexts and the restriction of words used in counting contexts only to counting words seems to be easily and successfully accomplished. The only intrusions seem to be of other "words," the letters of the alphabet, which are learned in a very similar way: as an arbitrary, long sequence having a conventional order and which adults and other children seem to love to ask one to recite.

Overall Structure of Sequences

The most common form of sequences up to thirty is the following: an initial group of words that is some beginning part of the conventional sequence (e.g., "one, two, three, four, five"), a next group of words, which deviates from the conventional sequence but which is produced with some consistency by a given child (e.g., "seven, nine, ten, twelve"), and a final group of words, which has little consistency over repeated productions (e.g., "fourteen, eighteen, thirteen, sixteen, twenty"). Identifying these three groups of words (the stable conventional, stable nonconventional, and nonstable portions) in the sequence of a given child requires repeated counting trials from that child. An example of such repeated trials is in Table 2.1. In this example, the stable, conventional sequence portion is "one two three four" and the stable nonconventional portion is "four six eight nine" (the linking member in each portion is recorded so that the structure with respect to omissions, reversals, etc. of the nonconventional portion is clear). The nonconventional portions vary from trial to trial and consist of the words following the "nine."

Table 2.1 Example of One Child's Repeated Counting Trials

one	two	three	four	six	eight	nine	fourteen	sixteen	thirteen	five
one	two	three	four	six	eight	nine	twelve	fifteen	sixteen	thirteen
one	two	three	four	six	eight	nine	fourteen			
one	two	three	four	six	seven	eight	nine	eleven		
one	two	three	four	six	eight	nine	fifteen	thirteen	eleventeen	
one	two	three	four	six	eight	nine	sixteen	eight	four	twelve
one	two	three	four	six	eight	nine	thirteen	two	six	
one	two	three	four	six	eight	nine	ten	thirteen	sixty	

Data Samples and Tasks

Data will be presented below concerning each of these sequence portions. The data come from two samples. The longitudinal sample consists of 33 3-, 4-, and 5-year-old middle class children attending an educational demonstration private school. At the first interview, six children in each half-year age group were included; three children had moved at the time of the second interview, so the sample dropped from 36 to 33. Word sequence data were collected twice (with a 5-month interval) on three different tasks: rote (nonobject) counting ("Count as high as you can for me"), counting a pile of 50 blocks ("How many blocks are in this pile?"), and counting a row of blocks that was lengthened on successive trials by the addition of one or two blocks ["I put down 1 (2) more block(s). How many blocks are there now?"]. On the final task the row was lengthened successively from 4 to 33 blocks. The cross-sectional sample consisted of 87 children aged 3 years 6 months to 5 years 11 months: the children in the Time 2 interview of the longitudinal sample who were of this age (27 of them) and 60 additional children—12 children balanced by sex in each half-year age group. These additional children attended a Chicago public school whose population was computer selected to match the population of the city racially and economically. They received the same tasks that had been used with the longitudinal sample.

The first data collection for the longitudinal sample was videotaped. Two coders transcribed these tapes; disagreements were resolved by a third person. The data collection from the cross-sectional sample was done by various pairs of trained collectors. Disagreements during training and during data collection were rare (less than 1% disagreement).

The Conventional Portion

Effects of Sex. Each sequence measure in each section below was examined for effects of sex and for interactions with this variable using analyses of variance. No main effects of sex and no interactions with this variable were found for any measure.

Cross-Age Variability. As might be expected, the conventional portion of the sequence increases considerably over this age range. Means, standard deviations, and ranges of the best rote count (i.e., no objects present) sequence produced by a child are given by half-year age groups for the cross-sectional sample in Table 2.2. One-way analyses of variance across age groups on these scores revealed a significant effect of age [$F(4, 81) = 5.93, p < .0003$]. Pairwise contrasts using the Newman-Keuls procedure indicated that the sequences of children in the two youngest groups differed significantly from those of the two oldest groups, whereas the sequences of the middle group (old fours) did not differ significantly from any of the others. Thus, the second half of the fourth year appears to be a time of considerable extension of the number word sequence.

The first five rows of Table 2.3 present the percent of each age group with sequences of given lengths. These data indicate that the largest percentage of the two youngest groups have sequences between ten and fourteen, the 4½- to 5-year-

Table 2.2 Means, Standard Deviations, and Ranges by Age for the Last Word Reached Accurately in the Conventional Sequence

Age	Counting rows of blocks		No object counting	
	100% of trials	Single best trial	Single best trial	Best trial with one omission[a]
3 years 6 months to 3 years 11 months				
Mean	8.00	14.06	14.17	16.56
SD	4.75	6.20	6.51	6.51
Range	(2-19)	(4-29)	(4-29)	(9-29)
4 years to 4 years 5 months				
Mean	9.47	14.00	17.18	18.71
SD	7.63	6.94	8.71	8.52
Range	(0-27)	(6-33)	(10-39)	(11-39)
4 years 6 months to 4 years 11 months				
Mean	19.23	20.77	29.59	36.47
SD	8.79	8.45	28.19	26.94
Range	(10-34)	(14-34)	(12-100)	(13-100)
5 years to 5 years 5 months				
Mean	22.38	27.63	40.19	44.81
SD	9.79	7.84	25.76	23.13
Range	(10-34)	(14-34)	(11-100)	(13-100)
5 years 6 months to 5 years 11 months				
Mean	25.00	26.94	38.17	43.00
SD	8.49	6.95	22.44	19.64
Range	(13-35)	(13-35)	(13-90)	(13-90)

[a] Sequence could omit one word; this sometimes was fairly far from the end of the otherwise accurate conventional sequence, for example, 1, 2, . . . , 13, 14, 16, 17, . . . , 29.

Table 2.3 Percentage of Age Groups Producing Accurate Sequences of Various Lengths

Age/grade[a]	$n<10$	$10 \leqslant n<14$	$14 \leqslant n<20$	$20 \leqslant n<30$	$30 \leqslant n<72$	$72 \leqslant n<101$	$101 \leqslant n<201$	$201 \leqslant n$
3 years 6 months to 3 years 11 months	17	44	22	17	0	0	0	0
4 years to 4 years 5 months	0	41	35	12	12	0	0	0
4 years 6 months to 4 years 11 months	0	12	47	18	12	12	0	0
5 years to 5 years 5 months	0	6	25	13	44	13	0	0
5 years 6 months to 5 years 11 months	0	6	22	17	44	11	0	0
Kindergarten	0	7	11	30	26	4	22	0
First grade	0	0	3	14	7	21	48	7
Second grade	0	0	0	0	8	3	31	58
Third grade	0	0	0	0	0	4	25	71

[a] The first five groups are from our cross-sectional sample. The last four are from Bell and Burns beginning of the year interviews.

olds have sequences between fourteen and twenty, and the two oldest groups have sequences between thirty and seventy-two. Table 2.3 also contains data from Bell and Burns (Notes 1 and 2) on the sequences of older children (kindergarten through second grade). These data come from a heterogeneous sample of children from a small city bordering Chicago. Children were asked to count to thirty, and they then were stopped and their sequence production was checked at certain key points (63-72, 98-101, 196-201, and even higher). These data indicate considerable sequence production ability by the first and second graders, even though teachers indicated that they did not teach such higher counting and that all of the children's computational work was with numbers less than 100.

An examination of the sequences produced by children revealed that some children would omit a single word in a sequence and then continue to produce many more correct words. These children thus seemed to be much more able than those who produced no correct portion past their first error. To examine this capability, a more lenient measure, "best with one omission," was devised; it is the last word in a sequence that is correct except for a single omission. The means, standard deviations, and ranges for this measure for the rote counting sequences are also given in Table 2.2. This measure indicates improved sequence production, especially for the three oldest groups. Thus, many of these children had productive knowledge about the sequence beyond the point of their first error. As before, a one-way analysis of variance revealed a significant effect of age on this measure [$F(4, 81) = 8.99, p < .0001$], but here the means for the two youngest age groups were significantly different from those for the three oldest age groups (Newman-Keuls $p < .05$).

Within-Age Variability. The very large ranges and standard deviations in Table 2.2 indicate considerable variability within age groups, also. Some 3-year-olds have longer conventional portions than do some 5-year-olds. This rather large within-age variability is indicated in more detail in the first five rows of Table 2.3, and the final three rows of Table 2.3 indicate that this extreme variability continues into the early grades of the elementary school (Bell & Burns, Notes 1 and 2).

Decade Structure. The big jump (from 17 to 30 to 40) in the means in Table 2.2 for the young 4-year-olds (age 4 years to 4 years 5 months), the old 4-year-olds (age 4 years 6 months to 4 years 11 months), and the young 5-year-olds (age 5 years to 5 years 5 months) and the similar jump in the percentage of 4-year-olds and 5-year-olds with sequences over thirty (Table 2.2) is the result of some old 4-year-olds and many young 5-year-olds at least partially solving what we termed in earlier articles (Fuson & Mierkiewicz, Note 3; Fuson & Richards, Note 4) the "decade problem." This problem arises from the repetitive decade structure of the sequence between twenty and one hundred. Many older children in our samples gave evidence that they understood this repetitive structure. Above the twenties their sequences showed the pattern of "x-ty, x-ty-one, x-ty-two, . . . , x-ty nine" followed by a different "x-ty to x-ty-nine" chunk. However, most of them had not yet learned the order of the x-ty words, the multiples of ten. The sequence would move, for example, from the twenties to the fifties, to eighties, to thirties, to the fifties again, to twenties, etc. As Tables 2.2 and 2.3 indicate, the full solution of this problem is not attained by almost all children until the beginning of second grade, though a significant portion of kindergarten children have solved it.

Siegler and Robinson (in press) asked children to produce a number word sequence once in each of four sessions. They differentiated three groups of children by the place in the sequence where word production stopped: the first group stopped between one and nineteen, the second, between twenty and ninety-nine, and the third, above one hundred. Siegler and Robinson (in press) reported that the nature of the stopping points differed in the three groups: no obvious stopping-point regularities for the first group, an absolute majority of children in the second group who stopped at a word ending in "nine" and a few who stopped on a word ending in "0", and for the third group many counts ending in "nine" but even more ending in "0". When we examined the stopping points in the cross-sectional sample on the two rote counting trials (administered at the beginning and at the end of the interview), we found somewhat different results. The stopping points for our first group were distributed fairly evenly over the words from one through seventeen, but one-third of the stopping points were at "eighteen" or "nineteen." For this group, our percentage of counts stopping at a word ending in "nine" was 26% compared with Siegler and Robinson's 14%. As did Siegler and Robinson, we found low percentages of counts and of children in this group with stopping points ending in "0" (4% and 8%), and we found a similar percentage of children ending a rote count with "nine" (38% compared to their 40%). In our second group (those with sequences between twenty and ninety-nine), we found much lower percentages of rote counts and percentages of children ending with a "nine" (31% vs. their 69% and 45% vs. their 96%) but higher percentages of rote counts and of children ending with a "0" (31% vs. their 4% and 43% vs. their 14%). Thus, our two groups of children do not differ in their rates of stopping at "nine," but they do differ in their rates of stopping at "0." We had only four children in the third group. They all stopped at one hundred on each trial.

Siegler and Robinson examined stopping points as a way to indicate children's knowledge of the decade structure. They inferred from their findings that the first group of children understood neither the structure of the teens nor that of the decades and that the many children in group two stopping at a "nine" word indicates that they know the decade structure but not the next decade word (and so they stop producing words). Our finding that as many of our children stopped at a 0 word as at a "nine" word contradicts the latter inference. However, we consider the use of stopping-point data to indicate knowledge of structure to be somewhat risky. The point at which children stop producing words in sequence is influenced by factors other than whether they, in fact, could produce additional words. They may make assumptions about stopping points preferred by the experimenter; they may tire; they may seek variety. In our sample, only 22% of the children stopped at the same word in their two rote counts, and the differences between the stopping points were often large. This variability is much larger than would be indicated by the consistency level differences that we found for the conventional sequences, and so other factors would seem to be influencing these stopping points. Some of Siegler and Robinson's (in press) findings of stopping-point differences in the three groups of children (especially those concerning words ending in "nine") do not seem to generalize to other samples. We do not interpret these differences, however, as necessarily contradicting their models but rather as indicating some other factors that might be affecting choice of stopping points.

The extent to which the "decade problem" is easily amenable to practice and to direct instruction is not clear at the moment. Three different training methods seem possible. One method would emphasize linking the first member of a cycle to the last member of the preceding cycle (e.g., practicing "thirty-nine, forty"). Another method would focus upon learning the list of decades as a new rote sequence ("ten, twenty, thirty, . . . , ninety") and then using this list to select the correct next cycle. Our informal interviewing of adults suggests that some adults use this method when learning a number word sequence in a foreign language. Finally, decade words might be connected to their corresponding digits (twenty to two, thirty to three, etc.) and the order of digits used to order the decades. The relative effectiveness of these alternatives might be examined in future research.

Within-Child Variability in a Single Session. We examined the extent to which a portion of the sequence, once learned, is reliably produced over trials. This was separated into reliability over short periods of time (variability within a single session) and over long periods of time. The latter is addressed by the longitudinal data in a later section. To assess the within-child variability at one session, children's repeated sequence productions in the rows task (in which blocks were added on each trial to make the row longer and longer) were examined. The number of sequences produced by a child varied from 3 to 24, with the 3 year 6 month to 4 year 11 month age groups producing a mean of about 16 trials, and the 5 year- to 5-year-11-month age groups producing means of about 10 trials. The lower number of trials for the older children resulted from their sometimes using the numerosity of a previous row to respond to the "How many?" question after one or two blocks had been added to the row (e.g., There were 13 blocks and 2 were added: "Fourteen, fifteen. There are fifteen now.").

Because we did not know at what level of consistency changes might be observed, several levels of sequence production were analyzed. The measure at each level was the last word in a correct portion of a sequence. For example, in the sequence "one, two, three, four, five, six, eight, nine, thirteen, nineteen," that measure would be "six." From highest to lowest consistency, the levels chosen are:

100%: the sequence was produced correctly up to that word on 100% of the sequence.

80%: the sequence was produced correctly up to that word on 80% of the trials on which the row was long enough to allow production of that sequence.

60%: . . . on 60% of . . .

40%: . . . on 40% of . . .

Best: the sequence was produced correctly up to that word on at least one trial.

The analyses of the levels 80%, 60%, and 40% above revealed some fluctuations by level and by age group within the extreme 100% and Best level performances, but these were fairly minor. Therefore the data presented here will be confined to the two extreme levels, 100% and Best. Additional data can be found in Fuson and Mierkiewicz (Note 3).

Means, standard deviations, and ranges for the Best and 100% scores of the cross-sectional sample are presented in Table 2.2 by age group. A 2 (Consistency Level) by 5 (Age) analysis of variance revealed significant main effects of Level [$F(1, 81)$ = 49.96, $p < .0001$], and of Age [$F(4, 81) = 16.73, p < .0001$], and a significant Level by Age interaction [$F(4, 81) = 2.77, p < .04$]. The interaction is a result of much closer means (two- to three-word difference) for the 100% and Best sequences for the old 4-year-olds and old 5-year-olds than for the other groups (about six-word differences). Thus, across this whole age range within-child variability in the sequences produced in one session clearly exists. The age differences in variability that appeared here (i.e., the interaction) should probably be replicated before any interpretation is made. Pairwise contrasts using the Newman-Keuls procedure indicated significant differences ($p < .05$) between the 100% sequences of the two youngest and the three oldest age groups and significant differences between the Best sequences of the two youngest, the middle, and the two oldest age groups.

Longitudinal Data: Age 3-5. The within-child variability of sequences produced over a 5-month period was examined at two extreme consistency levels: 100% and Best Overall (the single best sequence produced on any task). A 2 (Consistency Level) by 2 (Time) by 5 (Age) analysis of variance was conducted on scores consisting of the last word in the accurate portion of the sequence. Significant main effects were found for Consistency Level, an overall mean of 30.0 for 100% and 36.7 for Best Overall [$F(1, 26) = 15.80, p < .0005$]; for Time, an overall mean of 29.4 at Time 1 and of 37.4 at Time 2 [$F(1, 26) = 15.47, p < .0006$]; and for Age, overall means of 9.7, 13.7, 18.2, 29.3, 44.5, and 77.8 [$F(5, 26) = 6.93, p < .0003$]. A significant Consistency Level by Time interaction was also found [$F(1, 26) = 3.96, p < .05$] with a larger increase over the 5-month interval in the single Best Overall scores (from 31.0 to 42.4) than in the 100% consistent scores (from 27.7 to 32.4). For most age groups the 100% score at Time 2 was approximately equal to the Best Overall score at Time 1. Thus, the process of acquisition of longer correct sequences seems to have at least two aspects: extension of the sequence and consolidation of this extension so that it is always produced. In the five-month interval, the most recent extension (the Best Overall score) seems to become consolidated (becomes the 100% score) at the same time that a new longer extension is being made.

Stable Nonconventional Portions

Nature of the Stable Nonconventional Portions. Stable, nonconventional portions of a sequence consist of a group of two or more words that deviate from the conventional sequence and are produced consistently by an individual over several trials within a given session. In a later section we shall examine the extent to which these within-session stable portions remain stable over longer periods of time. As with the conventional portions, we did not know where important differences might occur in stable portions, and so we examined several consistency levels (stable over 40%, 60%, 80%, and 100% of the trials). In the example given in Table 2.1, the stable nonconventional portion "four, six, eight, nine" is stable over 80% of the trials (seven out of eight). None of the words following "nine" occurs more than 40% of the time. If "fourteen" had occurred after "nine" two more times, then the portion "four, six, eight, nine, fourteen" would have been a stable portion at the 40% consistency level (occurring four out of eight times). Similarly, if the "seven" had occurred within the stable portion three more times, the portion "four, six, seven, eight, nine" would have been a stable portion at the 40% level (four out of eight times). These examples illustrate the two major ways in which fluctuations in the stability of the nonconventional portion of words result: (a) the occasional insertion of correct words within the stable portion, and (b) the addition of a word or words at the end of the stable portion.

The nature of the stable portions produced by children is exactly what one would expect in a serial recall task: Almost all of the stable portions have the words in the conventional order, but they contain omissions. Of the stable portions in the two samples (longitudinal and cross sectional) of children aged 3 through 5, 88% contained omissions, 3% contained repetitions, and 9% contained reversals. All examples of the stable portions containing reversals and repetitions are given in Table 2.4. Two of the reversals involve "six" or "sixteen," three involve "seven" or "seventeen," two involve "eight" or "eighteen," and one involves "fifteen." The two repetitions are substitutions for the word "fifteen." Table 2.4 also contains the distribution of words that were omitted across all stable portions with words "twenty" and below. In those stable portions which consisted of two words (the last word in the conventional portion and a later word), "fifteen" was omitted more than all other words put together. This may be because of its irregular construction as "fifteen" rather than "fiveteen." In those stable portions consisting of three of more words, almost all words are represented in the omissions.

For the words between ten and twenty, the distribution of omissions resembles that of a typical serial position curve except that it is not bowed (i.e., its high point is not pushed toward the end of the distribution); rather it is quite symmetrical about the midpoint word, "fifteen." However, this symmetry may be an artifact of two different factors operating at each end of the teens distribution. First, because most of the youngest children in our samples could produce correct sequences up into the teens at least once (mean Best score for the 3½- to 4-year-olds was 14), data from younger children would be needed to reflect accurately omissions of "ten," "eleven," and "twelve." Second, for a word to appear in Table 2.4, some word following it in the sequence must have been produced. For example, each "eighteen" omission must have had a "nineteen" or a "twenty" or a "twenty-one," etc., consistently produced. However, Table 2.4 does not imply, as a serial position display does, that each of the words at the far right (the recency portion of the list) was produced. Data on the rate at which each word between ten and twenty was

Table 2.4 Number of Occurrences of Errors in Stable Sequence Portions

Omissions

	Consistency level (%)	4	5	6	7	8	9	10	11	12	13	14	15	16	17	18	19	20
Word omitted																		
Two-word portions	40[b]	1	1		1				1	3	10	10	16	3	1			1
	100	1	1		1				1	1	3	5	13	2	1			1
Three or more-word portions	40[b]		3	2	2			2	2				16	9	10	5	3	5
	100								1				8	4	6	2	1	2

Reversals

Portion	Consistency level[a] (%)
· · · , 15, 17, 19, 18	67
· · · , 9, 10, 11, 8	71
· · · , 12, 14, 18, 19, 16, 17	83
· · · , 14, 18, 19, 17	62
· · · , 4, 8, 9, 6, 7	53
· · · , 16, 18, 19, 15	75

Repetitions

Portion	Consistency level[a] (%)
· · · , 12, 14, 14, 16, . . . , 29	100
· · · , 14, 16, 16, 17	60

[a] Percentage of child's trials on which error was produced.
[b] Between 40% and 100%.

produced across the sample of 36 children producing stable portions between ten and twenty are given in Fig. 2.1. As in the omission data, there is a huge drop off for "fifteen," and here there is also a considerable dropoff from "nineteen" to "twenty." In the sequences produced 100% of the time, production of all of the teen words other than "fifteen" is approximately the same and somewhat less than that of "ten" through "twelve." In those produced less consistently, somewhat more fluctuation occurs among the teen words and the word "twelve."

The data from Table 2.4 and from Fig. 2.1 taken together seem to indicate that during the acquisition of the teen portion of the sequence, children initially produce stable, nonconventional portions with multiple word omissions most frequently in the thirteen to seventeen range. Some of these stable multiple word omissions contain the words "eighteen" and "nineteen" and others do not. Relatively few of these

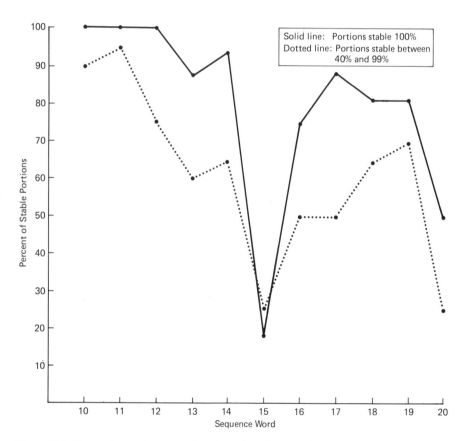

Figure 2.1 Percentage of conventional and stable portions containing words between ten and twenty. This figure includes words from the conventional portion preceding a stable portion (e.g., for 1, 2, . . . , 10, 11, 12, 13, 16, 18, 19, 1→13 is conventional and 13, 16, 18, 19 is stable; all words ten and above would have been entered in the table).

stable portions contain the word "twenty." Over time these multiple omissions become filled in with the correct words until the only remaining omission is the word "fifteen." The two children in the longitudinal sample whose stable portions moved from three or more words to two words followed this pattern. The omission of the word "fifteen" persisted in some children even after they produced a conventional sequence to "twenty-nine" or even into the thirties. It remains to be seen whether such a long-lasting omission has relatively trivial implications, that is, it is an easy one to correct, or whether it is more difficult to remedy.

Stable portions can have different lengths (i.e., contain a different number of words) and the gaps in them can be of different sizes (e.g., "twelve, fourteen" is a one-word gap, while "twelve, eighteen" is a five-word gap). For 100% stable portions of words below twenty, the mean length in the cross-sectional sample was 3.6 words, the range was 2-10 words, and the percentages of gaps of one, two, three, and four or more words were 71%, 0%, 7%, and 21%, respectively. Those figures for the stable portions at the 40% level are a mean of 3.13, range 2-10, and gap percentages of 59%, 11%, 9%, and 20%. Therefore, most of the gaps are of one word, but some gaps are of two and three words, and a sizable number (about 20%) are of four or more words.

Stable nonconventional portions containing words above twenty are of two kinds. Some (37.5% in our sample) end in a word between ten and twenty and then jump to a decade word (e.g., "eighteen, forty" or "seventeen, thirty") or to a decade-one word (e.g., "fourteen, forty-one" or "eighteen, eighty-one"). These confusions may stem from a misunderstanding of the decade structure or from acoustic confusion of "-ty" and "-teen" (e.g., fourteen and forty). Other stable nonconventional portions above twenty (37.5%) end in twenty-nine and jump to another decade ("twenty-nine, fifty, fifty-one, fifty-two, fifty-three"). Still others (25%) begin with the word "twenty" and then jump back into the teens words and produce several of them. Each of these types of stable portions seems to reflect partial knowledge of the decade word structure.

Do All Children Have Stable Portions? Our data indicate that stable, nonconventional portions are typical of sequences below thirty during the acquisition period, but our data for sequences longer than this are somewhat incomplete. Because stable, nonconventional portions occur after the conventional portion, it is necessary to obtain repeated productions of fairly long sequences. The task we used—successively adding one or two blocks to a long row of blocks (up to 34)—was successful in accomplishing this aim: Children seemed to enjoy seeing the row grow longer and longer and stuck with this repetitive and somewhat boring task fairly well. However, the ceiling of 34 blocks meant that we could not examine the existence of stable portions in those children who produced accurate sequences up to 34. Furthermore, some children made counting errors on the rows task (skipping blocks, pointing at blocks without producing words, and skimming along blocks while only producing occasional words) which meant that the last word they produced was always within the accurate portion of their sequence. Finally, a few children refused to continue the task although they were still producing entirely correct sequences. For the Time

1 interview of the longitudinal sample and for the additional children in the cross-sectional sample, 27 of the 96 children had accurate sequences up to 34, 11 made counting errors that resulted in the production only of short accurate sequences, and six stopped the task while still producing correct sequences. Of the remaining 52 children who had the opportunity to produce stable nonconventional portions, 46 or 88% of them did produce such portions, 28 at the 100% level (i.e., these stable portions were produced on every trial on which they could have been produced) and 18 at the 40%-80% levels. Thus, the production of stable nonconventional portions seems to be quite typical during the period of the acquisition of the number word sequence, at least for sequences below thirty. Children with accurate sequences to 34 also produced nonconventional portions higher than this that were stable over two or three rote counting trials, but because the number of repeated trials we have for these children is so low, we did not include them in the above stable analyses (they were included in the 27 children with accurate sequences up to 34).

Three of the six children who did not produce stable nonconventional portions produced sequences with what we characterized as "trouble spots": places in the sequence where each word in that trouble spot was produced on some trial but no trial contained all of the words and the productions varied enough that no stable portion was produced. This trouble spot pattern also characterized the sequences of some children with stable portions only at the 40% level; their other sequences contained other words from that troubled area, each with several different patterns of such production. Two examples are:

1. one, . . . , fourteen, sixteen, seventeen, eighteen
   or one, . . . , fifteen, seventeen, eighteen;
2. one, . . . , twelve, fourteen, fifteen
   or one, . . . , twelve, fourteen, sixteen
   or one, . . . , thirteen, fifteen
   or one, . . . , thirteen, fourteen.

This trouble spot pattern seems to be characterized more by an unequal and unpredictable production of certain words in the troubled area than by the consistent production of a sequence in that area.

Cross-Time Stability of Stable Portions. Are stable nonconventional portions really stable across different tasks and across several days, or are they just a temporary and misleading phenomenon resulting from a short-term fixation on certain patterns of words beyond the conventional portion of the sequence? We have tried to gather short-term (e.g., two-day or one-week intervals) data on this question, but we have had difficulty in developing a task that will quickly reach the portion of a child's sequence just beyond the conventional portion and will hold the child's interest during repeated productions of long word sequences. The only longitudinal data we have at this time is from our original longitudinal sample with a 5-month gap in interviews. Of the 11 children in this sample who had produced stable nonconventional portions at Time 1, one child was no longer at the school and four now produced sequences that were correct at the old stable portion. The other six all were still producing stable portions that were related to their old stable portions. Two children continued to produce the same stable portion that they had produced 5 months earlier ("thirteen, sixteen, twenty-one, twenty-two" and "four, six, seven, eight, nine, ten, eleven, twelve, fourteen, seventeen, eighteen"). Two children now gave stable portions that consisted of their old portions with all but one of the old omissions filled in (the stable sequence "twelve, fourteen, sixteen" had become "twelve, thirteen, fourteen, sixteen" and the stable sequence "ten, twelve, thirteen, seventeen, eighteen, nineteen, twenty-one, twenty-two, twenty-eight" had now become correct from ten to twenty-eight except for the omission of fifteen). Two children now produced a word they had omitted in the old stable portion but they also omitted the word next to it that formerly had been produced (a change from "five, six, eight" to "five, seven, eight" and a change from "twelve, fourteen, sixteen" to "twelve, fifteen, sixteen"). These data seem to indicate that the stable portions are not temporary stabilities, but rather they reflect ways in which the sequence is stored, remembered, and produced over fairly long periods of time. Words in multiple omissions get filled in over time, though sometimes an old contiguous word gets lost in this process.

The Stable-Order Principle. Gelman and Gallistel (1978) also reported stable nonconventional counting sequences produced by preschool children, but they characterized whole sequences, rather than parts of sequences, in this way, and they labeled such sequences "idiosyncratic." This word seems a bit too strong for such stable, nonconventional portions, for most of them in our data consist of the conventional sequence with omissions rather than more idiosyncratic creations. Gelman and Gallistel took the production of such stable, idiosyncratic sequences as evidence for what they called "the stable order principle." Their operational definition of this principle was the production of a stable list over repeated counting trials. However, if the stable order principle does not imply something beyond a description of the nature of the sequences produced by children, it is not clear why this is called a principle. Much of Gelman and Gallistel's discussion about this stable order counting principle seems to imply that children "honor this principle" (i.e., produce stable ordered sequences) from some understanding about the need for using a stable sequence in counting objects (e.g., to ensure that the numerosities obtained by repeated counts of the same set are the same).

Our data are in agreement with those of Gelman and Gallistel (1978) in that stable portions are typical of the sequence productions of children. However, the existence of such sequence portions does not, in our judgment, constitute evidence for possession of the stable order principle by children, if "principle" is meant to imply something more than the observation that stable, nonconventional sequences are produced. We rather consider stable, nonconventional sequences to result from the serial nature of the number-word sequence learning task. First, the existence in the nonstable sequence portions of so many forward ordered runs (see below) and the fact that most stable, nonconventional word groups differ from the conventional sequence only by omissions suggests that children learn the order of the words in the conventional counting word sequence along with the learning of the words. Second, the nonstable portions of many children's productions contain words from the earlier, produced conventional portion, and these repeated words most often are not consistent with the way those words were produced earlier. This repetition and its inconsistent nature would seem to constitute strong evidence that these children, in fact, do not understand the stable order principle. A possible caveat to this negative inference is that after "thirteen," the standard English word sequence does begin to display repetitions of parts of words (e.g., "four-teen," "twenty-five"). Until the nature of these repetition patterns become clear, they may confuse children and make it more difficult for them to observe that, in fact, each counting word is unique and that it occurs always in the same order in the sequence. In conclusion, it seems quite problematic to draw inferences about children's understanding of the need for using a stable sequence in counting only from the nature of their counting word productions. Direct evidence of such understanding is needed.

Nonstable Sequence Portions

Children did not always stop counting while in the conventional or stable portions of their word sequences. Many continued to produce words after their stable sequence, but these portions were not stable across repeated trials. Of the 46 children who produced stable portions, 28, or 61%, also produced nonstable portions. The remaining 18 children said words beyond their stable portion on fewer than four trials (usually only the rote counting and movable block tasks), making the stability of this extension of their word sequence impossible to determine. Eight of these children had conventional and stable portions sufficient for the rows task (i.e., of 33 or more words); eight others made errors in counting the rows (skipping objects, etc.) so that the last word uttered was always within the stable portion of their word sequence. Two children stopped the rows task while still within their stable portion. The data reported in this section come from those children on whom we had four or more trials of sufficient length to determine that their nonstable portions were indeed not stable.

Five examples of nonstable portions are given in Table 2.5. Nonstable portions are by definition irregular over repeated trials. However, they also possess some structure and some regularities, that is, they are not entirely random productions. Nonstable portions are composed largely of three different types of elements: (a) runs—from two to five words contiguous in the conventional sequence (e.g., "sixteen, seventeen, eighteen" or "twenty-one, twenty-two, twenty-three"); (b) runs with omissions—from two to five words in the conventional order but containing omissions (e.g., "twelve, fourteen, seventeen"); and (c) single unrelated words. The runs and runs with omissions are all forward directed (i.e., they are in sequence order), and these runs, runs with omissions, and the separate words are concatenated in a generally forward direction. For the longest nonstable portion of each child the ratio of contiguous word pairs that were in conventional sequence order ranged from 0.40 (more backward than forward) to 11.50, with a mean ratio of 4.52. The average nonstable portion therefore went forward four or five words, fell back to an

Table 2.5 Examples of Sequences with Nonstable Portions

Case L: Age 3 years 10 months
    1→12 14 18 19 15 19
    1→12 14 18 19 16 17 18
    1→12 14 18 19 15 17 18 19 17
    1→12 14 18 19 15 16 17 18 19 15 17
    1→12 14 18 19 16 17 12 14 18 19
    1→12 14 18 19 16 17 18 19 17 14 18
    1→12 14 18 19 16 17 18 19 16 17 18 19 16
    1→12 14 18 19 16 17 18 19 16 17 18 19 17 18
B[a] 1→12 14 18 19 13
R[b] 1→12 14 18 19 17 15

Case M: Age 3 years 6 months
    1→13 19 16 13 19
    1→13 16 19
    1→13 16 14 16 19
    1→13 16 19 16 13 14 19 16 19
    1→13 19 16 14
B 1→13 19 16 14 19 16 19 16
R 1→13 19 14 16 14
R 1→13 19 16 14 19

Case N: Age 4 years 2 months
    1→14 16→19 30 1
    1→14 16→19 30 40 60
    1→14 16→19 30 31 35 38 37 39
    1→14 16→19 30 40 60 800
    1→14 16→19 40 60 70 80 90 10 11 10 30
B 1→14 16→19 60 30 800
B 1→14 60 30 800 80 90 30 ten-eighty 60 31 38 39 32 31 34 35 thirty-ten 31
R 1→14 16→19 30 800 60
R 1→14 16→19 30 1 80 90 60 30 90 80 30

earlier word, and then went forward another four or five words, etc., or contained some other pattern of several forward and one backward word that would lead to the 4.5 ratio (e.g., nine forward words followed by two backward ones).

Some words in the nonstable portions were favorites across children. Table 2.6 contains the total number of times a word appeared in the longest nonstable portion of each child. The words "thirteen," "sixteen," "eighteen," "nineteen," and "twenty-nine" occurred with considerably higher frequency than other words.

"Favorite" words also appeared within the nonstable portions of individual children. For some children, certain elements (runs, runs with omissions, and words) were repeated within a given nonstable portion, but these repetitions did not form regular patterns: Random elements were inserted in between others, and the elements themselves were sometimes modified slightly (by omission or intrusion of a word). In addition, these "favorite" words or groups of words were not necessarily so favored in a later sequence production, though they frequently appeared once in other nonstable portions.

Table 2.5 (*continued*)

Case O: Age 4 years 1 month
      1→12 15 18 19
      1→10 12 14 18 19 16 11-teen
      1→10 14 15 19 1 2 3
      1→12 14 18 19 17 16
      1→10 12 14 18 19 16 11 12
  B 1→7 18 19 12 14 16 11-teen 12 15 17 18 19 12
  B 1→7 18 19 12 17 18 19 12 15 19 12 16 11-teen 14 18 19 14
  R 1→10 17 16 18 19 14 18 13 17 18 16
  R 1→10 11-teen 17
  R 1→6 11-teen 6 14 17 18 19 12 16 18 19 12 4 14

Case P: Age 4 years 4 months
      1→11 13 16 18 40 5 6
      1→11 13 16 18 40 5→8
      1→11 13 16 18 14 5→13
      1→11 13 16 18 14 5→13 16 18
      1→11 13 16 18 14 15 16 18 19 23 26 11 13 16 18
      1→11 13 16 18 40 16 18 10 11 13 16 18 24 26 28 24
      1→11 13 16 18 14 6 9 10 11 13 16 18 24 28 26 23
      1→11 13 16 18 24 28 22 3→11 13 16 18
      1→11 13 16 18 20 1→11 13 16 18 16 18
      1→11 13 16 18 20 21 26 24 28 1→5
      1→12 10 11 13 16 18 21 22 17 16 18 21 22 26 24 26 23 28 16 14 12 13 16
  B 1→11 13 16 18
  R 1→11 13 16 18

[a] B=Blocks trials: while counting a pile of 50 movable blocks.
[b] R=Rote trials: no objects.

The extent to which individual children repeated a word within a nonstable portion seems to vary somewhat with the location of that nonstable portion within the word sequence. If the single longest nonstable portion of each child is considered, the mean numbers of words repeated within that portion were 1.32 and 1.38 for portions with words only above twenty or only below ten, respectively. For nonstable portions with words only between ten and twenty and for those containing words from the teens as well as words above twenty, the mean numbers of repeated words were 1.52 and 1.63, respectively. The latter comparatively high figures may indicate that children producing nonstable portions within these ranges do not yet know either the decade pattern or very many of the decade words, so they repeat the teen and twenty words that they do know.

Children also vary in the relationship that the words in their nonstable portion have to those in their conventional and stable portions. For 25% of the subjects, the nonstable portion contained words from fairly early in their conventional portions. For all but one of these subjects, this seemed to be because they knew very few words outside their conventional portions: After these new words were produced, chunks from the conventional portion were emitted alternatingly with these new words. For the other subject, the production within the nonstable portion of the

Table 2.6 Total Number of Times a Number Word Appears in the Longest Non-stable Portion

Word	Number of times word appears	Word	Number of times word appears
One	3	Twenty-one	6
Two	6	Twenty-two	8
Three	5	Twenty-three	6
Four	7	Twenty-four	11
Five	8	Twenty-five	9
Six	8	Twenty-six	14
Seven	8	Twenty-seven	13
Eight	8	Twenty-eight	11
Nine	11	Twenty-nine	23
Ten	7	Thirty	12
Eleven	14	30-39[a]	11
Twelve	14	40-49[a]	7
Thirteen	30	50-59[a]	5
Fourteen	20	60-69[a]	8
Fifteen	10	70-79[a]	6
Sixteen	25	80-89[a]	8
Seventeen	15	90-99[a]	5
Eighteen	24		
Nineteen	31	Words used four or more times outside of decade pattern: sixty, sixty-two, sixty-one, eighty	
Twenty	22		

[a] Complete decade counts appearing in the nonstable portion (e.g., 30, 31, 32, 33, . . . , 38, 39).

conventional sequence from "one" or from "five" seemed rather to represent a hypothesis about repetitions in the structure of the word sequence (see example P in Table 2.5). Each repetition followed a word that "sensibly" preceded it (e.g., those repetitions beginning with five always followed a word with a "four" in it). For another 46% of the sample, the nonstable portion contained some words from earlier portions, but these came from near the end of the conventional portion or from the stable portion. For the remaining 29% of the subjects, the words in their nonstable portion were entirely new ones; none appeared earlier in the conventional or stable portions.

The data on nonstable portions are based on sequences produced in three different tasks: counting a row of fixed blocks, counting a large pile (50) of blocks, and rote (nonobject) counting. In many of our tasks, we intentionally gave children more objects to count than words they possessed in their conventional sequence. Children therefore had to make counting errors (skip objects, etc.), quit counting, or continue producing words past their conventional sequences. Most of them did the last, and no child seemed uncomfortable in doing this or verbalized less faith in those words produced beyond the conventional portion. The rote (nonobject) sequences that were produced were generally consistent with the object sequences, with one-third of the children who produced nonstable portions doing so on the first rote trial (the first counting trial overall) when no objects existed to extend sequence production. However, the possibility still remains that on the object trials the production of "incorrect" words was perceived by some children as a lesser evil than the other options (stopping or making correspondence errors), and that in fact children had differential faith in the conventional and nonconventional portions of the sequences they produced. This possibility needs to be examined in future work.

Models of the Number Word Sequence during the Acquisition Period

Greeno, Riley, and Gelman (Note 5) and Siegler and Robinson (in press) have proposed models of children's production of the number word sequence. Greeno and co-workers model the word sequence as separate words connected by a relation "next." This word sequence is then produced as part of the counting act. The Siegler and Robinson Model I (the model for sequences below twenty) has a beginning portion of the sequence consisting of single words connected by a "next" relation (these words are in the conventional order but may contain an omission) and one (or presumably more than one) later-occurring group of words connected by a "next" relation. In this model, when the last word in the first group of words connected by the "next" relation has been produced, a random choice "from the number list" (this is undefined) is made. This model thus incorporates the conventional and stable portion notions described in this chapter but views the nonstable portions as random productions. All of these features (a beginning portion followed by stably produced words with an omission, connected groups of words later in the sequence, random production of words and connected groups of words from the later part of the child's sequence) are actually consistent with parts of an earlier version of this chapter to which Siegler and Robinson refer (Fuson & Richards, Note 4). In that article, we termed the nonstable portions "spews" and described them as essentially random productions. Our subsequent analyses, however, have indicated that in fact they are not random, though not entirely regular, either. Thus, the Siegler and Robinson model does go a step beyond viewing the production of a number word sequence as involving only a simple "next" process, but it does not account for the nonrandom though irregular nature of the final nonstable portions nor for the probabilistic nature of the production of the end of the conventional and the stable portions. Sequences produced by Model I would consist of two parts: a conventional and stable part produced identically on every trial and a later part that differed on every trial. The data reported in this chapter obviously are inconsistent with both of these model productions: the ends of children's conventional and stable portions vary somewhat over trials (for this reason we needed the different consistency trials in our analyses), and the nonstable portions are not completely random. Models of each of these aspects obviously will need to involve some probabilistic process.

Siegler and Robinson proposed a more complicated model for sequences between twenty and ninety-nine. In the earlier draft of this chapter, which Siegler and Robinson referenced (Fuson & Richards, Note 4), we reported that children's sequences above twenty-nine often showed evidence of knowledge of the "*x*-ty to *x*-ty-nine" decade structure, and we noted that many children aged 4½-6 had what we labeled there (and here) "the decade problem," that is, children produced the decades out of order, frequently showing repetitions of these decades. Siegler and Robinson found similar patterns in their counting data, and their Model II incorporates these common findings. In that model, children produce a decade word (Siegler and Robinson term this a "rule applicability" word) and then cycle through adding each digit word to this word. When children do not know the order of the decades, the model postulates a random selection of a decade word. Again, our data indicate that though not entirely regular, this choice is also not random. "Favorite" and less favorite decades exist for particular children. Therefore, a probabilistic model again is probably more appropriate than a random model.

Modeling the number word sequence during its acquisition will obviously be a challenging task. As the Siegler and Robinson models make clear, such models will need to differentiate among sequences of different lengths (those that do and do not involve the decades, the hundreds, the thousands, etc.) because additional structure is involved in the higher word sequences. Such models also will need to account for the various probabilistic aspects of the sequence. After the sequence is acquired and is consistently produced, a simple model such as the one suggested by Greeno Riley & Gelman et al. is more appropriate, though after acquisition issues concerning the nature of the elaboration of various parts of the sequence (see later sections of this chapter) become important. At present we are considering two possibilities for models during the acquisition period. The first one is composed of probability trees for each number word. A tree connects a word to each word which may follow it, and each branch of such a tree is assigned a probability. Words in the portion of the sequence produced consistently have a single branch, and those occurring later in the more inconsistent portions have several branches. The other model involves two different memory stores. One consists of a connected "string" of number words that are produced one by one in sequence consistently from trial to trial. The other contains words and runs of words (with and without omissions), each of which has a probability attached to it. These probabilities determine which word or run will be produced, and the probabilities change with the production of a word or run.

Two important ultimate goals of any models of the production of the number word sequence are to model the processes involved in both the acquisition of new words and in the change from inconsistent to consistent production of words. First, however, we must be able to model how a given sequence is produced at one point in time, and we cannot yet do that adequately.

Invented Number Words

Some of the words in the nonstable portions are invented words. Twenty-seven percent of the cross-sectional sample produced at least one invented word. The mean number of different invented words produced by each of these children was 3.85 (SD = 3.78), and the mean number of such words produced including repetitions was 5.70 (SD = 5.74). Table 2.7 lists all of the invented words from the 96

3- through 6-year-old subjects in the cross-sectional and longitudinal samples. Almost all of these words continue a given decade above nine ("twenty-ten, twenty-eleven"), and a few continue the teen structure downwards (e.g., "eleventeen"). These "errors" obviously are not random but are based upon partial knowledge about structure within the number word sequence.

Very Early Word Sequences

A final point might be made about the very early acquisition of the counting word sequence. It is not clear whether all children start with at least the first word or two of the conventional sequence or whether some children first produce totally nonconventional sequences. In 140 children involved in our counting studies and pilot work for these studies, one 3-year-old and two 4-year-olds produced only non-stable nonconventional sequences. A few other children produced such sequences when they were tired or being silly, but produced sequences beginning with a conventional portion when told to "try hard" or to "shape up." This makes us somewhat reluctant to infer that the other three subjects could not produce a sequence of counting words that began with a conventional group of words. Gelman (Note 6) reported that retarded children produce only nonconventional sequences. Whether the very earliest counting word sequences of most children begin with a conventional portion is not yet settled. However, it is clear that most such sequences produced by 2-year-olds do begin with some conventional word or words.

Summary

The acquisition of the standard sequence of counting words up to one hundred begins in middle class American children before or soon after the age of 2 years and ends for most of them in first grade. The age of acquisition is extremely variable, with some 3-year-olds producing longer correct conventional sequences than some 5-year-olds. Most middle class children 3½ years or older can produce sequences to ten and are working on the teen part of the sequence, and children 4½ to 6 or 6½ are working on solving the decade problem. During the period of acquisition, the form of the sequences produced by most children is that of a conventional portion, followed by a stable, nonconventional portion containing omissions, followed by a nonstable portion that may be characterized in different ways for different children. Now that the nature of the sequences during the acquisition phase is beginning to be established, research is needed on ways by which new words are added and on factors that affect such additions.

Elaboration of the Sequence

After the number word sequence is acquired, it first functions as a unidirectional whole structure. The number words can be produced only by reciting the whole sequence. The elaboration of the sequence is a lengthy process of differentiating the

Table 2.7 Invented Number Words

Word	Number of children[a]	Number of times[b]	Mean use per child[c]	Range of use[d]
fiveteen	1	1	1.00	—
eleventeen	3	8	2.67	1-6
twelveteen	1	1	1.00	—
fivety	1	1	1.00	—
eleventy	1	1	1.00	—
ten-eighty	1	1	1.00	—
twelve-one	1	1	1.00	—
twelve-two	1	1	1.00	—
twelve-three	1	1	1.00	—
twelve-four	1	1	1.00	—
twenty-ten	8	22	2.75	1-8
twenty-eleven	7	16	2.28	1-6
twenty-twelve	9	11	1.22	1-2
twenty-thirteen	6	11	1.83	1-3
twenty-fourteen	6	6	1.00	—
twenty-fifteen	3	4	1.33	1-2
twenty-sixteen	3	3	1.00	—
twenty-seventeen	1	1	1.00	—
twenty-eighteen	4	4	1.00	—
twenty-nineteen	4	4	1.00	—
twenty-twenty	2	2	1.00	—
twenty-twenty two	1	1	1.00	—
twenty-thirty	5	7	1.40	1-2
twenty-forty	2	3	1.50	1-2
twenty-fifty	1	2	2.00	—
twenty-sixty	1	2	2.00	—
twenty-seventy	1	2	2.00	—
twenty-eighty	1	1	1.00	—
twenty-one hundred	1	1	1.00	—

words in the sequence and constructing relations among these words. We have divided this period of elaboration into five levels (see Table 2.8): (a) string level—the words are not objects of thought; they are produced but not "heard" or reflected upon as separate words; (b) unbreakable chain level—the separate words can be "heard" and they become objects of thought; (c) breakable chain level—parts of chain can be produced starting from arbitrary entry points rather than always starting at the beginning; (d) numerable chain level—the words are abstracted still further and become units in the mathematical sense in that segments of connected words can themselves be counted or kept track of (they are countable items in the terminology of Steffe, Richards, and von Glaserfeld, Note 7); (e) bidirectional chain level—words can be produced easily and flexibly in either direction. These different levels are marked by performance differences in more complex aspects of sequence

Table 2.7 (*continued*)

Word	Number of children[a]	Number of times[b]	Mean use per child[c]	Range of use[d]
thirty-ten	5	6	1.20	1-2
thirty-eleven	1	1	1.00	—
thirty-twelve	1	1	1.00	—
thirty-seventeen	1	1	1.00	—
thirty-eighteen	1	1	1.00	—
thirty-nineteen	1	1	1.00	—
thirty-thirty	2	3	1.50	1-2
fifty-ten	3	3	1.00	—
fifty-eleven	1	1	1.00	—
fifty-twelve	1	1	1.00	—
fifty-thirteen	1	1	1.00	—
sixty-ten	1	4	4.00	—
sixty-fifteen	1	1	1.00	—
sixty-twenty	1	1	1.00	—
sixty-twenty one	1	1	1.00	—
sixty-twenty two	1	1	1.00	—
sixty-twenty three	1	1	1.00	—
sixty-twenty four	1	1	1.00	—
sixty-twenty five	1	1	1.00	—
sixty-twenty six	1	1	1.00	—
sixty-twenty seven	1	1	1.00	—
sixty-twenty eight	1	1	1.00	—
sixty-twenty nine	1	1	1.00	—
eighty-twelve	1	1	1.00	—
eighty-nineteen	1	1	1.00	—

[a] Number of children who said the word at least once.
[b] Number of times word was said overall.
[c] Mean word use per child.
[d] Range of frequency use per child.

production, in the ability to comprehend or produce relations on the words in the sequence, and in uses of the sequence of words. The abilities at each level are presented schematically in Table 2.8.

Producing relations on and using the number word sequence in other contexts require knowledge in addition to the sequence skills themselves. Placement of relations or uses on the same horizontal line in Table 2.8 implies that the sequence skill is requisite for that relation or use. Developmentally, the lag between the acquisition of a sequence skill and a relation or use may be very small or fairly large, depending on the difficulty of the additional knowledge required. In some areas we know something about the nature and the difficulty of this additional knowledge; in other areas we know very little. Vertical placement of sequence skills within levels implies developmental lags except where specifically noted.

Table 2.8 Sequence Production Levels

Sequence levels	Forward sequence skills	Backward sequence skills	Relations	Counting, cardinal, ordinal, measure context uses
String ↑ 1	Produce word sequence from one; words may be undifferentiated			Count: no intentional one-to-one correspondences can be established
Unbreakable chain ●-o-o-o-o→ 1	Produce word sequence from one; words differentiated			Count: intentional one-to-one correspondences can be established Card: cardinality rule can be acquired (can count to find out "How many?") Ord.: ordinality rule can be acquired (can count to find out "What position?") Meas.: measure rule can be acquired (can count to find out "How many units?") Card. Op.[a]: simple addition problems if objects for the sum just need to be counted

to a

Breakable chain

Start counting up from a

o-o-o ●-o-o-o-o→
       a

the chain can be used to find these relations

Comes After, Comes Before: the chain can be used to find these relations

merosity "a"

Ord.: find the "ath" entity

Meas.: make (find) a quantity made up of n units

Card. Op.: Count-all and count-part procedures for addition and subtraction

And Then, And Then Before: these relations can be produced immediately

Comes After, Comes Before: these relations can be produced immediately

Between: partially correct solutions may be given by using And Then or And Then (Before) relations

Card. Op.: Count on without keeping track (addition)

Count up from a to b

Between: can produce all words between a and b going forward

Card. Op.: Count on from a to b without keeping track (subtraction)

Count down from b

Count down from b to a

Between: can produce all words between a and b going backward

Card. Op.: Count back from b without keeping track (subtraction)

Card. Op.: Count back from b to a without keeping track (subtraction)

Table 2.8 (*continued*)

Sequence levels	Forward sequence skills	Backward sequence skills	Relations	Counting, cardinal, ordinal, measure context uses
Numerable chain |-|-| •-|-|-|-|→ a	Count up n from a; give b as answer 1. $n = 1$ (And Then) 2. $n = 2, 3$ (4) 3. $n > 4$			Card. Op.: Count on with keeping track (addition)
	Count up from a to b, keeping track; give n as answer			Card. Op.: Count on from a to b keeping track (subtraction or missing addend problems)
		Count down n from b; give a as answer		Card. Op.: Count back with keeping track (subtraction)
		Count down from b to a; give n as answer		Card. Op.: Count back from b to a keeping track (subtraction)
Bidirectional chain ←-|-|-|-|→ a	Can count up or down quickly from any word; can shift directions easily			

[a] Card. Op.: Cardinal Operation—an operation on cardinal number words. We include the two earliest operations—addition and subtraction—here in Table 2.8.

String Level

At the string level the individual number words are completely embedded within the sequence. As sequence-number words, they are produced only within a recitation of the known sequence as a whole. The number word sequence for the young child at this level is just like any other recitation (e.g., nursery rhymes): The child "hears" the recitation only as a single whole and, if aware of the composing words, is so only to the extent of learning the correct recitation in some wholistic way. The individual words in some parts of the sequence may be inadequately differentiated, as, for example, in other sequences, "LMNO" or sweet "landaliberty."

The sequence-number words can be used in the act of counting at the string level, but because the words are not yet heard and reacted to as separate words, only a global correspondence can be established among the word sequence, the sequence of indicating acts (usually pointing), and the items being counted. The counting act at this level consists of the production of the string of number words and of a sequence of indicating acts roughly aimed at the entities to be counted. From the adult perspective, some one-to-one correspondences may occur, but the child has not made the requisite distinctions in its own behavior to make such a correspondence. Rather, these correspondences arise fortuitously or because of some human central nervous organization that makes it simpler to produce sequences of verbal and motoric acts in synchrony rather than completely in isolation. Over a period of two years, our experimenters have made records of over 40 2-year-olds counting various types of objects in various settings (homes, nursery schools, mother drop-in centers). We have found it difficult to obtain systematic data over various conditions (at least for object arrays of sufficient size to move beyond the child's accurate sequence) and difficult to describe the counting act at this level in any detail. Two impressions from this work might be noted for future research. First, the counting act seems to consist of the rather independent production of two separate sequences of behavior (the words and the pointing acts). Second, pointing at stationary objects seems to be a distinguishing feature of counting, for attempts to elicit imitation of counting that involved the movement of objects from an uncounted to a counted pile usually ended prematurely in some type of play with one of the piles of objects (i.e., such moving actions are part of "building with blocks," not part of "counting"). An exception to this is when the moved object is the child herself. Our observations and mother report data indicate that a frequent natural use of counting is in counting stairs as one walks up or down them.

Very few data presently exist about the string level. At the moment this level is characterized chiefly by what a child cannot do; these limitations will be more evident as the abilities on the higher levels are presented.

Unbreakable Chain Level

Differentiated Words. At the unbreakable chain level the sequence words are distinguishable, and can be "heard" or attended to, as words in the production of the sequence. However, the sequence must still be produced starting from the beginning; it cannot yet be "broken" and produced from an arbitrary entry point. Because each word has some separateness, intentional, as opposed to fortuitious, one-to-one correspondences among the words, indicating acts, and counted entities are now possible, thus laying the foundation for accurate counting (see Fuson & Mierkiewicz, Note 3, for data about age-related changes in counting accuracy). This distinguishing of words that appears at this level is simpler with counting sequences that begin with monosyllabic words. Israeli children fail initially to differentiate their sequence words and tend rather to make correspondences with each syllable of the first three two-syllable sequence words (echat, shtayim, shalosh) rather than with each word (Nesher, Note 8).

The clear differentiation of words in the unbreakable chain enables the child to establish the counting meaning of a number word (the meaning produced in the act of counting). It also enables the child to begin to establish a relationship (see Table 2.8) between the counting meaning and the meaning associated with the use of the final count word as an appropriate response to "How many?" (cardinal meanings), "Which position?" (ordinal meanings), or "How many units?" (measure meanings). This relationship between numerosity and the last word said in counting has (perhaps unfortunately) been termed the cardinality rule (Schaeffer, Eggleston, & Scott, 1974) or the cardinality principle (Gelman & Gallistel, 1978). Similar rules need to be constructed to relate counting to ordinal and measure meanings of number words (see Fuson & Hall, in press, for a more detailed discussion of this point). Such links with separate cardinal, ordinal, or measure number words are only possible when the number word sequence consists of differentiated words (e.g., one two three four five) rather than of a string of words (e.g., onetwothreefourfive).

A final use of the sequence skill of counting up from one is that children can begin to solve simple addition (and perhaps even subtraction) problems if objects representing each addend are provided and the total group of objects just needs to be counted.

Evidence for Unbreakable Chains. A chain is unbreakable if a person given a word from her chain cannot at once give the next word in the chain but must instead produce the sequence up to the given word before responding. The unbreakable chain is a whole structure that can only be produced from its starting point (or from some special starting points within the chain). Adults still have chains at the unbreakable chain level for at least the musical scale and the alphabet. For example, 19 of 20 adult self-reports in an informal study we did indicated that these adults had to say the whole musical scale (do, re, mi, . . .) up to a given word before they could tell the word that immediately followed it. Reaction time data also support such a "produce and search" process by adults with the alphabet (Hovancik, 1975; Lovelace, Powell, & Brooks, 1973; Lovelace & Spence, 1973; Klahr & Chase, Note 9). However, because of its length, the alphabet seems to differ somewhat from the musical scale: The common use of the rhyme, or song, of the alphabet tends to decompose it into unbreakable chunks (ABCDEFG HIJKLMNOP etc.). Consequently, the search process may involve only the production of one of these unbreakable chunks rather than the whole chain.

We examined whether the number word sequence of children had an unbreakable chain level in a study comparing the ability of 3- and 4-year-olds to produce the next word when given a single word versus two or three successive words from the sequence. The latter condition was designed to induce in the children a sequence recitation context similar to that induced by their own production of the sequence. The effect was to impose upon them the strategy adults use when they cannot immediately answer "comes right after" questions: They produce the sequence, stop at the given stimulus word, and then give the next word. Superiority of the sequence recitation context would indicate that the number word sequence in young children does go through an unbreakable chain level, but that many children do not think of using the sequence production strategy for questions involving the next word. Each of the 24 children in this study was given three presentation conditions which varied the number of successive number words said (one, two, and three words). Questions were of the form, "When you are counting, what word comes right after 6 (or 5, 6 or 4, 5, 6)?" The order of presentation of these conditions was completely counterbalanced. Number words of two different sizes were given: single digit (three through nine) and teens (between thirteen and eighteen). A 2 (Age) by 2 (Size of Number Word) by 2 (Number of Stimulus Words Said) analysis of variance was done on the percentage of correct responses for the two comparisons of single and multiple stimuli (one- versus two-word and one- versus three-word comparisons).

The percentage of correct responses in each condition is given in Table 2.9. For the one- versus two-word comparison, significant main effects were found for the Number of Stimulus Words [$F(1, 22) = 11.36, p < .01$], for the Size of Number, [$F(1, 22) = 5.45, p < .05$], and for Age [$F(1, 22) = 10.53, p < .01$]. The Age by Size of Number Word interaction was also significant [$F(1, 22) = 5.06, p < .05$]. More children gave correct responses to two-word than to one-word stimuli (69% vs. 45%). More correct responses were given by 4-year-old children than by 3-year-old children (73% vs. 41%). The 3-year-olds gave more correct responses for single-digit number words than for teens words (50% vs. 32%), while the 4-year-olds gave equal levels of correct responses for these different sizes (73% correct for both sizes). Almost identical results were obtained for the one- versus three-word comparison. The main effects and the interaction described above were all significant at the .01 level. The performance levels in the three-word condition were similar to those in the two-word conditions except that the 3-year-olds did slightly worse on teens in the three-word than in the two-word condition (33% vs. 48%).

The results of this experiment indicate that initially the number word sequence is in a recitation form, as a directed recited sequence, rather than as an associative

Table 2.9 Percentage of Correct Responses on Recitation Context Study

Age	One-word stimulus			Two-word stimulus			Three-word stimulus		
	Digit	Teens	Mean	Digit	Teens	Mean	Digit	Teens	Mean
3-years	39	15	27	62	48	55	63	33	48
4-years	64	63	63	82	83	82	83	81	82

chain of separable linked elements. The equal performance in the two- and the three-word conditions indicates that two words are sufficient to establish the directionality of a recitation context and enable a child to produce the next word.

Data from Siegler and Robinson (in press) also support an unbreakable chain level in the number word sequences of children. They reported that preschool children who were asked to start producing the number word sequence from a word well within their accurate counting range made a decade transition error (e.g., went from fifty-nine to seventy) or stopped at the end of a decade significantly more often than when they were producing the sequence from one. The total recitation context of the conventional sequence enabled children to produce a longer sequence than starting at some arbitrary point within it.

Additional evidence for the existence of an unbreakable chain level in the number word sequences of young children comes from reaction time studies of simple addition and subtraction problems given to 4- and 5-year-old children (Brainerd, Note 10). These problems required the children to increase or decrease the given addend by one. Such problems are quite easy to answer by using the number word sequence. Brainerd found reaction times supporting what he called a "drop back and count up" strategy. In order to produce the word following a given number word, some children produced the number word sequence starting from the beginning or very early in the sequence. In our terms, the children "drop back" to a piece of the sequence that is breakable and then count up, or they must begin at "one" in their unbreakable chain.

Counting up to "*a*". The main sequence skill to emerge at the unbreakable chain level is the ability to count up from one to a preselected word, "*a*." This is more difficult than simply producing the sequence, for the child must remember the word up to which she or he is counting and must create some way to stop counting when that word has been reached. The latter would seem to require some checking procedure. This might be instituted after each word is produced, or it might follow some estimate of where the designated word "*a*" is in the sequence and be used only when "close" to the designated word.

Emergence of "counting up to '*a*' " may be based on a combination of maturational and specific experiential factors. Case, Kurland, and Daneman (Note 11) have used a counting span task that shares characteristics with "counting up to '*a*'." In their task, a child must count a set, give its numerosity, then count a second set and give the numerosities of both sets in the order in which they were counted, etc. Thus, this task requires that a child remember a number word (the numerosity of the first set) while counting the second set. Case and co-workers found than 6-year-olds have a span of two (i.e., can count a second set and then give the numerosities of the first two sets), while 4-year-olds have a span of only one. Experience with counting does influence span. Several weeks of massive practice increased the span of 4-year-olds to that of the average 6-year-old, and adults using a new counting sequence have a span equal to that of 6-year-olds (Case, Kurland, & Daneman, Note 11). However, this additional experience must be quite extensive to have an effect, and Case and co-workers presented other data that implicated maturational factors as the chief source of this change in span. The same balance of factors would seem to be operating with the "counting up to '*a*' " skill.

The ability to count up to a prespecified word enables new counting uses of the word sequence to be made (see Table 2.8). In addition to the sequence skill, these uses all require specific knowledge about the context in which that skill is being applied. In cardinal ("How many?") contexts, a child can now find or make a group of objects of a prespecified numerosity. In ordinal contexts, children can find (or make) the "*a*th" entity. In measure contexts they can find (or make) quantities of "*a*" units.

The cardinal uses allow the child to develop general procedures for the solution of addition and subtraction problems. The count-all procedure for addition requires only the two sequence skills at the unbreakable chain level. In this procedure, items are counted out for one addend, then more are counted out for the other addend, and then all of the items are joined together and counted for the sum. For a count-part solution procedure for subtraction problems, items are counted out for the total, from which are separated items for the numerosity to be subtracted. Finally, what remains is counted (cf. Steffe, Thompson, & Richards, in press). The application of the word sequence skills to these cardinal operations of addition and subtraction requires that the child understand the relationship between counting meanings and numerosity (cardinal) meanings of number words in both directions; that is, the child must know that she or he can count a set of objects to find its numerosity and that, if a numerosity is known, a set of objects with the desired numerosity can be constructed by counting out objects. The child must also understand the fundamental meaning of addition as asking for a total of two different numerosities and of subtraction as asking for the remainder or the difference of two numerosities. Preschool children evidently have some basic understanding of "adding to" and "taking from" (Brush, 1978; Starkey & Gelman, in press), and school-aged children can use objects to model different types of addition or subtraction situations presented verbally (Carpenter, Hiebert, & Moser, 1981; Carpenter & Moser, in press; Moser, Note 12). When problems are presented symbolically, young children's abilities are not so clear, but even 4-year-olds apparently can easily learn the count-all procedure for addends of five or less (Groen & Resnick, 1977).

Relations on Sequence Words. At the unbreakable chain level the sequence skill "counting up to '*a*' " can be used to generate relationships between words in the sequence. One such relationship is "And Then," that is, " '*a*' and then ?" is the word immediately following "*a*" in the word sequence. Evidence was discussed above indicating that adults who have a chain at the unbreakable chain level (the alphabet or musical scale) do use their chain to answer And Then questions; that is, they produce the chain up to "*a*" and then give the next word as the answer. Some young children also seem to produce an unbreakable chain to find And Then relations in the number word sequence. Some children in a sample of 36 3-, 4-, and 5-year olds asked to produce words immediately following given words either said the word sequence aloud or gave visible lip movement evidence of subvocalizing the sequence before producing the required word. Far more children, however, did not use any observable procedure and simply replied quickly with a number word. These words were sometimes correct and sometimes not. The recitation context study reported earlier indicates that many children at these age levels can use the chain to answer And Then questions if successive words from the chain are spoken by the experimenter. It is not clear whether many children are not able to produce the chain from the beginning to answer an And Then question or whether children simply fail to think of using this strategy. The spontaneous use of it by some children supports the latter interpretation.

The sequence skill "counting up to 'a' " can also be used to answer questions about the general order relation "Comes After" (as in seven comes after four). In response to a question such as, "Does eight come after five?" two such procedures using the unbreakable chain are possible. One could produce the unbreakable chain listening and stopping at the sound of either word; this requires knowing that the word heard first does not come after the other word. Or one could produce words and stop at the sound of the second word; this requires only a direct use of the meaning of "Comes After." Again, in our studies, we have sometimes seen children producing an unbreakable chain (i.e., the sequence from its beginning) in response to "Comes After" questions, but, as with the "And Then" questions, a fairly quick response (sometimes correct and sometimes not) was much more common.

A brief note is necessary here on the choices we made for the names of the sequence relations we discuss in this chapter. We have at various times used different labels for these relations. None has been entirely satisfactory. Other possibilities for the relation which takes some word from the number word sequence and gives the next word (and which we have termed "And Then") are "Immediate Successor," "Comes Just After," and "Next." The problem with the first two (and similar variants) is that their usage requires that the normal sequence order be reversed: "7 is the Immediate Successor of 6." Because the forward linking relation is such a crucial one in the sequence, and because it depends so heavily on the forward recitation context, a term that would enable the relation to be stated in its forward recitation form seemed desirable. "And Then" was chosen because it met this requirement and because it implied only execution knowledge of the sequence and no further conceptual knowledge, as some of the other choices might have been inferred to involve. The awkwardness of the inverse of this relation ("And Then Before") is also then a positive characteristic, because it so accurately reflects the much more difficult nature of isolating in a forward directed sequence the word immediately preceding a given word. The terms "Comes After" and "Comes Before" were chosen for the general order relations on sequence words, because they seemed more general than "Comes Later Than" or "Comes Earlier Than," which refer only to time.

Other Comments. The unbreakable chain level may last for a considerable period of time in children even with a short chain and daily use. After the 5-year-old daughter of one of the authors learned the sequence of the days of the week, on her own she used the sequence at least once daily to solve relational questions about the sequence (e.g., "Today is Tuesday. What will tomorrow be?"). For at least four weeks, she was unable to answer And Then questions (i.e., to give the day following a given day) without running through the whole sequence to produce the answer.

Finally, evidence does exist about the relationship between two abilities (accurate counting and responses to "And Then" questions) at the unbreakable chain level. A sample of 14 3- and 4-year-old children (ages 3 years 6 months to 4 years 8 months) was selected from a larger sample on the basis of the length of their correct word sequences (these ranged from twelve to nineteen) and on their counting ability (over several trials they made a moderate number of word-object correspondence errors with accurate correspondence on at least one trial). These children were given words from their own conventional and stable word sequences and were asked to give the word that came immediately after these words. All children received the words between four and twelve, and children with 100% conventional and stable sequences above that received words up to "nineteen." Response scoring was based on a child's own stable sequence; for example, if the sequence was ". . . , fourteen, sixteen, seventeen," sixteen was scored as correct for the word following fourteen. The mean number of accurate responses was 49%, range 0-100% correct. Thus, while these children were capable of accurate object counting, they did not reliably or universally use the strategy of producing their word sequence in order to answer the "And Then" question.

Breakable Chain Level

Forward Sequence Skills. The breakable chain is a chain of connecting links that can be entered and produced beginning at any of its links (words). There are two new skills at this level: "counting up from '*a*' " and "counting up from '*a*' to '*b*.' " The latter is more difficult because the word to which one is counting-up must be remembered during the counting. The skill of counting up from "*a*" for "*a*" below ten seems to be acquired between age 3½ and 5 at about the time when children are acquiring correct sequences through the teens. We found that of 14 children aged 3½-4½ who had correct conventional sequences ending somewhere between twelve and nineteen, 6 were unable to start counting up from various words below ten, 3 did so on 60% of their trials, and 5 did so on 100% of their trials. Counting up from "*a*" for "*a*" in the teens seems to be well established for most children by age 6. Secada, Fuson, and Hall (Note 13) found only 6 out of 63 6½-year-olds who could not count up from "*a*" when "*a*" was a word in the teens. Data about counting up from "*a*" to "*b*" are reported in the later section "Counting Down from '*b*' to '*a*.' "

Forward And Then Relation. The ability to produce an immediate response to an And Then question appears to some extent in 3-year-olds and reaches fairly high levels in 5-year-olds. In the recitation context study described earlier, the correct response rate for 3-year-olds for And Then questions ("When you are counting, what word comes right after eight?") for words between two and nine was 39%, and for words between twelve and nineteen was 15% (see Table 2.9). Similar rates for the 4-year-olds were 64% and 63%, respectively. Success rates for words below 20 rose to 72%, 86%, and 100% for a sample of 36 middle class prekindergarteners (aged 4 years to 5 years 5 months), kindergarteners (aged 5½-6½), and first graders (aged 6½-7½). Correct item response times taken by digital stopwatch dropped from a mean of 2.56 seconds for the prekindergarteners to 1.67 and 1.38 seconds for the kindergarteners and first graders. Thus, most end-of-the-year kindergarteners seem to have these responses accurately and immediately available.

The sequence skill "counting up from 'a' " and the ability to respond immediately to an And Then relational question would seem to be closely related. If one successively produces And Then related words beginning at "a," one sounds as if one is counting up from "a," and vice versa. It is not clear whether the processes involved in these two procedures are the same, however. In the sample of 14 children for whom counting up from "a" data ("a" less than ten) were given above, data on responses to And Then questions were also gathered. Eight of the children performed better on the counting up from "a" task than on the And Then task; those performing moderately well on the And Then task counted up from "a" on all trials, and those giving only a very few correct And Then responses counted up to "a" on 60% of their trials. One of these eight children counted up from "a" in response to each And Then question about "a"; this child was the only one who responded accurately to every And Then question. Alternatively, four children did better on the And Then questions (success at a low—for one child—or at a moderate level—for three children) than on the count up from "a" task (they failed to count up on even a single trial). It is possible that this failure was a result of inadequately communicating the task to these children. However, some of them did seem to be trying to start counting up but they always finally had to begin at one. Thus, rather than these procedures developing together, it seems that children may begin to do fairly well on either one of these procedures before the other one.

These procedures also seem to be acquired in somewhat different patterns. Performance on And Then questions seems to improve continuously (scores for this sample ranged over the whole possible range), while that on "counting up from 'a' " appears at only two levels (around half the trials or on all of the trials). All of these data seem to implicate two different processes rather than a single one used for both tasks. Understanding of the processes involved in these two procedures and of the relationship between them must await more definitive research.

Backward Sequence Skills. Two new sequences appear at the breakable chain level: (a) the ability to produce a backward number word sequence beginning from an arbitrary number word (the sequence skill "counting down from 'b' ") and (b) the ability to start at and stop at arbitrary words ("counting down from 'b' to 'a' "). Each of these will be discussed in turn.

Producing Backward Sequences. Backward word sequences are sometimes learned as separate new word sequences, as in "ten, nine, eight, . . . , two, one, blast off!" However, except for the rocket example and for some nursery school songs, backward sequences are rarely required in our culture, especially above ten. They therefore seem rarely to be separately acquired but rather result from a slow and laborious production from the forward sequence. Vocalizing and subvocalizing patterns by the child subjects in the studies to be reported next indicated that many of them produced a two- to five-word forward sequence segment that included the word from which the backward sequence is to begin, then said this segment backward, and then repeated these two phases of (often subvocal) forward and overt backward chunks. Other children were not even this efficient; they always began their forward sequences from "one." This production of the backward from the forward sequence was especially evident for sequences between ten and twenty. For example, producing a backward sequence from eighteen might sound like "(silent lip movement: fourteen, fifteen, sixteen, seventeen, eighteen) eighteen, seventeen, sixteen, (lip movement: thirteen, fourteen, fifteen) fifteen, fourteen, thirteen, etc." This procedure requires the alternating use of two fairly difficult abilities: backward digit span (remembering several words and producing them in reverse order) and remembering the last word already produced in the backward sequence while finding and producing a forward segment that will end with the word just before that last word.

The ability to produce a backward sequence from twenty is relatively late to appear. More than half of a sample of 14 5-year-olds attending a heterogeneous urban school were unable to give a backward sequence beginning from a word between seven and twenty. Eleven of 32 6-year-olds were unable to produce such sequences from words between eleven and twenty, even though all of these could produce accurate forward sequences above twenty and at least one backward sequence beginning from a word below ten. The backward sequences were produced by the 6-year-olds with widely varying degrees of ease, with some children producing them smoothly and quickly and others doing so only very slowly and laboriously, with much subvocalization of forward segments. During this generation procedure by the latter children, the forward sequence was evidently so salient that occasional forward intrusions would occur within the backward sequence (e.g., "fourteen, thirteen, twelve, thirteen, eleven").

Bell and Burns (Notes 1 and 2) examined the ability of a heterogeneous sample of kindergarten and first, second, and third graders to produce backward sequences at various points from ten up to 3141. The percentage of correct performance at each testing point for each grade is given in Table 2.10. Producing a backwards sequence even from ten is a problem for a substantial number of the kindergarten sample and producing a backwards sequence from thirty remains a problem for almost two-thirds of the first graders and a third of the second graders. Performance within each of the first three grades is extremely varied, ranging over almost the entire range tested.

Bell and Burns also found a similar performance lag between backward and forward sequences for most children through third grade. In the same sample as above, they examined the production of both forward and backward sequences at seven levels: below thirty (Level 1), to thirty (Level 2), and then at certain higher key points: 68 to 72, 98 to 101, 197 to 203, 997 to 1003, and 3148 to 3151 (Levels 3-7). The range in the level differences between the forward and backward sequences of individual children was 0 (no difference) to 5 (forward sequences to 1003 and backward sequence less than thirty). The percentage of this kindergarten through third grade sample with no difference in the level of their forward and backward

Table 2.10 Percentage of Age Groups Producing Accurate Backward Sequences of Various Lengths[a]

	Not 10→1	10→1	30→20	72→62	101→91	203→193	1003 →999	3151 →3141
Kinder-garten	41	44	7	4	4	0	0	0
First grade	7	59	10	3	17	3	0	0
Second grade	3	30	15	10	13	15	0	15
Third grade	0	17	8	4	21	13	21	17

[a] These figures are computed from raw data generously made available to us by Bell and Burns. Each percentage is for children who were successful up through that length but no higher.

sequences was 38%, and the percentages with differences of one, two, three, four, and five levels between their forward and backward sequences were 20%, 18%, 16%, 8%, and 3%, respectively. These figures indicate that considerable individual differences exist in the ability to produce a backward sequence when a forward one is known. The percentage of children at each performance level whose backward sequence was at the same level as their forward sequence increased from 25% at Level 2 (in forward counting) to 50% at Level 5, indicating that producing a backward sequence once the forward one is known becomes relatively easier for children with longer sequences. The percentage with both forward and backward levels at Level 6 dropped to 14%, indicating perhaps that producing a sequence backwards over 1000 (i.e., from 1003 to 997) is particularly difficult. The percentages of children with no differences between forward and backward sequences were relatively high at Levels 1 and 7 (44% and 71%) due to floor and ceiling effects.

The types of errors the Bell and Burns children made at the decade words were of two types: they either omitted the decade word altogether (e.g., 72, 71, 69, 68, . . . , 62, 61, 59) or they began the backwards sequence within a decade with the decade word (72, 71, 60, 69, 68, 67, . . . , 62, 61, 50, 59, 58, etc.). Thus, for these children (and perhaps for all children at some developmental point) the decade word seemed to serve as the "starting signal" for the production of a decade-digit sequence; this "starting signal" was deemed necessary for a backward as well as for a forward production. Children also displayed similar difficulties with the hundreds and thousands words. The backward sequences for the most part maintained the structure within a decade (x-ty-nine, x-ty-eight, . . . , x-ty-one), however, indicating that children were using their knowledge of this forward structure to generate the backward sequences. Converging evidence on this point comes from Secada (Note 14): pauses in the hand signs made by deaf children producing backward sequences from thirty sometimes come between the production of a sign for twenty and that for the digit word accompanying that twenty (thirty, twenty-nine, twenty–pause–eight, twenty–pause–seven, twenty–pause–six, twenty," etc.). These children seem to know that each word will be a "twenty-x" word, but they need to stop and think to produce the correct digit word.

Our data indicate that children initially produce backward sequences through the use of the echoic memory technique adults report using with the alphabet: The generation of parts of the forward sequence and the production of these parts backward while the forward part is still in short-term memory. The ability to do this would seem to be dependent upon a child's processing capacity (in the sense used by Case, Kurland, & Daneman, Note 11) and on the level of the word sequence (i.e., at least at the breakable chain level). Later, as suggested by Bell and Burns, children use their ability to produce a backward digit sequence (from nine to one) and their knowledge of the structure of the forward sequence to produce backward sequences above twenty. Children's knowledge of the forward structure dictates how they will produce the backward digit sequence. Problems occur at the transitional points in the structure and reflect either inadequate knowledge of the forward structure or a representation of this structure that is inadequate to support the backward production at that point (as the auditory short-term memory supported the earlier productions). The situation with respect to the teens is not entirely clear. There was no evidence in any of our data that children were aware of or used the digit pattern present in the teens to produce a backward sequence. Rather they exhibited alternating forward-backward partial productions, indicating that the same echoic memory process used below ten was being used in the teens. Eventual facility in producing teen backward sequences rapidly may come from one of two sources: After they can produce it, children learn the backward sequence from twenty by rote (much as they do the sequence from ten) or they may later learn the digit structure in the teens (perhaps as a result of learning the symbols for those words) and then use this structure to produce the backwards sequence rapidly. An alternative with all backward sequences, of course, is that they may be acquired independently as the forward sequence is, but this seems to occur rarely except for the sequence from ten to one.

Counting down from "b" to "a." Counting down from "b" to "a" (i.e., from one arbitrary word to another) is the backward skill analogous to counting up from "a" to "b." To assess the relative difficulty of counting up from "a" to "b" and counting down from "b" to "a," both of these tasks were administered to 16 children from a university laboratory preschool. The children ranged in age from 4 years 2 months to 5 years 6 months (mean age 4 years 8 months). The order of presentation of tasks was counterbalanced, with the counting up and counting down tasks administered on separate days to reduce interference between them. Each testing session began with an explanation of the task and two practice trials. For example, the counting up task was described as follows: "To count up from two to five, you start counting at two and count up to five, like this: two, three, four, five. Start at two; stop at five." Practice trials of counting up from three to six and four to seven followed. An analogous description and practice trials were given for the counting down task. Six counting trials were then presented. Five, five, seven, eight, eleven, and thirteen were used as starting numbers for counting up; eleven, twelve, thirteen, sixteen, eighteen, and twenty were used for counting down, with "b" differing from "a" by either seven or fourteen numbers. "Twenty-one" was the largest number appearing in these trials. Consequently, only children with conventional word strings exceeding that number were used in this study. The assessment of children's conventional word strings revealed that our subjects were divided into two groups: Nine children had conventional strings of at least fifty (rote counts were stopped at fifty), while the other seven had conventional strings below thirty-nine, with most ranging from twenty-nine to thirty-four. As a result, the length of a child's conventional sequence was included as a variable in the following analyses. This allowed an examination of the relationship between the degree of acquisition of the conventional word sequence and its elaboration, as evidence by performance on the counting up and counting down task. In general, children exhibited the behaviors observed in the counting up and counting down studies described earlier, like getting a "running start" to count up from "a" by surreptitiously counting from one, determining the next number when counting down by counting forward from a lower number, and intruding forward counts while counting down (e.g., "fifteen, fourteen, thirteen, fourteen, fifteen, sixteen, . . .")

The number of correct trials per child was measured by two criteria: In strict scoring, only flawless counts were considered correct, while lenient scoring included as correct those sequences with mistakes that were spontaneously corrected (such as lapsing into counting forward while trying to count backwards). A 2 (Direction of Sequence) by 2 (Conventional Sequence Length: to 50 or below 39) by 2 (Number to be Counted Up or Down: seven or fouteen) analysis of variance was done on each of the scores (strict and lenient). As expected, counting up from "a" to "b" was clearly easier than counting down from "b" to "a." The main effect of Direction of Sequence was significant for both types of scoring: $F(1, 14) = 13.73, p < .01$ for strict scoring and $F(1, 14) = 8.06, p < .02$ for lenient scoring. The mean number of correct counting up and counting down trials was 4.25 (out of 6) and 2.58 trials, respectively, for the strict scoring, and 4.56 and 3.19 for the lenient scoring. The length of the conventional sequence produced by a child had a significant effect on performance with the lenient scores, $F(1, 14) = 7.97, p < .02$, and this effect approached significance with the strict scores, $F(1, 14) = 4.13, p < .06$. Children with sequences to fifty had lenient score means of 4.56 correct trials per task compared to a lenient score mean of 3.00 for children with shorter conventional sequences; these means for strict scores were 4.06 and 2.57, respectively. This effect of conventional sequence length indicates that children with longer conventional word sequences have elaborated the earlier parts of their word sequences more than children with shorter conventional sequences as measured by the possession of these two sequence skills. The interaction of direction of count and conventional sequence length was not significant with either type of score, indicating that the backward sequence elaboration was delayed similarly in both groups of children. The main effect of number counted up or down was significant for the strict criterion scores [$F(1, 14) = 4.63, p < .05$], but not for the lenient scores, indicating that spontaneously corrected mistakes were more likely to occur on the longer sequences than on the shorter ones. With the strict scores, 60% of the trials in which seven words were counted up or down were correct, while 50% of those requiring fourteen words counted up or down were correct.

Errors made on these tasks revealed more details about the development of word sequence skills. The most common mistakes were sequence errors (selecting an incorrect next word, usually due to omission) and forgetting the stopping point, thereby producing a correct sequence that was too long or too short. In counting up from "*a*" to "*b*," sequence mistakes were made on only 5% of the trials, while 20% of the trials contained stopping-point errors. Thus, the major difficulty in counting up from "*a*" to "*b*" was stopping the word sequence at the appropriate point, with 80% of the mistakes being of this type. On the counting-down task, 27% and 28% of the trials contained counting mistakes and stopping-point errors, respectively. The difference between tasks in the number of sequence mistakes was significant $[F(1, 14) = 8.16, p < .02]$, again indicating that backwards sequences are more difficult to produce. The difference between counting up and down in the number of stopping-point errors was not significant. However, it seemed possible that this was attributable to the smaller number of counting-down trials that were actually completed. To test this, a second analysis compared the percentage of completed trials containing stopping-point errors on each task. This analysis revealed significant main effects of both Direction of Count $[F(1, 14) = 5.29, p < .05]$, and Length of Conventional Sequence $[F(1, 14) = 5.29, p < .05]$. The mean stopping-point error rate was 20% for counting up and 39% for counting down. The children with longer and shorter conventional sequences made stopping errors on an average of 20% and 41% of their completed counts, respectively.

These results are consistent with a model of short-term memory having limited capacity (Case, Kurland, & Daneman, Note 11). According to such a model, more difficult tasks require more processing capacity, leaving less space available for retaining other information or for executing other cognitive processes. At least two sources of stopping-point errors seem possible: difficulty in remembering the stopping point and difficulty in using an adequate checking procedure for determining when this number has been reached. Both of these require space in short-term memory. Because producing a backward sequence is more difficult than producing a forward one, as indicated by the greater number of sequence errors and the number of trials not completed, producing a backward sequence requires more short-term memory capacity. More backward stopping-point errors would then be expected because less space is available for retaining the stopping number or for executing the checking procedure. Similarly, the significant effect of length of conventional sequence suggests that the sequence skills are more effortful (or take more space in memory) for children with shorter conventional sequences. Consequently, these children are more likely either to forget the stopping-point word or to fail to execute their checking procedure than are children with longer conventional sequences.

And Then Before Relations. The first step toward the production of a backward word sequence is the ability to answer And Then Before questions for a given number word, for example, given "eight" to produce "seven." Performance on And Then Before questions ("When you are counting, what number comes just before eight?") is considerably lower than that for And Then questions ("When you are counting, what number comes just after eight?") until about age 5½. For two samples of 24 children aged 3½-4½ and 4½-5½, the percentages of correct performance on these two types of questions were 13% versus 49% and 57% versus 81%, respectively. Accuracy levels for these two relations were roughly equivalent for 12 kindergarteners aged 5½-6½ (80% vs. 86%), and performance was at ceiling for 12 end-of-the-year, middle class first graders aged 6½-7½ (100% accuracy for both relations). Response times taken by a digital stop-watch for producing correct And Then Before responses were slower for all age groups than times for producing correct And Then responses (7.9 vs. 2.6 seconds, 4.3 vs. 1.7 seconds, and 2.1 vs. 1.4 seconds for the three oldest groups described above).

Use of And Then and And Then Before Relations. The And Then and And Then Before sequence relations have analogous relations on cardinal words: One Smaller Than and One Bigger Than. It was not evident whether these sequence and cardinal relations developed independently or whether one type of relation was used to construct the other. We examined this question in a study with 72 prekindergarten, kindergarten, and first grade children. At each age children were randomly assigned to cardinal or sequence conditions and given one of the following types of questions: sequence: "When you are counting, what number comes right after (comes right before) seven?" or cardinal: "What number is one bigger than (one smaller than) seven?" Subjects in both conditions were given both after and before (or bigger and smaller) questions. In all the Age by Number Word Size (below ten and between ten and twenty) cells, responses to the And Then/And Then Before sequence questions and the One Greater Than/Smaller Than cardinal questions were approximately the same, with two exceptions. For words between ten and twenty, correct responses to the sequence questions exceeded those for the cardinal questions for the prekindergarteners in the forward direction (And Then responses 78% correct and One Greater Than responses 56% correct) and for the kindergarteners in the backward direction (And Then Before 78% and One Smaller Than 50% correct). Data reported in earlier sections indicated that 4-year-olds are just becoming able to answer And Then questions for words in their sequence, and 5-year-olds are becoming able to do so quite well for And Then Before questions. These are therefore exactly the ages at which one would expect performance on cardinal questions to be lower than that on sequence questions, if children do use the latter to answer the former. That is, one would not expect children just acquiring sequence relations to use them for cardinal relational questions. However, after the And Then or the And Then Before relations have been acquired, they could be used to respond to verbal questions involving the corresponding relations in cardinal contexts. At the latter point, performance in sequence and cardinal conditions would be equivalent. This is the pattern observed in the data. Thus children seem to use these sequence relations to determine the cardinal relations.

Comes After and Comes Before Relations. In a preliminary exploration of performance on Comes After and Comes Before relational questions, 36 middle class children aged 4½-7½ were given questions such as, "In counting, which comes later, five or nine?" or "In counting, which comes earlier, five or nine?" All pairs of words were four words aparts; words "two" through "nine" and "twelve" through "nineteen" were used. The form of the questions (Comes Later Than or Comes Earlier

Than), order of the words within the word pair, and size of the pair of words (single digits or in the teens) were all counterbalanced. Mean correct response rates for both question forms and both sizes of number word pairs fell (in no particular pattern) between 61% and 72% for children aged 4½-6½ and rose for those aged 6½-7½ to 98% and 92% for single-digit and teens responses, respectively.

Three possible derivations of the Comes After and Comes Before relations seem plausible. One of these involves the use of other sequence relations, one depends on the use of analogous cardinal relations, and the third requires the use of some mental process on some representation of the sequence. These three derivations are: (1) that the Comes After (Comes Before) relation results from the application of transitivity to successive iterations of the And Then (And Then Before) sequence relation; (2) that the Comes After (Before) relation is derived from the isomorphic Greater Than (Less Than) relation defined on the cardinal number words (or vice versa); and (3) that the Comes After (Before) relation is derived from the sequence itself by some sort of direct mental process with psychophysical properties. We shall discuss each of these in turn. During this discussion, it should be kept in mind that, in fact, it is possible that either different children use different ones of these methods or that different mixtures of these methods are used, perhaps depending upon the size of number involved.

The first possible derivation of the Comes After relation is the most mathematical and perhaps the most obvious. It predicts that a child first learns And Then for words in her or his sequence and uses these successively to find Comes After relations. An example is: "5 And Then 6" and "6 And Then 7" and "7 And Then 8" and "8 And Then 9"; therefore, 5 is followed by 9 (or 9 Comes After 5). If And Then is so used to construct Comes After, the response to an And Then question should be faster than that to the derived Comes After relation. One would also expect that some children could answer And Then questions but would not be able to answer Comes After questions.

We examined this in a preliminary way by giving to 36 first graders, kindergarteners, and prekindergarteners Comes After questions for number word pairs that differed by four ("In counting, which comes later, 2 or 5?") and And Then questions for the smallest number in the Comes After pair ("In counting, which comes later, 2 or 3?"). The scores of the first graders reached ceiling. For the kindergarteners and prekindergarteners, there were no significant differences between these conditions in the error scores (all scores were between 61% and 72% correct). Response time data taken by digital stopwatch showed different patterns for number pairs above and below ten. For the former, the mean response times of correct judgments (based only on those item pairs for which both And Then and Comes After responses were correct) for And Then responses were slower than the times for Comes After responses (1.9 vs. 1.5 seconds, 2.1 vs. 1.5 seconds, and 3.5 vs. 1.4 seconds for the first grade, kindergarten, and prekindergarten groups). For the number words less than ten, neither type of pairs was consistently better across all age groups. These response time data indicate that the first proposed derivation of the Comes After relation—from the composition of contiguous And Then relations—is inaccurate. Transitive application of the And Then relation does not seem to be the process by which the Comes After relation is determined.

The second alternative for the source of the Comes After (Comes Before) sequence relations is that they are derived from the Greater Than (Less Than) cardinal relations. Fuson and Hall (in press) discussed this possibility and presented data that were not definitive with respect to the relationship between the two types of relations for words below ten but found that for words between ten and twenty, the cardinal relations seemed to be derived from the sequence relations. In their study they compared the performance of children aged 4-7 years old on questions involving the order relations on sequence and on cardinal words [the Comes After (Comes Before) and the Greater Than (Less Than) relations]. These data supported the conclusion that below the age of 6½, the order relations on cardinal (numerosity) words less than ten develop earlier than (or at least are more accurate than) those on sequence words, that a single process for deriving the order relations on sequence words is used over the whole range of sequence words from one to twenty, and that this same sequence process is used for order relations on cardinal words between ten and twenty. By age 6½ a ceiling effect is reached for all questions of this type for words below twenty. These data thus support the opposite of Alternative 2 above for number words between ten and twenty and are not definitive with respect to it for words below ten.

Some authors in the literature have, in fact, argued for the opposite of the second alternative above, that is, they have argued for derivation of the cardinal relations from the sequence relations. Parkman (1971), for example, describes a model in which sequence words are produced covertly and very quickly and are used to decide Greater Than relational questions. Some of the kindergarten subjects on some items in the Sekuler and Mierkiewicz (1977) study overtly used such a sequence production procedure: The child would count from one until she or he reached one of the number words and then said that the other word was the bigger one (Mierkiewicz, Note 15). Although we also observed the overt use of this procedure, most children gave no evidence of using it. It may be that this is a "fail-safe" procedure, used when the more usual process fails.

The third possible source of performance on Comes After relational questions is that this relation on a given pair of number words is "read off" an internal representation of the number word sequence by a process with psychophysical characteristics. Such processes are characterized by an inverse relationship between reaction time and the distance between two stimuli (reaction time increases as the distance decreases) and are assumed to occur by some sort of analog process in which items become decreasingly discriminable as they become more similar on some physical scale. There is considerable literature on the existence of these relations in adults. The linear order literature and the digit and alphabet comparison literature are particularly relevant to the Comes After (Comes Before) sequence relations. These are reviewed by Fuson and Hall (in press) with respect to their implications for understanding relationships between the order relations on sequence words (Comes After/Comes Before) and those on cardinal words (Greater Than/Less Than). In spite of the considerable amount of research on the Greater Than (Less Than) order relations on cardinal words, the process used in producing these relations is still not clear. Nor is it clear whether the Comes After (Comes Before) order relations on sequence words below ten are derived from those on cardinal words or whether the sequence order relations involve a different (though possibly similar) representation and an independent processing of this sequence representation.

The Between Relation. The adult Between relation on sequence words (e.g., "Six is between five and eight") is equivalent to the conjunction of the Comes Before and the Comes After relations. For example, "Six is between five and eight" is equivalent to "Six comes after five and six comes before eight." The Between relation is also related (somewhat more primitively) to And Then and And Then Before relations, for the proper use of either of these will give at least one word between two given words (e.g., "five And Then" will be a word between five and eight as will "And Then Before eight"). The Between relation is also related to two word sequence skills at the breakable chain level: counting up from "a" to "b" and counting down from "b" to "a." The use of either of these will generate not only some but exactly all of the words between "a" and "b." The Between relation also possesses a spatial meaning. A request for a number word between five and nine might then elicit the use of a representation of the number word sequence that has a spatial aspect, with the resulting answer "seven," the "most" between word. If the Between relation is instead initially linked to counting up or down or to the And Then/And Then Before relations, such a request might produce the words "six" or "eight." Very little empirical work has been done on any of these aspects of the Between relation.

Using the Between Relation. The Between relation on sequence words also has a counterpart relation in cardinal or numerosity contexts. The Between relation in cardinal contexts is defined by counterparts of the Comes After and Comes Before relations on sequence words: a word is between (in the cardinal sense) five and nine if it is "Bigger Than five" and "Smaller Than nine." We examined the nature of the relationship between the Between relation on sequence words and that on cardinal words. Forty-eight kindergarten and first grade children were asked to respond to cardinal or to sequence questions that gave the boundaries for the Between relation in two separate phrases. The questions asked were of the form, "Tell me two numbers that come after three and before seven when you are counting" (sequence) and "Tell me two numbers that are bigger than three and smaller than seven" (cardinal). The number word pairs given in the questions always had three words between them to provide an opportunity for different strategies of response as described above. Steffe, Spikes, and Hirstein (Note 16) used such pairs for Between questions for that reason; we adapted their between questions to our two-phrase forms. In each condition of this study half of the questions involved pairs ten and below and half used pairs between ten and twenty. These pairs were used in the same random order for all subjects. For each condition the phrases within each question were ordered so that half of the questions had the number word pairs in ascending and half in descending order (e.g., "Tell me two numbers that are smaller than nine and bigger than five"). Half of the subjects began with each order. Grade, Word Context (sequence or cardinal), and Order of First Pair were between-subjects variables and Size of Number Word was a within-subjects variable.

Preliminary analyses indicated no main effect and no interaction with Order of First Pair on the number of correct responses, so further analyses collapsed over this variable. A 2 (Grade) by 2 (Word Context) by 2 (Size of Number Word) repeated measure analysis of variance on correct responses revealed significant main effects of Grade [$F(1, 44) = 14.73, p < .001$], Word Context [$F(1, 44) = 5.01, p < .03$], and Size of Number Word [$F(1, 44) = 12.66, p < .001$], and a significant Grade by Word Context interaction [$F(1, 44) = 16.62, p < .001$]. The percentage of correct performance is given in Table 2.11. The kindergarten and first grade children performed equally well on the sequence questions (78% and 76%), but on the cardinal questions the kindergarten children did much worse than did the first graders (37% vs. 88%). In three of the four Grade by Word Context cells the children did slightly (about 10%) better on the pairs below ten than on those above ten.

The two responses to each question were classified according to their location within the word sequence with respect to the given word pair (examples will be given for the pair "five and nine"). Three major types of response patterns depending upon the sequence were identified. The first type consisted of a two-part strategy in which a single response was given to each of the two questions asked. These responses used the And Then relation on the smaller number and the And Then Before relation on the larger number. The classification of the responses in the Cardinal condition as And Then and And Then Before responses was based on the earlier reported evidence of children's performance in sequence and cardinal conditions. Supporting evidence that this strategy in fact did consist of answering each of two questions separately was that many children paused between their two responses and some also then asked for a verification of one of the questions ("Was that 'after five'?") or subvocalized the question to themselves (e.g., lip movement for "comes after five" and then vocalization of "six"). The other two strategies used on the between questions required the integration of the two responses together into the sequence. The first consisted of simple count up or count down strategies (responses were "six, seven" or "eight, seven"). In the second, the first word given was the "middle" spatial response discussed earlier (giving the word exactly in between the question pair); then the next word up or down from that middle word was given (responses were "seven, eight" or "seven, six"). Note that both of these sequence types had both forward and backward counterparts. Over all the condi-

Table 2.11 Percentage of Correct Responses to Two-Phase "Between" Questions

	Kindergarten		First grade	
	Single digits	Teens	Single digits	Teens
Sequence condition	85	70	76	76
Cardinal condition	42	32	93	83

tions and over all subjects, the responses of these two types going up outnumbered the down responses by a ratio of five to one.

Table 2.12 contains the percentage of uses of these strategies by age and by number word question asked. There is very little difference in the strategies used by the two age levels in the sequence conditions (i.e., with the Comes After and Comes Before questions) but considerable difference between the two age levels in the strategies used in the cardinal condition (with the Bigger Than and Smaller Than questions). More first grade than kindergarten children used or tried to use the two-part strategy in the cardinal condition (59% vs. 27%) and a higher proportion of those who used it were able to use it successfully (75% vs. 23%). Earlier findings had indicated that kindergarten children could successfully use the And Then sequence relation in a cardinal context but that they were experiencing difficulty in using the And Then Before relations. The correct two-part responses given by the kindergarten children were consistent with this earlier finding: 70% were words immediately following the given word (And Then responses) and only 30% were And Then Before responses. By the first grade, correct And Then and And Then Before responses were evenly balanced (49% and 51%). In addition to this difference in the use of the two-part strategy, the kindergarten children seemed to have particular difficulty with the directionality of the words in the cardinal conditions; many of their incorrect two-part strategy responses were in the wrong direction (e.g., smaller than rather than larger than the word). They did not show the same directional difficulty in the sequence condition. There was also a considerable difference between the sequence and the cardinal condition in the kindergarteners' percentage of errors that were close errors (within two words of the given number word pair): 69% of the errors in the sequence condition were of these close errors while only 43% of the errors in the cardinal condition were close. A final difference between the two age groups was that the first grade children were also somewhat more advanced than the kindergarten children in their use of the integrated sequence strategies in the cardinal condition (38% vs. 17%).

The order in which the number word pair was presented in the very first question seemed to influence the answer strategy used over all the questions by the first

Table 2.12 Percentage of Strategy Use by Grade and Question Type on Two-Phrase "Between" Questions

| | Two-part strategy | | | Integrated sequence strategies | | | |
	Both correct	One correct	Total	Count up/ down two words	Middle and then up/ down	Total	Other
Sequence							
Kinderg.	28	17	45	36	6	43	13
First	28	20	48	26	13	39	14
Cardinal							
Kinderg.	6	21	27	10	7	17	55
First	44	15	59	23	15	38	4

graders. In the sequence condition, if the words were given in their sequence order (e.g., "Give two words that come after five and come before nine"), children were more likely to use the integrated sequence strategies than the two-part strategy (25 vs. 4 occurrences). If the words were given in reverse sequence order (e.g., "Give two words that come before nine and come after five"), the two-part strategy was more likely to be used than an integrated sequence strategy (23 vs. 12 occurrences). In the cardinal conditions, the children responded to the order in which they heard the number pair in the opposite way, presumably because they responded first to the last number word they heard. If the words were given in nonsequence order, they would respond to the last question first (by giving the word that was bigger than five: "six") and then would continue with the word following six ("seven"), that is, they used an integrated sequence strategy rather than the two-part strategy by 28 to 9 occurrences. If the words were given in their sequence order, a number smaller than nine would first be given and then a response to the second part of the question (bigger than five) would be given; that is, the two-part responses outnumbered the integrated sequence responses 33 to 8. This finding would seem to indicate that children, in fact, possess both the integrated sequence and the two-part strategies, and they employ the one that seems best to fit their initial view of a task. Task variables seem to present particularly tricky problems here, and such variables may be responsible for underestimating the extent to which children have in fact coordinated sequence and cardinal meanings and can use one type of meaning to respond to a question in the opposite context.

This study, of course, was only a very preliminary step toward understanding the development of the sequence and the cardinal Between relations. Studies which compare the two-part terminology used here with the use of the word "between" obviously need to be done. The end of the year kindergarteners in the present study seemed to have much greater difficulty with the cardinal Greater Than/Less Than questions than with the sequence Comes After/Comes Before questions. These cardinal difficulties may have been exacerbated by the juxtaposition of two Greater Than/Less Than questions in the opposite direction when no concept of "between" was present to impose constraints on these directions. The sequence relations may have been simpler because the sequence itself may have imposed some sense of "betweeness" on the two relational statements.

Use of Counting Up and Down Skills in Addition and Subtraction. At the breakable chain level the ability to count up from "a" to "b" may be used in addition situations such as "8 + ? = 13." Such users will begin counting up at eight and will stop at thirteen. However, children at this level fail to keep track of how many words they have counted up, and so they cannot give any accurate answer at the end of this procedure. Steffe, Richards, and von Glasersfeld (Notes 7 and 17) reported such failures by some children. Such performances occurred in the studies that we report in the next section. The breakable chain level also seems to occur in other cultures. New Guinea Oksapmin children and adults unfamiliar with economic transactions also use counting up from "a" to "b" without keeping track on their body parts counting system (see Saxe, Chapter 5 of this volume). They say and point to the body parts from "*a*" to "*b*" (e.g., from elbow to ear), but fail to count or match these parts with any other set, and so they also fail to produce any answer. What is required for all of these problems in any culture is that the words of the sequence be taken as units that represent the missing addend and that some means of assessing the numerosity of these units be used. Both of these occur at the next level, the numerable chain level.

Numerable Chain Level

Forward and Backward Sequence Skills. At the numerable chain level, the number words in the sequence can be taken as distinct units, and the numerosity of word segments (words contiguous in the sequence: seven, eight, nine, ten, eleven, twelve) can be ascertained. At this level, the number words are not just produced— they can also be counted or matched to a set of items of known numerosity (e.g., five fingers). Two new forward sequence skills exist at this level: "count up a specified number '*n*' from '*a*' " and "count up from '*a*' to '*b*' to find the number of words from '*a*' to '*b*.' " Parallel skills for the backward sequence become evident some time later: "count down '*n*' from '*b*' " and "count down from '*b*' to '*a*' to find the number of words from '*b*' to '*a*.' "

Counting up from "*a*" to "*b*" and counting down from "*b*" to "*a*" while keeping track of how many words are counted up or down require one to remember the word to which one is counting up (or down) while keeping track in some way of the number of words being produced. Counting up or down by "*n*" requires one to remember the number of words that one is counting up or down while also keeping track of the number of words that one has already produced. Both types of skills require both the memory of a number while one is counting up or down and some method of keeping track of how many one is counting up or down. We have done research on three of the four sequence skills and on keeping-track methods. The first study compared performance on counting up and down by "*n*" and the second compared the two counting-up skills using larger second numbers than were used in the first study. Each of these studies and the work on keeping-track methods will be discussed in turn.

Our own research and the research of Steffe, Richards, and von Glaserfeld (Note 17) has indicated a considerable delay between the ability to count up or down with small numbers (one, two, three, and perhaps four) and with larger numbers. Counting up or down two or three seems able to be done with methods that are used relatively early and do not generalize to larger numbers. For a particular chain to be at the numerable chain level, we therefore require performances on one of the word sequence skills with "*a*" and "*b*" differing by five or more.

Counting Up or Down by "*n*". We investigated the approximate age of acquisition of the skills of counting up and counting back by "*n*" and also explored the effects on this skill of the size of "*n*" and of the word being counted from. Initial piloting in an urban school with a heterogeneous population indicated that many 5-year-olds had considerable trouble counting up with second addends of five or more, and some of them could not even produce a backward counting sequence. Therefore, a sample of 32 randomly selected 6-year-olds (half aged 6 years to 6 years 5 months and half, 6 years 6 months to 6 years 11 months) from this school was given matched counting up and counting down problems. Three sizes of number words counted up or down were used (two, five, and eight), and three starting points in the word sequence were employed (three, seven, and fourteen). Instructions of the form, "Start counting with 'a' and count up (or back) 'n' more numbers," were provided, and repeated demonstrations were given if necessasy. Experimenters recorded any "keeping-track" behavior exhibited, and after the final problem they asked children who had displayed no observable strategies how they had known when to stop counting. The order of the counting-up/counting-down sets of problems was counterbalanced. Sex was balanced within each age by order cell. Two scoring systems were used to evaluate the responses. The strict system gave a point only for a correct answer; this system thus identified problems for which a correct keeping-track method had been selected and been used properly. The lenient scoring system gave credit for any answer that was within one number of being correct.

Most of the children could do some, but not all, of the problems. Four children performed perfectly on the counting up tasks, while none did perfectly on the counting down tasks (although one child overcounted by one on one problem and had the rest correct). Only two of the 32 subjects could not do any of the counting up tasks correctly, while five did not get any of the counting down problems correct. A 2 (Age: young sixes and old sixes) by 2 (Direction: counting up and counting down) by 3 (Size of number word counted up or down: two, five, and eight) analysis of variance was done on the strict and on the lenient criterion scores. For the strict criterion scores, the main effects of Direction $[F(1, 30) = 14.73, p < .01]$ and Size $[F(2, 60) = 42.74, p < .01]$ were significant. None of the interactions nor the main effect of Age attained significance. Counting up was significantly easier than counting down; performance was 51% correct for counting up and 33% correct for counting down. Many children were still having difficulty producing a backward word sequence, and some still had to produce it piece by piece from the forward sequence. With respect to the size of number counted up or down, children did much better when they had to count up or count down two than when they had to count up or count down five or eight, and they did somewhat better for five than for eight. A Newman-Keuls test on the means for each size indicated that each of these size differences was significant. The percentages of correct responses for counting up two, five, and eight were 79%, 45%, and 30%, respectively, and for counting down by these amounts were 68%, 18%, and 13%, respectively.

The strict criterion scores assessed correct procedures correctly carried out. The lenient criterion scores (correct score +1 or -1) gave credit to children who were using a basically correct procedure but who made some minor error. A 2 (Age) by 2 (Direction) by 3 (Size) analysis of variance on the lenient criterion scores revealed several more subtle effects. As with the strict criterion scores, the main effects of Direction $[F(1, 30) = 21.57, p < .001]$ and Size $[F(2, 60) = 28.57, p < .001]$ were significant. Counting up was still significantly easier than counting down (74% vs. 52% correct). A Newman-Keuls test on the means for each size of number word counted up or down indicated that the difference between counting up or down by two and by five and the difference between counting up or down five and eight were each significant. A significant Size by Direction interaction [$F(2, 60) = 6.83$, $p < .005$] indicated that the difference in performance between counting up and counting down was very small for two (80% vs. 74%), but was larger for five (83% vs. 47%) and for eight (59% vs. 34%). A significant Size by Age interaction [$F(2, 60)$ $= 6.83, p < .005$] indicated that the difference in performance between counting up and counting down was very small for two (80% vs. 74%), but was larger for five (83% vs. 47%) and for eight (59% vs. 34%). A significant Size by Age interaction [$F(2, 60) = 5.18, p < .01$] indicated that the difference in the performance of younger (6-6½) versus older (6½-7) children on the problems involving counting up or down eight was much greater than was the age difference for counting up or down five or two (35% vs. 57% correct for eight, 63% vs. 68% for five, and 79% vs. 75% for two). A Direction by Age interaction that approached significance [$F(1, 30) = 3.03, p < .10$] revealed a tendency for the younger children to perform the same as the older children on counting up (74% correct vs. 74%) but to do much more poorly on counting down (44% vs. 60% correct). These results on this narrow age range (6-6½ vs. 6½-7) seem to indicate that the ability to count down develops fairly rapidly from early to late in the seventh year and that the young 6-year-olds are working on, but have not yet mastered, ways to keep accurate track of the number words. The findings of significant Direction and Size of Number Word effects with both criterion scores emphasizes the relative difficulty of counting down as compared with counting up and of keeping track of eight versus five versus two number words counted up or down.

There seemed to be no difference in the accuracy of counting up or counting down as a function of the magnitude of the first number word (three, seven, or fourteen). By age 6, these children seemed to be about equally proficient at counting up from fourteen as from three. However, this result may be partially a result of a lack of complete counterbalancing of these items; the larger number words tended to come somewhat later, and so a practice effect may have been operating. In addition, only the number of errors and not the speed of response was recorded. Different measures might have indicated differences due to location in the number word sequence. The effect of the place in the number word sequence where the counting up/counting down occurs needs further study.

Forward Sequence Skills. Twenty first graders attending a school whose population was computer selected to reflect the racial and economic composition of the city of Chicago participated in this end-of-the-year study. Because the difference between "a" and "b" was larger than in the previous study, young 7-year-olds were selected for the sample (age range 7 years 1 month to 7 years 5 months, mean 7 years, 3.4 months). The "count up 'n' from 'a' " questions were of the same form as the last study: "Start counting with 'a' and count up 'n' more number words." The question employed for the number of words from "a" to "b" skill was of the form, "Count up from 'a' to 'b' and tell me how many number words you counted up." The difference between "a" and "b" was either medium (six and seven) or large (thirteen and fourteen), and "*a*" ranged from two to twelve ("*b*" was always less than twenty). The questions for each skill were blocked, and the order in which the blocks were given was counterbalanced. As in the earlier counting up "*n*" study, some children (in this study, about half) counted the starting word as one of the "*n*" words and thus produced an answer one word before (one less than) the correct answer. This occurred even more frequently for the "count up from '*a*' to '*b*' " questions (in 70% of the sample) and was probably exacerbated by the form of the question used here. In future studies a question form more directly parallel to the other question should be tried (i.e., one that begins, "Start counting with '*a*' ''). Overall, performance on these two skills was roughly the same. If both exact answers and those subject to the "one less than" error noted above are pooled and if responses obtained by the use of number facts are also included, 73% of the "Count up from '*a*' to '*b*' " medium responses were correct, and 65% of those for the "Count up '*n*' from '*a*' " were correct. Number facts were only used in response to the latter questions—7% of the time. Performance for the large numbers "*n*" (thirteen, fourteen) was much poorer, 15% and 20%, respectively. This difference resulted chiefly from the fact that most subjects used their fingers to keep track of the number of words they were producing, and they could not figure out how to use their fingers for numbers which exceeded their own ten fingers. Though overall performance for these two skills was generally at about the same level, for individual children it was not always so. Five of the subjects performed better on the "Count up from '*a*' to '*b*' " tasks than on the "Count up '*n*' from '*a*' " task, and eight performed better on the latter than on the former. Seven children performed equally well on both tasks, but three of these reflected ceiling effects and one, a floor effect. This finding of individual children showing superiority in one or the other of these skills should be explored in the future with tasks that have small differences between "*a*" and "*b*" (as well as larger ones) to ensure that subjects understand each type of task.

Procedures for Keeping Track of *n*. All of the skills at this level require that one keep track of the number of words uttered in a given counting up or counting down production. Fuson (in press) developed a classification of the keeping-track methods observed both with word sequences and addition situations in her studies and those of others (e.g., Carpenter, Hiebert, & Moser, 1981; Carpenter & Moser, in press; Moser, Note 12; Steffe, Spikes, & Hirstein, Note 16; Steffe, Richards & von Glaserfeld, Note 17). This classification appears in Fuson (in press) and is presented in Table 2.13. The first type of keeping track of the second addend (counting entities) is used in addition situations and requires only a word sequence at the breakable chain level. Objects, not words, are used for each addend, and it is objects that are counted. In the last two major types of keeping track methods ("matching the count" and "counting the count"), the word sequence must be at the numerable chain level, for words now form the addends which are matched with other types of countable units (e.g., fingers or "beats" in an auditory pattern) or are counted to assess the numerosity of the second addend.

The use of these various keeping-track methods has not been studied very systematically. The "counting real entities" method is the first one to develop; it

Table 2.13 Keeping-Track Methods

Example: 8 + 5 = 13

COUNTING ENTITIES

Real

"E* N TN EL TV TH"

Represented

"E N TN EL

TV TH"

MATCHING THE COUNT

Match count to estimate

"E N TN EL TV"

Match count to fingers

"E N TN EL TV TH"

Match count to auditory pattern

"E N-TN-EL TV-TH"

COUNTING THE COUNT

Auditory count of fingers
(Chisenbop)

"Eight" "One" "Two"

(X means that finger is pressed
down on the table)

"Three" "Four" "Five"

Fingers say thirteen.

1 2 3 4 5 6 7 8 9 10 11 12 13

Auditory count of visual-
symbolic (number line)

"ONE | THREE | FIVE"

TWO FOUR

Auditory count of auditory
(double counting)

"EIGHT. NINE IS ONE, TEN IS TWO, ELEVEN IS
THREE, TWELVE IS FOUR, THIRTEEN IS FIVE."

Visual count of visual
(slide rule)

0 1 2 3 4 5 6 7 8 9 10 11 12 13 14 15 16 17

0 1 2 3 4 5 6 7 8 9

8 + 5 = 13

* Abbreviations represent auditory counting words:

E N TN EL TV TH
(8, 9, 10, 11, 12, 13)

may involve the use of real entities already present or the use of readily available entities such as fingers. After that, for "n" four or greater, some children seem to use the "counting represented entities" (counting a mental representation of entities which may or may not be in a figural pattern), while others use the "match count to estimate" method, the "match count to fingers" method (successively producing a finger with each word until a given number of fingers has been produced), or the "match count to auditory pattern" method (producing words in a rhythmic pattern). Three of these are fairly accurate, but the "match count to estimate" method is not. It entails no visible means of keeping track and seems to consist of the production of additional words until "about enough" of these have been produced. It thus is probably only a breakable chain level production: a child may simply be counting up some approximate number of words with no well-defined notion of each word as a separate unit. The "match count to auditory" pattern is the method that was seemingly used by most children for $n = 2$ in our counting-up/counting-down study; the sound of the next two words seemed to be sufficient to stop further production. All of the "counting the count" methods need to be learned in school, with the possible exception of the "auditory count of auditory words," which has been observed by all of the above researchers in a few children when there was no evidence that this method had been taught in school. For more details concerning these methods, see Fuson (in press).

Uses of Sequence Skills in Addition and Subtraction. The word sequence skills at the numerable chain level permit tremendous advances to be made in the solution procedures available for addition and subtraction problems (see Table 2.8). A child can now solve problems like "8 + 6 = ?" by counting up six words from "eight," problems like "8 + ? = 14" by counting up from eight to fourteen or by counting down from fourteen to eight while keeping track of how many words have been produced, problems like "14 - 6 = ?" by counting up from six to fourteen or counting down from fourteen to six while keeping track, problems like "? + 6 = 14" by trial-and-error counting up six from arbitrary numbers or by counting down six from fourteen while keeping track. Some first and many second grade children have been observed to use all of these word sequence solution procedures (Carpenter, Hiebert, & Moser, 1981; Carpenter & Moser, in press; Houlihan & Ginsburg, 1981; Moser, Note 12; Secada, Note 18; Steffe, Richards, & von Glaserfeld, Note 17), with the particular solution procedure used dependent upon the sizes of the numbers involved and, for verbal story problem versions, upon the situation portrayed in the story. These solution procedures all involve beginning the counting up or down with one of the addends rather than with one. They are called "counting on" and "counting back." For discussions of the additional concepts involved in these procedures see Fuson (in press), Steffe, Thompson, and Richards (in press), Briars and Larkin (Note 19), Davydov and Andronov (Note 20), and Steffe, Richards, and von Glaserfeld (Note 17).

The discrepancy between the ability to count up with small and with large numbers has its counterpart in the use of counting up in addition situations. When the second addend is one or two and objects clearly portray a counting-up addition situation (i.e., the number of objects is known and then one object is added), even some 3-year-olds can use counting up one word to find the total number of objects. In the word sequence acquisition studies reported in the earlier sections, children ascertained the number of blocks in a row and then one or two more blocks were added to the end of the row. When only one block was added, on at least one trial 3 out of 12 3-year-olds uttered the word that had been the number of the row of blocks on the last trial and then its immediate successor. They said, for example, "Eleven, twelve. There are twelve blocks now." Six out of 12 5-year-olds, for at least 60% of their trials, counted on from their previous response when one or two blocks were added, and two more 5-year-olds counted on for at least 40% of their trials. Five months later 6 of those 12 children counted on for at least 90% of their trials and four more did so for at least 60% of their trials. However, when "n" is five or greater, we have seen that most 5-year-olds and many 6-year-olds do not even possess the numerable chain level word sequence skills, let alone being able to apply them in addition and subtraction situations.

More Complex Sequence Skills. Counting up or down can be done by tens and by ones. These more advanced counting up and counting down skills permit the solution of two-place addition and subtraction problems. For example, 54 + 37 could be solved by counting up from 54 three more tens and then seven more ones: "Fifty-four. Sixty-four, seventy-four, eighty-four. Eighty-five, eighty-six, eighty-seven, eighty-eight, eighty-nine, ninety, ninety-one." Or this problem could be solved by counting up three decades from fifty and then counting up the ones: "Fifty. Sixty, seventy, eighty. Eighty-seven, eighty-eight, eighty-nine, ninety, ninety-one." The extent to which such counting up or down could be used to measure or to facilitate understanding of our base ten system of numeration or of the usual addition and subtraction computational procedures might be examined in future research.

Counting up or down repeatedly by the same number (e.g., counting up by eight: "Eight, sixteen, twenty-four, thirty-two, forty, forty-eight, fifty-six, sixty-four, seventy-two") will yield the multiplication or division sequence (the "facts") for that number. Such sequences might be used in at least four ways. First, they might be studied for patterns which could facilitate the remembering of facts. Second, the lists for the larger numbers (say, six through nine) could be memorized as a first step in remembering the multiplication facts; the various lists would serve to organize all of the separate multiplication facts. Then factors that went with each product would need to be learned. Something like this happens now with the fives: The list "five, ten, fifteen, twenty, . . ." serves to circumscribe the "fives facts" and then one needs only to sort out a few particulars. Third, learning that one could generate multiplication and division answers by such counting up and counting down might add to a child's understanding of multiplication and division. Fourth, such generation procedures might be used in more limited ways—in the production of one fact from another. For example, 3 X 6 might be found from 2 X 6 by counting up six from twelve. Houlihan and Ginsburg (1981) reported the use of such counting up from known facts by second graders in addition and subtraction problems.

Bidirectional Chain Level

The sequences below the numerable chain level are all strongly unidirectional. Each word is a vector—an entity with direction. The forward or backward recitation context in which each sequence is produced strongly influences the production. We have seen this directional influence earlier in forward intrusions when backward sequences are beginning to be produced. In our studies we have also observed backward intrusions in forward tasks when the forward tasks followed a backward condition. That is, a child seems to set a particular recitation context and then has some difficulty shifting out of it. A sequence at the bidirectional chain level possesses two attributes that distinguish it from other levels: (a) strongly automatized forward and backward sequences that contain no directional intrusions, and (b) the ability to change directions rapidly and flexibly. At the moment the developmental relationship between the bidirectional chain and the numerable chain is not known. The bidirectional chain level may develop independently of the numerable chain level, or it may follow the latter. If these levels develop independently, some children will be at the bidirectional level without being at the numerable level and vice versa.

Steffe, Richards, and von Glaserfeld (Note 17) discussed two uses of bidirectional word sequences: bidirectional counting and reversible counting. In bidirectional counting a child can indicate the counting number of a particular object in a row by counting backwards from a given counting word. For Steffe and co-workers, this bidirectional counting indicates that a child has connected the forward and backward counting actions and knows that they will result in the same counting word for that object. In reversible counting, a child makes a conceptual abstraction and can use backward counting from a known number in a row of objects to determine the numerosity of a group of those objects hidden under a cloth.

The bidirectional level ability to change word production direction rapidly and flexibly enables a child to select the most efficient direction to use to solve a particular problem. It also can lead to an understanding of the inverse relationship between addition and subtraction through either one of two routes: through relating forward and backward counting of the same set of objects or through relating counting up and counting down sequence skills. With respect to the former, children as young as 3 and 4 evidently understand in an intuitive way that "putting together" and "taking away" are inverse operations in the sense that, if the number of objects in a set has been altered, a child will, by "taking away" or "putting together," attempt to recover the original set (Brush, 1978; Gelman & Gallistel, 1978; Starkey & Gelman, in press; Blevins, Mace, Cooper, & Leitner, Note 21). However, these operations are not quantified at this point; children will do the correct replacement operation but will not use the correct amount. A bidirectional chain used in counting objects would seem to be one way to lead to such quantification of the inverse operation. The relating of the forward and backward counting up/counting back sequence skills in order to understand the inverse nature of the addition and subtraction operations may occur in several situations: in verbal problems, in object situations, and in symbolic situations (e.g., $8 + 5 = 13$ is related to $13 - 5 = 8$ and to $13 - 8 = 5$), and thus these may differ considerably. Most present models of addition and subtraction problem solving place understanding of this inverse relationship at the highest level (Riley, Greeno & Heller, in press; Briars & Larkin, Note 19; Nesher, Note 22; Steffe, Richards, & von Glaserfeld, Note 17). Future research may uncover ways in which the number word sequence at the bidirectional level contributes to the understanding of this inverse relationship.

Conclusion

The sequence of counting words is one of the most important tools of early mathematics learning. Its acquisition is a structured process, with children showing consistent individual patterns before the full conventional sequence is learned. After acquiring initial segments of the conventional number word sequence, there is a period of elaboration during which various sequence skills are acquired and relations between words in the sequence are established. The sequence is first used as a problem-solving tool in the act of counting objects and then later the counting words themselves become the objects that are counted. This elaborated, flexible, and easily produced sequence can then become a representational tool that is used in sophisticated counting procedures. In this chapter we have provided an outline of the acquisition and elaboration of the number word sequence. Further work is required for fuller and more detailed understanding of many parts of this developmental learning process.

Our preliminary efforts at examining sequence number words have consisted largely of isolated studies of certain aspects of these changes. Such intensive and isolated efforts are needed in the future, but they need to be complemented by research that involves performance by the same child across many tasks and across longer periods of time. The developmental sequence proposed in this paper is a description of levels, of static states. To date there has been little focus upon the processes by which a child moves from level to level. It is hoped that future work will be able to move from attempting to verify performance at certain levels to explicating the transitions between levels. We also wish to reiterate our caveat at the beginning of the paper about our use of the word "levels." These levels surely are "messier" than Table 2.8 implies. However, they do seem to be useful conceptual distinctions which can facilitate our consideration of changes in children's acquisition and elaboration of the sequence of number words.

References Notes

1. Bell, M., & Burns, J. Personal communication, May, 1981.
2. Bell, M., & Burns, J. *Counting, numeration, and arithmetic capabilities of primary school children.* Proposal submitted to National Science Foundation, April, 1981.

3. Fuson, K. C., & Mierkiewicz, D. *A detailed analysis of the act of counting.* Paper presented at the Annual Meeting of the American Educational Research Association, Boston, April, 1980.

4. Fuson, K. C., & Richards, J. *Children's construction of the counting numbers: From a spew to a bidirectional chain.* Unpublished manuscript, Northwestern University, 1979, and paper presented at the Annual Meeting of the American Educational Research Association, Boston, April, 1980.

5. Greeno, J. G., Riley, M. S., & Gelman, R. *Young children's counting and understanding of principles.* Unpublished manuscript.

6. Gelman, R. Personal communication, March, 1979.

7. Steffe, L. P., Richards, J., & von Glasersfeld, E. *Children's counting types.* Unpublished manuscript, University of Georgia, 1980.

8. Nesher, P. Personal communication, February, 1980, April, 1981.

9. Klahr, D., & Chase, W. G. *Developmental changes in latency patterns for access to the alphabet.* Paper presented at the Annual Meeting of the Psychonomic Society. San Antonio, November, 1978.

10. Brainerd, C. J. *Working-memory analyses of children's mental arithmetic.* Paper presented at the Biennial Meeting of the Society for Research in Child Development, Boston, April, 1981.

11. Case, R., Kurland, M., & Daneman, M. *Operational efficiency and the growth of M-space.* Paper presented at the Biennial Meeting of the Society for Research in Child Development, San Francisco, March, 1979.

12. Moser, J. *A longitudinal study of the effect of number size and presence of manipulative materials on children's processes in solving addition and subtraction verbal problems.* Paper presented at the Annual Meeting of the American Educational Research Association, Boston, April, 1980.

13. Secada, W., Fuson, K. C., & Hall, J. W. *The development of counting-on from counting-all in cardinal addition.* In progress.

14. Secada, W. Personal communication, January, 1981.

15. Mierkiewicz (Briars), D. J., personal communication, July, 1978.

16. Steffe, L. P., Spikes, W. C., & Hirstein, J. J. *Summary of quantitive comparisons and class inclusion as readiness variables for learning first grade arithmetical content.* Working Paper 1, University of Georgia, Center for Research in the Learning and Teaching of Mathematics, 1976.

17. Steffe, L., Richards, J., & von Glasersfeld, E. *Children's counting types: Philosophy, theory, & case studies.* Monograph presented at the Interdisciplinary Conference on Counting Types. Athens, Georgia, April, 1981.

18. Secada, W. *Counting solution procedures spontaneously employed on an addition task.* Unpublished manuscript, Northwestern University, 1980.

19. Briars, D., & Larkin, J. *An integrated model of skill in solving elementary word problems.* Paper presented at the Biennial Meeting of the Society for Research in Child Development, Boston, April, 1981.

20. Davydov, V. V., & Andronov, V. P. *Psychological conditions of the origination of ideal actions* (English translation). Madison, WI: (Project Paper 81-2) Madison, Wisconsin: Wisconsin Research and Development Center for Individualized Schooling, The University of Wisconsin, 1981.

21. Blevins, B., Mace, P. G., Cooper, R. G., & Leitner, E. *What do children know about addition and subtraction?* Paper presented at the Biennial Meeting of the Society for Research in Child Development, Boston, April, 1981.

22. Nesher, P. *An analysis and review of addition and subtraction verbal problems*. Paper given at the Research Presession to the Annual Meeting of the National Council of Teachers of Mathematics, St. Louis, April, 1981.

References

Bewley, W. L. The functional stimulus in serial learning. In R. F. Thompson & J. F. Voss (Eds.), *Topics in learning and performance*. New York: Academic Press, 1972.

Brush, L. Preschool children's knowledge of addition and subtraction. *Journal for Research in Mathematics Education*, 1978, *9*(1), 44-54.

Carpenter, T., Hiebert, J., & Moser, F. The effect of problem structure on first grader's initial solution procedures for simple addition and subtraction problems. *Journal for Research in Mathematics Education*, 1981, *12*, 27-39.

Carpenter, T., & Moser, J. The development of addition and subtraction problem solving skills. In T. Romberg, T. Carpenter, & J. Moser (Eds.), *Addition and subtraction: A developmental perspective*. Hillsdale, New Jersey: Erlbaum Assoc., in press.

Fuson, K. C. An analysis of the counting-on solution procedure in addition. In T. Romberg, T. Carpenter, & J. Moser (Eds.), *Addition and subtraction: A developmental perspective*. Hillsdale, New Jersey: Erlbaum Assoc., in press.

Fuson, K. C., & Hall, J. W. The acquisition of early number word meanings. In H. Ginsburg (Ed.), *The development of children's mathematical thinking*. New York: Academic Press, in press.

Gelman, R., & Gallistel, C. R. *The child's understanding of number*. Cambridge, Massachusetts: Harvard University Press, 1978.

Groen, G. J., & Resnick, L. B. Can preschool children invent addition algorithms? *Journal of Educational Psychology*, 1977, *69*(6), 645-652.

Hamilton, J. M. E., & Sanford, A. J. The symbolic distance effect for alphabetic order judgements: A subjective report and reaction time analysis. *Quarterly Journal of Experimental Psychology*, 1978, *30*, 33-43.

Harcum, E. R. *Serial learning and paralearning*. New York: Wiley, 1975.

Hovancik, J. R. Reaction times for naming the first next and second next letters of the alphabet. *American Journal of Psychology*, 1975, *88*(4), 643-647.

Houlihan, D. M., & Ginsburg, H. P. The addition methods of first- and second-grade children. *Journal for Research in Mathematics Education*, 1981, *2*, 95-106.

Lovelace, E. A., Powell, C. M., & Brooks, R. J. Alphabetic position effects in covert and overt alphabetic recitation times. *Journal of Experimental Psychology*, 1973, *99*(3), 405-408.

Lovelace, E. A., & Spence, W. A. Reaction times for naming successive letters of the alphabet. *Journal of Experimental Psychology*, 1972, *94*, 231-233.

Parkman, J. M. Temporal aspects of digit and letter inequality judgments. *Journal of Experimental Psychology*, 1971, *91*, 191-205.

Riley, M., Greeno, J., & Heller, J. Development of children's problem-solving ability in arithmetic. In H. Ginsburg (Ed.), *The development of children's mathematical thinking*. New York: Academic Press, in press.

Schaeffer, B., Eggleston, V. H., & Scott, J. L. Number development in young children. *Cognitive Psychology*, 1974, *6*, 357-379.

Sekuler, R., & Mierkiewicz, D. Children's judgments of numerical inequality. *Child Development*, 1977, *48*, 630-633.

Siegler, R. S., & Robinson, M. The development of numerical understandings. In H. W. Reese & L. P. Lipsitt (Eds.), *Advances in child development and behavior* (Vol. 16). New York: Academic Press, in press.

Slobin, D. I. *Psycholinguistics*. Glenview, Illinois: Scott, Foresman, 1976.

Starkey, P., & Gelman, R. Addition and subtraction algorithms in preschool children. In T. Romberg, T. Carpenter, & J. Moser (Eds.), *Addition and subtraction: A developmental perspective*. Hillsdale, New Jersey: Erlbaum Assoc., in press.

Steffe, L., Thompson, P., & Richards, J. Children's counting and arithmetical problem solving. In T. Romberg, T. Carpenter, & J. Moser (Eds.), *Addition and subtraction: A developmental perspective*. Hillsdale, New Jersey: Erlbaum Assoc., in press.

3. Children's Concepts of Chance and Probability

Harry W. Hoemann and Bruce M. Ross

Interest in children's concepts of chance and probability has been prompted by several questions. Assuming that the development of a concept of chance and probability is influenced by experience, what are the conditions that bring it about? What are its precursors? Is it acquired all at once, or is it acquired gradually over a relatively long period of time? At what age is its development complete? Does every mature adult have a similarly functioning concept of chance, or are there individual differences? If so, how are they to be explained? To what extent is a concept of chance a result of formal instruction in school? What kinds of training are likely to improve upon immature or deficient concepts of chance or probability? When making probability judgments, is there one optimum strategy that can be said to be correct in each type of situation, or is there a variety of strategies more or less adequate or appropriate? To what extent is performance in a probability setting controlled by the reinforcing consequences of previous outcomes? What is the relationship between chance and probability concepts, on the one hand, and the development of linguistic ability to articulate them, on the other? In what ways are various probability tasks alike, and how do they differ? What makes some tasks seem harder than others? What is the relationship between the development of concepts of chance or probability and cognitive development in general?

These do not seem to be trivial questions. Indeed, many of them have been addressed in published research reports and monographs. The purpose of this chapter is to review procedures that have been devised to investigate some of these questions and to evaluate the conclusions that have tentatively been drawn. We

Special support for writing this chapter was furnished by the Boys Town Center for Youth Research, Catholic University of America, Washington, D.C. 20064.

hope that this survey of empirical studies and their accompanying theorizing may help to establish probability concept development as an important and intriguing topic for psychological research.

Piagetian Theory

Piaget and Inhelder (1975), whose work stimulated much of the interest in this area, viewed children's understanding of chance as complementary to their understanding of cause and effect. Without some comprehension of caused events, there is no frame of reference for identifying events that are due to chance. Thus, Piaget and Inhelder concluded that children's concepts of chance and probability are secondary and derived concepts, emerging out of their search for order and its causes. This hypothesis is consistent with the cornerstone of Piagetian theory, which is that the main task of the intelligent mind is to construct logical means for structuring and, thereby, understanding reality. If chance is the domain where logic does not apply, then chance events are those that are left over when logic has had its day.

We have come to expect Piaget and his associates to invent ingenious tasks to investigate children's cognitive capacities. Their work in the area of chance and probability does not disappoint us. Their devices and procedures enable an examiner to produce mixtures, to rig outcomes, to generate normal, skewed, and uniform distributions, to work miracles, to permit random draws, and to elicit combinations, permutations, and arrangements of elements. The tasks are intrinsically interesting to children across a wide age range, and the results are ordinarily obtained relatively quickly, so that neither the subject nor the examiner is likely to lose interest.

As in other Piagetian studies, the clinical method was employed, and the data consist of protocols derived from exposing children to a variety of contrived events and questioning them about their understanding of what they experienced. For example, in one protocol a child was presented with a sack of six red and two blue counters and asked, "If you remove a counter from the sack, but do not look inside, what color do you think it is likely to be?" *"Red."* "Why?" *"Because I like red a lot."* The question is repeated with six blue and two red counters. *"Red."* "But there are a lot of blue ones; don't you think that it will be more likely to be a blue one?" *"Yes."* The question is repeated with six blue counters and one white counter. *"White."* "Why?" *"Because white is the first."* The interview is continued until the examiner is satisfied that the limits of the child's reasoning have been established.

The protocols are recorded as nearly verbatim as possible, and they are subsequently classified as to the type of reasoning they reflect. For example, predicting that red will be the color drawn because it is the child's favorite color is indicative of a rather immature mode of thinking. It does not take into account the odds favoring red. This protocol would be classified as belonging to the first and earliest stage of development of a concept of chance.

Piaget and Inhelder's analysis of the protocols that they gathered yielded three stages of development corresponding to the now familiar preoperatory, concrete operatory, and formal operatory periods. Prior to about age 6, children have no well-defined concept of cause and effect; therefore, they have no way to conceptualize what is fortuitous. For preoperatory children, everything is more or less caused, more or less fortuitous, and more or less miraculous. Concrete operatory children, from ages 6 to about 12, are able to discriminate two classes of events, one governed by the laws of cause and effect and bound by logical consequences and another characterized as random, mixed, unpredictable, and subject to chance. As long as the probability task is not too complex, they are able to calculate or at least to estimate the relative probability of alternative outcomes, and their performance in probability tasks tends to take into account the prevailing odds. In the formal operatory period, beginning about age 12, the arithmetical tools of combinations and permutations come into service, and the set of all possible chance outcomes for a given situation can be calculated or, at least, conceptualized. In addition, the law of large numbers provides a logical basis for making individual predictions, since choosing the most favorable odds at least guarantees that one will maximize gains across large numbers of trials. Thus, in the three stages outlined above we see, first, a lack of differentiation between caused and chance events, second, a differentiation and the beginnings of the quantification of probabilities, but an incomplete set of strategies for calculating odds in complex situations and for defining or enumerating all possible outcomes, and, finally, an integration of deductive logic and concepts of chance as formal structures are developed for dealing deductively with chance events.

The natural inclincation of the human mind to search for order and structure may be implicated in young children's inability to respond appropriately to chance events. They tend to see order where it does not exist and to deny the reality of disorder even when they see it happening before their eyes. Given a tray with a row of marbles on one end, eight white and eight red, one can tilt the tray so that the marbles will roll to the opposite side of the tray. As they do, they will collide and, sometimes, exchange places. Gradually, after many trials, they will be thoroughly and irrevocably mixed. In the first stage of the development of a concept of chance, children predict that the marbles will eventually return to their original places, or that the whole set of red will find its way to the side originally occupied by white, and vice versa. The original, ordered condition of the mixture has a privileged status in the minds of preoperatory children, and they believe it will sooner or later be restored. They do not recognize that a random mixture, like Humpty Dumpty, will not be put back together again.

According to Piaget and Inhelder (1975), preoperatory children do not understand the irreversible nature of the random mixture because they have not yet discovered operatory reversibility. Consequently, they have no logical frame of reference for interpreting something as irreversible. When preoperatory children are asked to draw one marble out of a sack containing a mixture of marbles, they do not realize that their hand could by chance come into contact with any one of the marbles at any one time and with any of a large number of possible sequences if they came into contact with several of the marbles. Preoperatory children tend to see a correspondence between aspects of the situation that, in fact, have no causal connection. In the example cited above, it was predicted that red would be the color drawn because red was the child's favorite color. Another common basis for young children's predictions is the unique status of the marble that they happen to be thinking of. For example, if there is one red marble in the sack among many others of different colors, the preoperatory child may predict red because there is exactly one red marble in the sack and he or she was asked to draw out exactly one marble. These errors reflect a different concept of what is in the sack than that held by older children, who understand that the mixture is irreversible, and who realize that on a blind draw any of the colors could occur but not for reasons such as those cited by the younger children.

Weisz (1980) has recently documented preschool children's inability to recognize the noncontingency of unrelated aspects of a chance event. In a card game whose outcome depended solely on the luck of the draw, kindergarten children uniformly explained high or low winnings as a result of skill or concentration, and the kindergarteners predicted that older, practiced, and smarter children would do better than younger children, who had less practice and were not as smart. Even fourth graders had some lingering doubts about the irrelevance of these factors, though the game had been designed to produce outcomes solely due to chance.

Piaget and Inhelder (1975) also relate young children's failure to quantify probabilities to their inability to deal with part-whole relations in the classic class-inclusion task. Given a display of three tulips and two daisies, preoperatory children will argue that there are more tulips than flowers. Once the tulips are thought of as tulips, they are no longer thought to be flowers. Probabilities also involve part-whole relations. The whole is the set of all possible outcomes, the denominator of the probability fracton, and the important part of that whole is the set of favorable cases, which goes in the numerator. Thus, the quantification of probabilities requires decomposing all possible outcomes into favorable and unfavorable cases, so that the favorable cases can be assigned to the numerator, and then recombining the outcomes into a whole, all possible outcomes, so that they can serve as the denominator. However, these operations are carried out simultaneously rather than consecutively. The probability of an event is seen as the resulting fraction. But to think simultaneously of the favorable cases both as the numerator and as a part of the denominator of a fraction is precisely what preoperatory children are unable to do.

Piaget and Inhelder concede that young children sometimes make predictions that appear to be based on logical considerations. For example, they seem to know that each of two or more alternatives may sometimes occur. Thus, if they predicted a draw of a red counter from a pouch on the first trial, they may predict blue on the second trial. But they make this prediction not because they have weighed the odds and consider what is probable, but because they feel a need to compensate for the previous outcome. When asked why they predicted blue, they may reply, "Because it is blue's turn." The colors, like children, must share. It is only fair. What appears at first blush to be a precursor of a concept of probability, since it involves distributing predictions across the possible outcomes, turns out in the end to be a denial of chance and probability, since it imposes an orderliness on the outcomes that is derived from ethical necessity.

Young children also sometimes make predictions that appear to be the result of their experience with previous outcomes. For example, they may base their predictions on the frequency of previous occurrences. If red has been drawn more frequently than any other color on several draws from a sack, the young child may predict red, explaining that red has occurred most often before. Again, this would appear to be a precursor of a concept of probability, since frequency over larger numbers of cases is an appropriate empirical approach to determining probability. The greatest frequency is associated with the highest probability. But here too Piaget and Inhelder caution that the behavior is deceptive. For the very young child, frequency is an attribute of a particular outcome (red) that may attract the young child's attention and serve as the basis for a prediction, but so may other attributes, such as the fact that red goes very well with pink, or that a red marble is the first marble in the display that has been placed nearby as a memory aid for what is in the sack. The child's mention of frequency would be impressive if this were the only attribute that the child was prone to use as a basis for prediction and if there were objective grounds for predicting red in addition to frequency across a small number of trials. According to Piaget and Inhelder, the child is merely reflecting a belief in a hidden order or regularity, which is manifesting itself in the frequency with which a given event has occurred. It would be gratuitous to call this the beginnings of a concept of chance.

Piaget and Inhelder also investigated children's understanding of normal, skewed, and uniform distributions. To study children's understanding of normal and skewed distributions they devised an apparatus which funneled balls into slanted boxes with partitions at the base to catch the balls. When the funnel was placed in the middle of a box, the balls could be expected to fall on either side of the center with approximately equal frequency, yielding a symmetrical distribution. When the funnel was placed off center, near the side of the box, the balls should pile up on that side in a skewed distribution. Young children's predictions as to where the balls would go when dropped into the funnel reflected no concept at all of a symmetrical or skewed distribution. In the same vein, Piaget and Inhelder devised an apparatus simulating the falling of rain drops on squares of pavement. Older children, as expected, predicted that the squares of pavement would receive approximately equal numbers of drops as the rain continued to fall. Young children distributed the drops either markedly unevenly, with one or two squares receiving far too many drops as the rest of the squares were ignored, or much too uniformly, with each square receiving exactly one drop after the other, as if the drops were forced to treat the squares like children and give each one a turn.

The limitations of young children's understanding of chance and probability are especially apparent when both caused and chance events are made to occur in the same setting. Piaget and Inhelder devised a spinner apparatus with colored sections of equal size to yield a uniform distribution of equally probable outcomes. As a second step, they added match boxes loaded with unequal weights, and they rigged one of the match boxes with a magnet so as to produce biased outcomes with the apparatus. In the first condition, when the apparatus was fair, young children believed inappropriately that they could predict a chance outcome or that they could control the outcome by aiming or thinking hard or by spinning it just hard enough to make it stop on a predicted color. They saw causal relations where none existed, for example, between adjacent spaces or successive trials ("It will land on green because that is next to red") or between the spinner's outcome and some hidden intent ("It will land on red because it wants to"). In the second condition, when the apparatus was rigged, they were not as surprised as they should have been that the bar kept stopping at the same place. When they were asked whether it did that by chance or whether there was a reason, they sometimes decided that it was chance.

By the same token, young children are not as impressed as they should be by an event so improbable as to be miraculous, such as 15 out of 15 heads or the same color counter drawn from a sack time after time even though the sack is supposed to contain other colored counters. It is only in contrast to lawful regularity that something is seen as a miracle, that is, contrary to natural law. For young children the absence of a system of deductive logic leaves everything more or less miraculous. In a probability setting virtually anything can happen, and many things do.

According to Piaget and Inhelder (1975), the development of a concept of chance and the ability to quantify probabilities takes a long time. During the 6–12-year age range, the concrete operatory period, children are more likely to base their predictions on the odds, especially when the number of possible outcomes is limited and when the odds are long and easy to estimate. Statistics replace fairness as the basis for making alternative predictions, and the more idiosyncratic bases for making predictions, such as color preferences, are no longer observed.

Still lacking at the concrete operatory stage is a complete system for dealing with complex probability situations and with large numbers of possible outcomes. The enumeration of all possible outcomes may require the operations of combinations or permutations to exhaust the possibilities. The ability to quantify probabilities in complex cases requires formal, combinational thinking.

Even when combinational operations are not worked out in detail so as to yield a numerical result, the ability to conceptualize the class of all possible outcomes still provides a logical basis for coping with experiences that would otherwise lie outside the realm of deductive reasoning. For example, in the case of the tray of marbles that are rolled back and forth to create an irreversible mixture, children in the formal operatory period are able to consider each possible arrangement of the marbles as one out of a very large number of possible arrangements. Armed with that concept, they can concede that the original, ordered array may reoccur, but only as one very rare event out of a very large number of possible alternative events. Moreover, formal reasoning provides a frame of reference for understanding chance events in general. One can appeal to the law of large numbers to make a prediction of a single chance event, since choosing the outcome with the most favorable odds insures the best results "in the long run."

It is the unique capacity of formal thought to elevate the realm of the possible to a status even more important than what is real that gives it a special talent for resolving a rather basic question, namely, how can one deal deductively with events that are unpredictable? Operatory logic cannot assimilate one fortuitous event, but it can assimilate the class of all fortuitous events, which taken together comprise the totality of what is possible. Moreover, the law of large numbers can be invoked to infer that the frequency of an event is *governed* by the probability of the occurrence of that event. Now chance has lost its character as the realm of the unpredictable. It is no longer true that anything can happen and many things do. Everything that happens, even what happens by chance, is reducible to one of the outcomes among the many that are possible by chance. Nothing is new. Everything must of necessity remain within the framework of deduced possibilities. Thus, operatory intelligence assimilates chance.

Subsequent Studies

Task Analysis

One of the first studies reported in the English language dealing with probability concepts was by Goodnow (1955). She compared a two-choice gambling task and a two-choice probability-learning task with comparable apparatus. Probability-learning tasks also typically involve two choices, but the payoff ratio is not divulged to the subject nor are they given any information as to what factors may govern payoffs at either alternative. Goodnow found that subjects tended to follow different strategies in the two tasks. In the probability-learning setting, subjects were dissatisfied with less than 100% success, and they accepted initial losses as they searched for a system that might eventually lead to a solution. In the gambling task, subjects were willing to accept a payoff of less than 100% as long as the gains outweighed the losses.

Ross (1966) placed a small number of balls of two colors in an opaque box and required subjects to predict sequential draws with and without replacement. The subjects were instructed to respond nonverbally by pointing to the color they predicted. Correct responses when only one ball remained in the box indicated that subjects were able to keep track of its contents even when draws were made without replacement. Ross' subjects, whose ages corresponded to the age ranges normally considered to be in the concrete operatory and formal operatory periods, made predictions against the odds when the odds were not too long against the predicted outcome, but they tended to go with the odds when they were clearly uneven.

[We recognize that the assignment of children to preoperatory, concrete operatory, and formal operatory periods on the basis of their chronological age is not always defensible. The age norms for these periods allow for considerable variability even within the same cultural setting and especially between subjects from a different socioeconomic status or from a different culture. Except when the context requires the operatory level as a theoretical (Piagetian) assumption, we shall use more specific labeling and refer to their school level or the age level of the children.]

Studies of Preoperatory Children

Yost, Siegel, and Andrews (1962) took issue with Piaget's characterization of preoperatory children as having no concept of chance or probability. They cited five factors that they felt might account for Piaget's negative results: (a) Piaget relied heavily on verbal tasks; (b) he did not control for color preferences; (c) the model that served as a memory aid proved to be a distracting influence; (d) no reinforcements were given for correct responses to provide motivation; and (e) no provision was made for statistical treatment of results.

To contrast results obtained under the conditions enumerated above with results obtained in a setting designed to overcome these limitations, Yost and co-workers prepared a two-choice decision-making task with provision for reinforcements, for nonverbal responding, and for controls for color preferences. Significant differences were obtained between results in the decision-making task and results in a prediction task patterned after a study described by Piaget (1950). Five of nine subjects in the decision-making task performed above chance. In a second session, in which subjects were assigned to the opposite task from the one to which they had previously been assigned, at least half the subjects in both groups performed above chance.

Davies (1965) compared threshold ages for demonstrating a concept of probability with verbal and nonverbal responses. With nonverbal responses 3-year-old children showed some evidence of a grasp of probability, and all of the 6-year-old subjects responded appropriately. Not until age 9, however, were all of the children able to verbalize their understanding of the concept.

Davies' apparatus eliminated the need for a model of the contents of a closed container. She designed a two-choice lever-pressing apparatus that appeared to be attached to two gum ball machines containing colored marbles—one-fifth red and four-fifths white in one jar and four-fifths red and one-fifth white in the other. The visual display also made preliminary mathematical calculation of the odds unnecessary, since they could be estimated on the basis of a casual visual comparison of red and white marbles in the two containers.

Goldberg (1966) modified slightly the procedures of Yost, Siegel, and Andrews (1962) by providing equivalent reinforcing conditions (knowledge of results) for the two-choice, decision-making task and the prediction task. Of 16 subjects ranging in age from 3 years 10 months to 5 years 1 month, 6 performed above chance levels in the prediction task, and 12 performed above chance levels in the two-choice decision-making task. These results are consistent with the findings of Yost and co-workers, but they show further that the absence of reinforcement in Piaget's procedures does not account for children's superior performance in the task requiring a choice between two alternatives.

The studies of Yost, Siegel, and Andrews (1962), Davies (1965), and Goldberg (1966) have in common the conclusion that when preoperatory children are given a fair test of their probability concepts, many of them perform above chance levels, suggesting that they have acquired some understanding of chance and probability. But neither they nor Piaget (1950) provided any evidence that probability concepts were required for successful performance on their tasks. In spite of their high face validity, some probability tasks may generate successful performance on the part of subjects who have no understanding at all of probability. For example, if a child who likes licorice jelly beans is offered two handfuls, one in which there are many black beans (e.g., four-fifths black and one-fifth other colors) and one in which there are only a few (e.g., one-fifth black and four-fifths other colors), one would expect that the child could choose the hand with the greater number of black jelly beans without invoking a concept of probability.

Estimating Magnitudes and Probabilities

To ascertain whether commonly used probability tasks require an understanding of probability concepts for above-chance performance, a series of studies was carried out using tasks requiring a choice between two alternative odds and tasks requiring predictions with a single set of prevailing odds (Hoemann & Ross, 1971). Identical situations were presented to preoperatory and concrete operatory children with two types of instructions, one requiring a probability judgment and the other requiring a magnitude estimation. In the first two experiments, spinners with black and white wedges were used to present relative proportions of black and white areas. In the probability instruction for the two-choice, alternative odds task, subjects were asked, "If black is a winner (white for half the trials), where will you spin to win, here (the spinner on the right) or here (the spinner on the left)?" The position of the correct response was right for half the trials and left for half the trials. In the magnitude estimation instruction subjects were asked, "Which circle has the most black in it (white for half the trials)?" In the probability instruction for the prediction task, subjects were shown a single spinner and asked, "What do you think the pointer will point to when it stops, white or black?" In the magnitude estimation instruction, subjects were asked, "Which color is the most, white or black?"

If performance in the two types of instructions yielded the same result, it would appear that comparing proportions and estimating odds was not required for a correct response. In the two-choice, alternative odds task this was the outcome observed. The differences in performance in the probability task and in the magnitude estimation task were very small at all age levels tested, regardless of the difference between the proportions presented in the two alternatives. It was concluded that probability concepts do not contribute to correct solutions in the two-choice task. In the prediction task, on the other hand, errors in the probability instruction were significantly higher than errors in the magnitude estimation instruction at all age levels. Moreover, children 5 years old and older were sensitive to the prevailing odds, that is, they made more accurate predictions as the odds differences increased. Four-year-old children, on the other hand, performed similarly, regardless of the magnitude of the odds, and their mean performance was only 56% correct, which is not significantly above chance. It was concluded that probability concepts are required for successful performance in a prediction task. Moreover, in support of Piaget and Inhelder's (1975) analysis, it was concluded that the 4-year-old children showed no evidence of a concept of probability.

Ordinarily one would not want to draw too strong a conclusion from a no-difference finding. As a matter of fact, the conclusion drawn from the data was not that the two-choice task fails to measure probability concepts. It may in a mature sub-

ject who evaluates the alternatives and chooses the more favorable odds. The conclusion drawn was that children may perform at better than chance levels without
using (or having) a concept of probability. They may be simply choosing the alternative with the greater amount of the specified color. The question is one of task
validity rather than one of hypothesis testing. The burden of proof is on researchers
who use the two-choice task for the purpose of measuring probability concepts to
show that the task measures what it is supposed to measure.

Piaget and Inhelder (1975, pp. 146-148) offer an explanation for the relative
difficulty of the one-choice prediction task compared to the two-choice, alternative
odds task. To perform correctly in the prediction task, it is argued, children must
decompose all possible outcomes into favorable and unfavorable cases, and then
construct a fraction that uses the favorable outcomes in the numerator and the
total number of possible outcomes in the denominator. With the two-choice task,
on the other hand, no decomposition of possible outcomes is necessary as long as
either the numerator or the denominator remains the same in both of the alternative odds. In a spinner task the sum of the sectors of the circles are always equivalent; consequently, all that the children had to do to make a correct response was
to compare the relative size of the black areas when black was the favorable outcome or the relative size of the white areas when white was the favorable outcome.
The larger amount would be the correct response. This is exactly the same demand
made of children in the magnitude estimation task.

Is there a way to make the two-choice task a probability task? Following Piaget
and Inhelder's reasoning, the answer would appear to be "Yes." If colored marbles
were used instead of spinners, one could arrange that neither the number of favorable cases, nor the number of unfavorable cases, nor the number of total possible
outcomes was the same in either alternative. For example, one could offer one red
counter and two blue counters in one alternative, and two red counters and five
blue counters in the other alternative. If red were designated a favorable outcome,
it is highly unlikely that 4-year-old subjects would perform successfully at better
than chance levels in such trials. Chapman (1975) designed an experiment including such trials and examined children in grades 1, 3, and 5 and college students.
The results showed that even fifth grade children did not fully understand proportionality.

Even with spinners one can arrange that the sums of the favorable and the
unfavorable outcomes is not the same in the two circles by designating a "spin
again" area in one of the circles. An outcome in that area could be treated as
though it did not count. With such an apparatus one could offer alternatives in
which the smaller of two areas of color was the correct choice from a probability
standpoint because it offered better odds. Consistent with Chapman's (1975)
results, it was determined (Ross & Hoemann, 1975) that such a task is not performed successfully without some coaching.

Even when whole circles are used as spinners, it might still be possible to offer a
task that requires some notion of probability. Subjects may be required to compare
different colored alternatives, as in the questions, "Where will you spin to win?"
"Will you spin here (on the right) for black or here (on the left) for white?" A direct
comparison of the magnitude of these different colored areas can be justified only

if one recognizes that there is a logical basis for equating the possible outcomes in the denominator of the compared fractions. One cannot test such implicit under-standing, but if performance in a two-spinner task comparing black in the one circle and white in the other circle proves to be similar to performance in a one-spinner prediction task, this would provide some evidence that this two-spinner task, like the one-spinner prediction task, requires some understanding of probability concepts for a correct performance. A third experiment was conducted (Hoemann & Ross, 1971) in which such a two-spinner task and a comparable one-spinner task were administered to 7-year-old subjects. The results in the two tasks proved to be quite similar, leaving open the possibility that the two-spinner task with different colored alternatives, unlike the standard two-spinner task, might require some knowledge of probability for its solution.

Alternative Hypotheses

Not all researchers have accepted the magnitude estimation hypothesis for young children's success in the two-choice task. Perner (1979a) proposed two alternative hypotheses for the "double spinner facilitation effect." He cited Chapman (1975) and his own previous study (Perner, 1979b) as examples of studies that had failed to replicate the effect. He noted that both of these studies had induced a problem solving set in their subjects either by having subjects solve problems prior to engaging in the probability task or by recruiting subjects from a museum environment in which they had been engaged in problem-solving tasks. Studies showing superior performance in the two-choice task, on the other hand, had induced a different kind of set, namely to express a preference. Perner hypothesized that subjects primed to express a preference would perform better in a two-spinner task than in a one-spinner task, while subjects primed to analyze the situation and "figure out" which was the better choice would perform similarly in both tasks. Moreover, preferentially primed subjects were expected to be misled by spinners with decep-tive disks in which the shorter segment was made fatter so that it presented a larger area of the minority color.

A second alternative hypothesis proposed by Perner (1979a) focused on the amount of variability in the displays representing the odds in studies showing better performance in the two-choice task. The greater variability in the num-ber of elements or in the sizes of the areas may have attracted attention to these features of the display. Perner hypothesized that subjects exposed to more across-trial and between-trial variation would perform better on the two-spinner task than the one-spinner task, but subjects exposed to homogeneous trials would perform similarly in both tasks.

The hypotheses were not supported by the data. Neither preferential priming nor more variability in odds differences produced the predicted results. Perner con-cluded that previously reported differences favoring the two-choice task are the result of idiosyncratic differences in procedures and cannot be replicated.

Close scrutiny of Perner's data, however, lend considerable support to the mag-nitude estimation hypothesis proposed by Hoemann and Ross (1971) and extended to school-age children by Chapman (1975) and to adolescents by Ross and Hoemann

(1975). Perner tested two age levels, 4-5 and 6-7. He also presented long (7:1) and short (5:3) odds. Of course, it is the younger subjects at preoperatory age levels whose performance is of special interest. At close odds (5:3) they performed at or near chance levels in both tasks (61.0% and 55.6%). At long odds (7:1) their performance was near chance in the one-spinner task (58.8%) but much improved in the two-spinner task (74.8%). At close odds the older subjects scored 72% in the one-spinner task and 70% in the two-spinner task. At long odds their scores were 83% (one spinner) and 75% (two spinner). These data are consistent with the conclusion drawn by Piaget and Inhelder (1975) that preschool children do not have a sufficient understanding of probability to make predictions based on the odds even when the odds are very discrepant. The results replicate previous studies in that the 4- to 5-year-old children at 7:1 odds performed much better in the two-spinner task. The fact that their performance was best when the odds were most discrepant supports the magnitude estimation hypothesis for their success on this task.

Even stronger support for the magnitude estimation hypothesis was generated by Perner's ingenious deceptive disk manipulation. If preschool children tend to choose the larger area of color rather than the better odds in the two-spinner task, then Perner's deceptive disks should induce them to prefer the alternative with the poorer odds because of the illusion of greater area. Thus, they should perform at or below chance levels in the two-spinner task when given the deceptive disks. In the one-spinner tasks with deceptive disks the preschool children's scores were 53.7% at long (7:1) odds and 36.0% at close (5:3) odds, and in the two-spinner task they were 38.0% at long odds and 46.8% at close odds. The older subjects were also somewhat misled by deceptive disks at close odds (58.4% in the one-spinner task and 30.6% in the two-spinner task), but less so at long odds (78.8% in the one-spinner task and 73.2% in the two-spinner task).

Thus, although Perner was unable to find confirmation for the alternative explanations that he had proposed for preoperatory children's success in the two-spinner task, preferential priming and odds variability, his data are consistent with the view of Piaget and Inhelder that preschool children perform at or below chance levels in prediction tasks. His data also support the magnitude estimation hypothesis for preschool children's success when they perform above chance levels in two-choice tasks. Since this hypothesis makes it unnecessary to invoke complex probabilistic reasoning or to attribute to young children advanced cognitive concepts, it should be preferred over alternatives that are less parsimonious. But what about the studies cited by Perner (1979a) that failed to find a difference between one-choice and two-choice tasks, for example, Perner (1979b) and Chapman (1975)?

First, it needs to be mentioned that Chapman's conclusions are consistent with the position that it is not until the formal operatory period that children evaluate proportions in order to make probabilistic judgments. Prior to that, when the larger number of favorable outcomes was found in the alternative offering poorer odds (e.g., 2 blue, 1 yellow versus 3 blue, 3 yellow, with blue as the target color), children made many errors and showed only gradual improvement across Grades 1-5.

Chapman (1975) reported that his subjects' verbal reports revealed a relatively unsophisticated strategy for solving probability tasks. His subjects based their choice of alternatives on differences in the quantity of items rather than on the prevailing odds. This strategy leads to a correct response in both one-choice and two-choice tasks except when the two-choice task presents the kinds of alternatives described above, namely, 2 blue, 1 yellow versus 3 blue, 3 yellow—blue target. Finally, it must be argued that Chapman's data are not relevant to the issue Perner raised, since it is preschool children's above-chance performance in the two-choice task that is hard to explain if it is a valid test of their probability concepts. None of Chapman's subjects was younger than first grade.

Given Chapman's data, it is, perhaps, more productive to ask why preschool children do not use magnitude estimation in the one-choice task, since it seems to work so well for older children in most circumstances. Piagetian reasoning would call attention to the fact that the outcome of the probability event is specified in the two-choice task, for example, a target color. The subjects' responses are limited to a choice of which bag or spinner they prefer in order to obtain the specified outcome. In the one-choice task, on the other hand, it is the outcome itself that must be predicted. If preschool children believe that these outcomes are influenced by a variety of hidden causes, from their own color preferences to the obligations of the colors to take turns, there is nothing to prevent them from finding an intellectually gratifying basis for predicting any of the possible outcomes. But concrete operatory children are constrained by their newly acquired logical framework to consider some of these grounds for a prediction to be irrational. This leaves magnitude estimation as a plausible basis for a prediction. It is easy to do, especially when the odds discrepancy is great. No computations are necessary. Also in the one-choice task it always leads to the best chance of success, since the larger number of elements or the larger area of a standard disk always offers the preferred odds. Perner's data support this interpretation. The highest score found in any of the eight cells of his data for standard disks (two tasks $\times$ two age levels $\times$ two odds differences) was the score earned by the older children in the one-spinner task at long (7:1) odds, 83.2%.

There is, in reality, only one study reporting no "double spinner facilitation effect," namely, Perner's own prior investigation (1979b). Perhaps, as Perner (1979a) suggested, there were idiosyncratic procedures involved in that study leading to the discrepant finding. But those are not sufficient grounds to conclude that the phenomenon cannot be reliably replicated, since it has already been replicated at least three times (Goldberg, 1966; Hoemann & Ross, 1971; Yost, Siegel, & Andrews, 1962), and since it is supported by Perner's own data (1979a) for preschool children at 7:1 odds.

On the basis of existing data, there does not seem to be any compelling reason to give up the magnitude estimation hypothesis for young children's successes in two-choice probability tasks. It is parsimonious, that is, it makes the fewest assumptions about the level of ability required by subjects for a successful performance. It is testable in that if young children are making probability choices on the basis of relative quantity, they ought to be misled by deceptive disks in which the area that appears to be larger offers poorer odds. This prediction has been verified independently by Ross and Hoemann (1975) and by Perner (1979a). Further, the magnitude estimation hypothesis calls into question the validity of the usual two-choice task as a measure of probability concepts. If subjects not only do not need to have a concept of probability to succeed but actually have a tendency to choose the larger number of favorable cases or the larger area of a favorable outcome, regardless of the odds, one cannot draw inferences about their probability concepts from their success in such a task.

If one excludes preschool children's success in the two-choice task from consideration, the conclusion drawn by Piaget and Inhelder (1975) that preoperatory children do not have a concept of probability appears to have been replicated repeatedly, inasmuch as children prior to age 6 not only do not perform above chance in the one-choice task but they do not even seem to be sensitive to odds differences. Their performance is almost as poor in trials with heavy odds favoring a particular outcome as in trials offering nearly even odds. Moreover, Perner (1979b) combined subjects from ages 3.9 to 9.9. It is unclear from the results whether the preschool children did or did not show superior performances in the two-spinner task, since the percentage scores (75%, double spinner; 74%, single spinner) are not reported separately for each age level. There was one condition in which results were broken down by age, a single spinner with two pointers; in that condition the 4-year-old subjects simply spun the top pointer 19 out of 20 times, regardless of the odds. This "two-pointer" spinner was designed to create a one-spinner task somewhat comparable to a two-spinner task in that two events could be conceptualized, one for each pointer, even though there was only one spinner. But the tendency of the younger subjects to spin the top pointer resulted in lower scores in this condition (70%) than in any of the other spinner conditions.

Alternative Theories

Up to now we have considered studies largely stemming from Piaget and Inhelder's theorizing. This is the case even when results have been found that are interpreted as contradictory to the ideas of Piaget and Inhelder. Other approaches have been advanced, however, that put the interpretation of children's probability performance on altogether different bases. We shall single out two of these alternative conceptual approaches for consideration here.

Fischbein (1975) in a book-length summary and interpretation of the child probability literature (including four experiments of his own) has put forward an intuitional basis as the key to probability understanding:

> We have defined an intuition as an action programme which is partially autonomous within cognition, and which is a synthesis of individual experience in a given domain. Its global, immediate nature enables it to control action instantaneously. According to this view, probability matching is the expression of a particular intuition, the *intuition of relative frequency*. (Fischbein, 1975, p. 58)

(The emphasis here and in subsequent quotations is Fischbein's.) At the same time, *"Intuitions themselves become more 'rational' with age, in that they adopt strategies and solutions which are based on rational grounds"* (Fischbein, 1975, p. 65). But Fischbein immediately acknowledges that subjects do not necessarily reach correct conclusions, an example being negative recency (gambler's fallacy).

Fischbein's lumping of probability learning experiments with their large number of consecutive trials (sometimes hundreds) together with probability concept experiments is a different approach from that taken by the present writers, who have consistently maintained (Ross, 1966) that probability learning experiments do not do much to elucidate probability understanding. A considerable theoretical difficulty in giving probability learning experiments a developmental interpretation is that probability matching results tend to bear a curvilinear relationship to age. This finding was first pointed out by Weir (1964), and Fischbein makes some attempt to explain this striking result. It is necessary that Fischbein do this since he claims that the *"primary intuition* of chance is present in the everyday behavior of the child, even before the age of 7. Chance is equivalent to unpredictability, and not necessarily to the smallness of odds" (Fischbein, 1975, p. 118). One of Fischbein's explanations is that the

> pre-school child grasps more readily than the adult that the maximum of correct predictions can be obtained by adopting the 'pure' strategy, i.e. constant prediction. This is not a far-fetched explanation; it accords with results we have obtained which demonstrate the superior ability of small children to estimate odds (in certain experimental conditions). (Fischbein, 1975, p. 119)

We disagree with the interpetation that young children have a superior ability to estimate odds, but we have substantiated Weir's results and analyzed probability learning results in some detail (Sullivan & Ross, 1969). It was found that with an 80:20 probability ratio for a two-choice probability task, majority choice as an overall percentage was more alike for 5-year-olds and 17-year-olds than for either 9-year-olds or 13-year-olds. With a 67:33 probability ratio the 5-year-olds preferred the majority choice more and were closer to probability matching than children at any other age including 17-year-olds. Needless to say, our interpretation of these counterintuitive results are on other bases than probability intuitions.

Probability concept experiments have also been extensively considered by Fischbein. His proposition that young children have intuitions of chance and relative probability is incompatible with the conclusions drawn by Hoemann and Ross (1971), and he considers their experiments to be flawed both in procedure and interpretation of results. The argument is made that since each of the probability judgment tasks is dependent on perception, the differences obtained between the several Hoemann and Ross experimental procedures result from differences in perceptual complexity rather than children's variations in ideas about chance and probability. Hoemann and Ross (1971) did not, however, claim, as Fischbein suggests, that no probability component is involved in tasks where simple perceptual comparisons can produce a correct solution.

With regard to the finding that perceptual judgments and probability instruction tasks give similar results with young children if no ratio formulation is necessary, Fischbein makes an argument that strikes us as distinctly odd: "The problem as posed is in terms of estimating odds, and a correct response indicates that the child really does (although no doubt implicitly) make use of the idea of chance. Otherwise the child could not respond to this question as it is posed!" (author's exclamation mark, Fischbein, 1975, p. 88). If such a validity criterion is to be used when subjects' responses are far from being uniformly correct, there must be many more intuitions that young children possess that are just waiting to be enumerated.

It is evident that while we appreciate the novelty of Fischbein's approach, our interpretation has not been a sympathetic one. This may result from the biases of the present authors, who have an opposed point of view. With its comprehensive summary of the child probability literature, the Fischbein book deserves to be better known. The question that Fischbein raises as to the young child's early detection of uncertainty might be an interesting one for investigation. But we remain unconvinced that this detection of uncertainty by the young child mediates probability performance, particularly when Piaget and Inhelder (1975) have shown that at a somewhat older age children commonly tend to find causal explanations for randomized mixtures.

In the information-processing tradition, a familiar one to contemporary psychologists, Brainerd (1981) has performed a series of experiments on probability judgments using 5-year-olds and 8-year-olds as subjects. Brainerd has attempted to exploit the idea of "working memory" (a somewhat different concept than short-term memory) to demonstrate that probability choice errors are more a product of limited retention capacity than a conceptual deficit. The claim is made that accurate retrieval of frequencies is the processing operation most at fault when errors are made. Further, age changes in performance accuracy are directly related to age changes in frequency retrieval, while such retrieval is itself dependent on the constraints of working memory that characterize different ages.

Thus, like Fischbein, Brainerd (1981) finds that nonconceptual processes mediate success in probability tasks. Fischbein maintains that obtained age differences reflect differences in the perceptual complexity of a task, while Brainerd finds that age differences are a function of memory differences. Yet these two points of view are in some ways polar opposites. Brainerd's younger children do not achieve like Fischbein's; they make memory errors in the simplest of situations. For example, with 5-year-olds, 18% of their memory responses are in error when the children recall the starting frequency differential, even though there is replacement after each drawing, while 8-year-olds are practically perfect in their recalls. Thus, owing to the retention inadequacy of the younger children, it is possible to show that there is major dependency on memory accuracy in performing probability judgments. It would seem more difficult to extrapolate the memory constraint viewpoint to older ages where, as we have delineated, probability errors continue to be plentiful. Although this initial attempt to give children's probability understanding an information-processing explanation presents a developmentally limited endeavor, models of this kind could prove useful. Potentially, they could permit more accurate descriptions of specific probability situations. It is the belief of the writers, however, that a number of the Piagetian interpretations would have to be incorporated as decision-rule formulations in order to maximize the success of any such model.

Gender Differences

Gender differences have sometimes been observed in probability studies (Chapman, 1975; Perner, 1979b; Pire, 1958; Ross, 1966), but only with school age children. When they occur, they favor boys. Quantitative ability in general is an area in which gender differences have been observed in children, and they too are not found in preschool children but only children aged 9 and older (Maccoby & Jacklin, 1974). They favor boys. It is noteworthy that in all of the areas of behavior in which gender differences have been consistently observed, namely, quantitative ability, visual spatial, and field articulation (all favoring boys) and verbal ability (favoring girls), the proportion of the total variance accounted for by these gender differences is relatively small, ranging from .010 to .043 in studies in these four areas reporting ω^2 values (Hyde, 1981). Moreover, gender differences must be interpreted with caution when the male and female subjects have not been matched for cognitive level prior to the experiment. This precaution does not seem to have been taken in any of the published research in the area of chance and probability.

Studies of Deaf Subjects

Studies of deaf children's probability concepts are interesting in their own right for the light that they may shed on deaf children's cognitive development. Deaf subjects also offer an opportunity to observe the development of probability concepts in children who lack specific educational experiences with probability theory and wide experience with games of chance. Thus, they provide a useful control group to compare to the more widely experienced and diversely educated hearing groups.

Ross (1966) found that 11- and 13-year-old deaf subjects lagged behind hearing subjects in solving simple probability tasks, but by age 15 they caught up. Later it was determined (Ross & Hoemann, 1975) that unselected deaf subjects showed a deficit at age 15 in more difficult probability problems. However, in that same study (Experiment 2), a select group of deaf subjects who had been given prior training in nonverbal logic performed as well as hearing subjects about the same age.

The "catch-up" effect noted above and the equivalent performance of selected deaf subjects and hearing age peers suggest that the poorer performances that are sometimes observed in deaf subjects are not the result of a cumulative cognitive deficit but, rather, a lack of experience or practice in solving probability problems. This means that their deficiencies can be prevented or perhaps remedied by appropriate training.

The effects of training on deaf subjects' probability performance in middle and late childhood were evaluated as part of a larger study of deaf children's intellectual functioning (Furth, 1971). The training group in the study attended a Thinking Laboratory five days a week for the greater part of two school terms. A variety of "thinking games" was used in the laboratory, including sorting tasks, memory tasks, nonverbal logic, and manipulative tasks with blocks and clay. Probability training made use of one-choice prediction tasks with a spinner and with marbles in a can as well as two-choice alternative odds tasks with both marbles and spinners. The control group in the larger study consisted of children approximately the same age and ability as measured by school achievement who were assigned to a Language Laboratory for the same period of time that the experimental subjects attended the Thinking Laboratory. Activities involved the functional use of language in story telling and picture description as well as work on vocabulary, sentence construction, and grammar.

Ten two-choice problems were administered periodically to the trained and untrained subjects. The ten-problem test was administered at 5-month intervals except that seven months separated the third and fourth administrations. Eight months after the fourth test, a transfer test was administered with 12 easy problems in one session and 18 hard problems in another session. Training took place over a period of 16 months spanning a summer recess. The transfer tests were given 25 months after the beginning of the program.

In order to examine the effects of training as a function of age, subjects were divided into two age levels. The mean ages of the younger subjects were 8 years, 6 months for the experimental group and 8 years, 9 months for the control group. The mean ages for the older subjects were 11 years, 6 months for both groups.

The results of the study were straightforward. Both training groups improved significantly from Test 1 to Test 4. Scores were 60% and 63%, respectively, for younger and older subjects on Test 1. They improved steadily across sessions and were 81% and 92%, respectively, on Test 4. The older control group showed some spontaneous improvement ($p < .05$) from Test 1 (65%) to Test 4 (86%), but the younger control group did not (53%-59%). On the easy transfer test, both the younger and the older training groups had scores significantly superior to their corresponding control groups. The spontaneous improvement of the older control subjects was not as generalizable as the improvement observed in the older trained subjects.

The hard transfer problems were too difficult for all groups. The highest score was earned by the older training group, but it was only 64%. The effects of training were limited to problems that could be solved without constructing and comparing proportions.

Deaf subjects were also included in two advanced probability tasks (Experiment 4) designed to tap formal operatory thinking in adolescents (Ross & Hoemann, 1975). The outcomes of a one-choice task were assigned different values, that is, a pink outcome was worth one point and a green outcome was worth two points. In a trial offering three pink and two green balls in the container, green would be the better choice from the standpoint of maximizing points within the constraints of the prevailing odds. Some trials had two outcomes and some had three outcomes. It was arranged that in some trials, like the example above, the less frequent color was the correct choice.

Somewhat surprisingly, none of the subjects, whether deaf or hearing, did well when the less frequent color was the correct response. Apparently the subjects were not combining point values with the odds but were simply choosing the most frequent color. Either maximizing winning outcomes was more important to them than maximizing points, or else they did not know how to evaluate their best chance of winning the most points.

To investigate these two possibilities further, a second version of the task was devised as a limited follow-up study with ten 15-year-old deaf boys in which points were subtracted from the subjects' score when a ball was drawn of the predicted color. If subjects predicted the smallest number of balls in order to minimize the number of losing trials (the reverse of the strategy used before), this could be costly when the predicted outcome was worth three points. In this avoidance task, subjects might predict the outcome with a point value of one, regardless of the odds. Either way, winning was no advantage; the only way to avoid a loss of points was to draw a ball that was not the predicted color. It was expected that these procedures would encourage subjects to pay attention both to point values and to the number of balls of each color.

The avoidance paradigm met with only limited success. Some subjects based their predictions on point value instead of frequency, but no subject consistently combined both point values and frequencies to weight the odds so as to minimize their loss of points.

Do deaf adults display formal operatory thinking in probability situations? Data are lacking. The performance of deaf adolescents hints that they probably have the potential to do so, but that they may need coaching or practice before they will do so habitually. But this may be true of hearing persons as well as deaf persons. Meanwhile, anyone who has frequent contact with the deaf community of any major city undoubtedly knows persons deaf from birth or early childhood who do as well as the next man at the race track and who make as worthy an opponent as one might want in a game of stud poker.

Studies of Adolescents

Only a limited amount of research was conducted by Piaget and Inhelder (1975) on concepts of probability found in adolescents. They went beyond the ages of 12-13 in only one study of permutations. In a later publication (Inhelder & Piaget, 1958) they examined a few older subjects' understanding of distributions containing chance elements as a part of their study of random variations and correlations.

Given Chapman's (1975) finding that concrete operatory children continue to use a magnitude estimation strategy throughout most of the concrete operatory period, it is appropriate to consider what kinds of strategies are used by adolescents to solve probability problems, especially two-choice problems, and whether these strategies reflect formal operatory reasoning. Piaget (1972) has conceded that not all adolescents develop formal operations at the same rate and that some individuals may never reach the level of formal thought. Most people, however, are expected to be able to engage in formal reasoning by age 20 at least in their areas of interest or aptitude. One does not have to be a university-trained scientist to test hypotheses systematically. A good auto mechanic does the same thing, and so does a farmer striving for the best possible yield. At the same time one cannot assume that subjects have attained formal operations simply because they are 12 years old or older.

Before considering adolescents a word about school-age children assigned by Piagetian theory to the concrete operatory period is in order. These children are inclined to choose on the basis of the odds as long as they are not too difficult to estimate. But they estimate the odds using strategies that do not require the construction of proportions, and they lack the ability to calculate mentally the least common denominator of unlike fractions, to convert to decimals, or to compare fractions with different denominators that are not far apart in value. They learn at a young age to estimate the odds when they are discrepant. When the odds are close, they appear to prefer to guess rather than try to carry out the necessary computations in their heads. At close odds, it is less important to choose the more favorable odds. Eventually, attention to the number of favorable and unfavorable cases in each alternative will lead to the development of a trade-off strategy, to be described shortly as the most effective strategy available for dealing with dissimilar fractions without calculating their value as a proportion. Another strategy that evolves during the concrete operatory period is to use a familiar fraction, such as one-half or one-fourth as a standard, and to judge the other fractions relative to the standard. If one or both of the fractions is a familiar one, that makes the task especially simple. But if one of the fractions is unusual, such as four-sevenths, the familiar fraction strategy often leads to errors.

In order to extend Piaget and Inhelder's (1975) research well into the period of adolescence and to explore the various strategies that older subjects might use to solve simple probability tasks, 32 15-year-old subjects were given 20 two-choice problems using poker chips as counters (Ross & Hoemann, 1975). None of the problems had an equal number of favorable or unfavorable chips in the alternatives from which subjects were to choose. After the problems were completed, the subjects were asked how they made their choices. In addition to any other question, the subjects were always asked if they used a specific method in making choices, whether there were any alternative methods of making choices, and whether some problems were easier than others. Frequently one or two problems were repeated and the subjects were asked to think aloud as they came to a decision.

Fourteen subjects used a trade-off procedure in which they took the number of favorable (good) chips in one alternative and matched them one for one with the number of favorable chips in the other alternative. In the same way the subjects then matched the number of unfavorable (bad) chips in the two alternatives. The subjects then compared the good with the bad remainders to make a prediction. If a particular alternative had a remainder of one good chip but two bad chips, the bad chips outnumbered the good chip in that alternative, and subjects would avoid it, choosing the other alternative. Ten subjects used such a trade-off strategy *across* alternatives and then compared the remainders. Four subjects compared good and bad chips *within* each alternative and compared those remainders across alternatives to make their choice. The outcome is the same in both procedures, and, unless the final result is a tie, the procedure always yields an appropriate choice from a probability standpoint.

The trade-off strategy seems to be the favorite of adolescents, even though it sometimes results in a tie, requiring another strategy for breaking ties. This strategy is impressively systematic. Both the favorable cases and the unfavorable cases have to be taken into account, and the differences between alternatives have to be derived and compared before a decision is made. The fact that it does seem to be systematic and that it does lead, except in ties, to a definitive outcome makes it a candidate for consideration as an example of a formal operatory solution to a probability task, even though it does not mandate constructing proportions. As a matter of fact, Piaget and Inhelder (1975) accepted a trade-off strategy as indicative of third level or formal functioning. In Chapter 6, they present partial protocols of four subjects given 19 problems, eight of which were hard problems in that the favorable and unfavorable cases were unequal. One subject, whose protocols were judged to be a good example of the third stage of development, solved five of the hard problems using a trade-off strategy with occasional reliance on a familiar fraction. On the basis of this criterion, Piaget and Inhelder classified children as belonging to the third stage who are somewhat younger than one expects for the formal operatory period unless the children are unusually precocious. The one subject mentioned earlier was 12 years 5 months of age, but the other three were 11 years, 10 years 3 months, and 10 years 2 months of age, respectively.

Four subjects used an incomplete trade-off strategy. They compared good chips found in the two alternatives and chose the alternative with the most good chips, regardless of the number of bad chips. This, of course, will lead to a wrong choice in the special case where the most good chips are found in the alternative with the poorest odds (2 blue, 1 white versus 3 blue, 3 white; target, blue). Since anyone who can count and compare sums can make use of this strategy, it clearly does not require formal operatory thinking. Subjects using this strategy will score "above chance" in any probability task that does not have very many problems of the type detailed above. Since mean percentage scores on probability tasks with heterogeneous problems are directly affected by the types of problems included in the task and the relative proportion of them that mislead subjects using a particular strategy, such scores are uninterpretable unless they are broken down by problem type (Chapman, 1975) or unless the subjects' strategies are identified (Ross & Hoemann, 1975).

Four subjects also followed a rule involving counting and comparing sums, but they were attending to the total number of chips in each alternative, some favoring the larger total and some the smaller. If a probability task were designed in such a way that the larger group of elements was correct half the time, subjects using this strategy would perform at chance levels.

Six subjects claimed that they took both good and bad chips into account, comparing the good chips with the total chips in each alternative and then comparing them. If these subjects had used this procedure consistently and made no mistakes, they should have had perfect scores. But there is a mathematical problem involved in comparing fractions. Unless one calculates the least common denominator of two fractions or converts both fractions to decimal fractions, the comparison may not be easy to make. It is not all that obvious which fraction offers the better odds, 3/7 or 4/10.

Two subjects used a method of comparing proportions that relied on the fact that some fractions are relatively familiar, such as 1/4 or 1/2. If both of the alternatives were familiar values or easily reducible to them (e.g., 2/4) this method was almost always successful. But many errors occurred when, for example, 2/3 was "felt" to be larger than 5/7.

One subject followed the textbook procedure of calculating the odds in each alternative and then choosing the more favorable odds. Not surprisingly, that subject's score was considerably higher (88%) than the rest of the subjects (61%-66%).

To summarize, of the 32 subjects tested one used the optimum strategy of calculating and comparing proportions, two made frequent use of a familiar ratio to make the comparison, six claimed to be taking favorable and unfavorable cases into account, but on an intuitive level rather than on the basis of mathematical calculations. Four used a rule that was correct when there were more good chips in the alternative with better odds. Four went with the alternative with either the most or the least number of elements (an inferior strategy to be sure). Finally, 14 used a trade-off strategy that took note of differences between both favorable and unfavorable cases, comparing the alternative by means of any remainders after differences were compared. This worked except when the result was a tie. In that case, subjects had to come up with another strategy (two said that they did), or they had to guess.

There are some problems with this classification scheme. Some strategies worked with one kind of problem but not with another. Also, even though subjects described a strategy as one that they characteristically used, there is no way of knowing from the data how consistently they used it. For example, the four subjects who used the partial trade-off strategy and the four subjects who went with the most or the least number of elements scored too well to have been using this strategy on every trial. Nevertheless, it is apparent that the subjects in this study made only minimal use of probability theory to solve the problems that were put to them. Even subjects who attempted to compare the proportions had some difficulty doing this using only mental arithmetic. Most of the subjects used a variety of ad hoc approaches, depending on the nature of the problem, and sometimes they applied more than one rule to the same problem.

Given this variety of strategies, some clearly inadequate for certain kinds of problems, is there any evidence that adolescents differ qualitatively from children who are in the concrete operatory age level? One study reported by Ross and Hoemann (1975) suggests that there is (Experiment 5A and B). Like Perner's (1979a) investigation, this study used deceptive spinners. They differed from Perner's approach in that they made the better odds unattractive by constructing one of the spinner backgrounds with a large white area that did not count. When subjects' pointer landed on white, they were required to spin again until they obtained a red or a blue outcome. When three-fourths of the circle was white, a red outcome in that circle could be represented by an area of one-eighth of the circle and yet be more probable than a blue sector one-fourth of the area of the other circle. Different colors were used as alternative outcomes to discourage magnitude estimation as a strategy.

The subjects in one experiment (5A) were given training in area comparison: "Look at the circle on the left. Is the red more than the blue or less than the blue, or are they about the same? Look at the circle on the right. Is the red more than the blue or less than the blue or are they about the same?" Only correct answers were accepted for these questions. Then the experimenter asked, "Which is the better choice?" During training wrong answers were corrected. In the problems where the smaller area was the correct choice, the experimenter followed the correct (or the corrected) response with the statement, "That is a good choice, because white doesn't count, and the red (blue) gives you a better chance of winning."

Eight problems were given before and after coaching. Before coaching, children in the 7-11 year age range consistently failed in the four problems in which the smaller area was the correct choice. Their scores were around 20% with 50% being chance. After coaching the 7-year-old subjects scored at chance levels (50%), but subjects 8 years old and older scored over 75% correct. Thus, the coaching was effective for all but the youngest children in the concrete operatory period. Preteen and teenage deaf children also scored above 75% following area comparison coaching.

Another group of children was given the same set of problems before and after coaching, but they were given odds training instead of area comparison training. They were asked, "What are your chances of getting red (blue)? Are they even, less than even, or more than even?" As before, incorrect answers were corrected. Subjects evaluated the odds in each alternative with the help of the experimenter. They were reminded of their answers as to the odds for each alternative, and then asked, "Which is the better choice?"

Precoaching performance was the same as in Experiment 5A, around 20%. Postcoaching performance for children at ages 10 and 12 remained below chance. Mean scores were well below 50%. But older subjects at ages 14 and 15½ scored well above chance. It could be argued that these results constitute evidence that the older subjects had attained the level of formal operatory thinking, since very little coaching was required for their success, and the coaching that was used did not appeal to concrete features, such as colored areas, but invited attention to "better chances." The possibility was considered that increased vocabulary comprehension accounted for the coaching effect, but it does not seem plausible that such a pronounced effect could be due to improved linguistic skills between ages 12 and 14, especially since "better chances" did not have to be defined in any formal sense.

In order to develop our understanding of the probability performances and abilities of older subjects further, it might be useful to establish more stringent criteria for a higher level of formal operatory thinking as it is applied to probability problems. Higher levels of formal thought may be inferred from previous studies (Ross & Hoemann, 1975) by deaf subjects trained in nonverbal logic who, later, solved hard probability problems, by 14- and 15-year-old hearing subjects who benefitted from odds training with a deceptive spinner, and certainly by the one subject who explained verbally that he calculated the proportions in each alternative and then compared them.

Another way to elaborate upon older subjects' performance is to observe their preferred strategy as a function of different types of problems. The strategy that they report following a test with heterogeneous items may belie a variability in approaches that takes into account the difficulty of the task. It would be useful, for example, to discover whether subjects at the concrete operatory level are able to discriminate problems that are too difficult for them as compared to problems that are within their grasp.

Already some interesting results have been obtained with two different types of deceptive spinners. Additional variations of this type on now-familiar tasks may provide insight into the reasons why some children fail in certain kinds of tasks even though they enunciate a strategy that would appear to give them a basis for a correct response. Additional research is also needed to explore the effects of different instructions (Perner, 1979a), different kinds of coaching (Ross & Hoemann, 1975), and different types of training. More complex tasks, such as the one assigning different point values to different outcomes, requiring subjects to combine information from two sources, will also be helpful for exploring the limits of subjects' abilities who fall into the "higher level" of formal thought discussed earlier.

The search for a valid test of formal operatory strategies to the solution of probability problems is not over, nor is the search for adolescents who habitually use them. The strategies that they invoke are intriguing, and there are grounds for optimism that various coaching or training procedures might bring about considerable improvement in their performance on a variety of tasks. Complicating the issue is the fact that simplistic strategies are appropriate for some probability tasks. The textbook strategy may be "correct" in all circumstances but cumbersome and unnecessary when comparing familiar proportions. A comprehensive survey of formal approaches to probability problems must allow for unsophisticated strategies when they work.

Theoretical Implications

One is liable to lose the forest for the trees, or in this case the conclusions for the colored balls and spinners, in detailing experimental procedures and the inferences that arise from them. There are, nevertheless, wider conclusions to be reached. Why should it be important whether young children act on the basis of magnitude estimation or some other guiding hypothesis? The issue is clear; either the young child does or does not have a primitive conception of probability. Our conclusion, on the basis of the convoluted strands of evidence we have just discussed, is that young children have no such system of concepts. From our point of view then, probability is not like perceptual constancies and other perceptual phenomena that have clear precursors in early childhood. There is a discontinuity, since probability reasoning in recognizable and consistent form does not arise till the concrete operatory period. It seems to us that even if one were to accept some of the special hypotheses controverting our experimental conclusions that we have detailed above, this crucial point is not challenged. We reiterate this conclusion with particular obstinacy because some of our own earliest efforts started with the assumption that there at least ought to be a glimmer of probability understanding in young children.

Results are generally in agreement with the predictions of Piaget, but at the same time Piaget has presented a specific and seemingly dogmatic conception of probability achievement that would almost by definition make probability understanding by young children impossible, whatever one's theoretical persuasion. It is no accident that Piaget's (1975) book dealing with probabilities names "chance" but not "probability," and indeed in the book he places experiments on children's conception of chance ahead of those on probability conception. This order is appropriate, because for Piaget one must have a notion of chance to be able to handle probability reasoning. For Piaget, the young child goes through a first stage in which there is a failure to differentiate between the possible and the necessary, followed by a second stage in which there is the discovery of chance as a noncomposable reality and as the antithesis of cognitive operations. The terminal third stage allows probabilistic composition by a synthesis of chance and deductive operations.

In Piaget's view, and specifically in opposition to the mathematician Borel, there is no such thing as an isolated probability event unrelated to a distribution, whether the distribution is explicit or implicit. As Matalon (1966) has pointed out —in an honorary volume to Piaget—this approach scarcely accords with the emphases by most later writers on the foundations of the probability calculus (such as Carnap, Nagel, and Savage), who largely ignore the definition and interpretation of chance events. Of course, the axiomatic treatment of probability need not accord with the psychological, but a concept of chance in any rigorous sense can hardly be a concept within the grasp of preoperative children. Thus, we might conclude that a strict adherence to Piaget's point of view would scarcely need experimentation to demonstrate young children's failure to reason probabilistically.

It is to Piaget's credit that he attempts a full-fledged interpretation of how the concept of chance emerges during the concrete operatory period. The difficulty is that several interpretations are given that are not necessarily congruent with each other, while the experimental data base is very small. Piaget and Inhelder (1975) tell us that the child who has become capable of deduction takes into account indetermination, and this discovery is then the source of the idea of chance. Understanding of chance can occur on two levels, the spatiotemporal and logicoarithmetical. An example of the former might be predicting where a spinner would stop, while the latter would be exemplified by blindly drawing balls of several colors out of a container. One might expect that for Piaget a concept of physical chance would appear earlier than that for logical or numerical ensembles, but he does not explicitly state this. Rather, both types of chance are brought about in the same way, usually either by insufficient determination (including lack of adequate data) or the intervention of another independent causal series in a fortuitous (uncorrelated) way.

As Matalon (1966) emphasizes, however, this is a model of chance that has as its foundation physical phenomena such as those derived from classical thermodynamics, and the model is complex in that these formulations are based on unobservable occurrences. Piaget boldly tries to bridge the gap between the physical and mental:

> Chance which is proper to psychic phenomena is due to the fact that consciousness can never bring together all the data into one united field except precisely in the logical or deductive domain. Consciousness proceeds then by successive centrations around a center motivated by the interest of the moment which stimulates them, but is more or less fortuitous in the points of their application and, therefore, intersecting the data at more or less uncertain points. (Piaget & Inhelder, 1975, pp. 240-241)

This kind of centration explanation is a shift in perspective from the previously expressed idea of chance as the separation of incommensurable events from those that are deductible. Piaget also makes play with the idea that chance (specifically in thermodynamics and entropic functions) is an irreversible process, but it takes reversible operations to understand the concept of chance. Hence, a conception of chance or at least its limits can only be fully encompassed by the attainment of formal operations.

The conceptual apparatus appears to be at best only partially illustrated by the mere handful of demonstration experiments that Piaget and Inhelder have performed. Apart from the Piaget and Inhelder studies on mixtures and distributions, the development of children's chance concepts, whether in terms of sequences, visual displays, physical events, or unfathomable probabilities has scarcely been studied empirically by anyone. In setting apart the child's separation of the certain from the incalculable Piaget is pointing out a division that children must inevitably make at some point in their development. But the period during which a conception of chance originates is hypothesized as occurring at the time that concrete operations are developing in the individual. Therefore, the concept of chance must have its greatest extension when it is first grasped. As the acquisition of operations increases what is calculable, the range of chance phenomena decreases. A seeming paradox occurs in that the period during which chance appears to have its greatest scope follows the preoperatory period when the child adheres to an almost total belief in causal determinism. By this reasoning the switch from a belief in determinism to chance is very abrupt. It is likely, though, that younger children more weakly hold their belief in chance than the older child and adolescent, who can define a relatively more circumscribed field for chance occurrences. We offer these considerations as an example of an interesting area for research whether one follows or disavows Piaget's specific hypotheses.

Probability problems have the virtue of being intrinsically motivating for children as well as adults and of possessing properties that are not duplicated by other test materials. A unique characteristic is that the probability problem solver can be right though wrong, and vice versa. That is, acting on a wrong hypothesis or on an arbitrary basis, a subject can be fortuitously correct while a reasoned correct choice can be wrong. At least this is the case in the usual probability experiment, where trial-by-trial outcomes are not under the control of the experimenter. Even though knowledge of results is often misleading, the sedulous experimenter must continue to congratulate the young child who makes long strings of wrong "correct" choices because of pure luck. If one were to consider reinforcement of prime importance for making choices, not only would administered reinforcement frequently be misleading, but each subject would be on a different reinforcement schedule. Correct probability concepts must instead be held in the face of some lack of success, while consistent errors can sometimes be correlated with success. It is hard to think of any other commonly administered cognitive task in which this is the case.

Another property of probability tasks, but a less unique one in that it is common to the problem solving literature, is that children and adults need not reach correct solutions in order to produce revealing results. A notable example was our earlier work with the gambler's fallacy (Ross & Levy, 1958), where 13-year-olds did not evidence the gambler's fallacy but 15-year-olds did, and adults did so to an even greater degree. In other words, even the acquisition of a fallacy may be a developmental achievement. Again one may note that the gambler's fallacy can hardly be a function of differential reinforcement, yet it is pervasive.

In that Piaget has set the agenda for probability concept studies, it comes as no surprise that the turning points are seen to correspond to the shifts from preoperatory to concrete operations and from concrete to formal operations. The importance of the shift from concrete to formal operations remains somewhat problematic. As detailed above, a variety of strategies can be used by adolescents even with straightforward odds variation problems. And, as just mentioned, the indirect index of probability achievement given by a shift to use of the gambler's fallacy is not attained at age 13 when on average some use of formal operations might be assumed to have occurred. On the other hand, a gain in knowledge of simple permutations and combinations appears to take place around ages 12-13 in line with Inhelder and Piaget's (1958) results. But in our experience knowledge of simple permutations is often strikingly unintegrated with other conceptions that a subject holds about probability.

What developments can we look for in the future that will more closely integrate the study of children's probability concepts with more mainstream areas of psychology? At the adolescent period there is the not-yet-achieved possibility of linking developmental questions with the large and growing literature on decision making. But one can easily be overly optimistic about the theoretical yield for developmental psychology to be gained from the hypotheses and theories derived from decision-making studies. This is so because much decision-making research is concerned with applied problems and with compound decisions in which it is not easy to disentangle the basic knowledge that subjects possess from situational factors.

Putting these considerations to one side, it is also the case that with unselected adolescents probability achievement has quite a low performance ceiling. In some as yet unpublished research from our laboratory we have found that in attempting to combine probabilities, adolescents even at age 15 do not clearly distinguish between conjunctive probability multiplication and disjunctive probability addition. In particular, they cannot figure out whether combining probabilities should produce odds more or less favorable than the original odds before probabilities were combined. It is our prejudice that decision-making studies often imply a level of probability literacy higher than can be found in the average educated adult population. This overestimation is not just due to subject selection or some limited special instructions subjects are given, but even more to problem arrangements, and answer alternatives that do not permit the low-level (sometimes even stupid) answers that many subjects would give if left to their own devices. Instead, answer alternatives tend to be all more or less plausible. This view may be too pessimistic; certainly much empirical work would have to be done to justify our speculative hunch.

We would emphasize—perhaps we can speak here only for ourselves—that we do not view experiments on children's probability concepts as mainly hypothesis-testing experiments performed to verify or invalidate Piaget's theory. Empirical investigators have been less theoretical than Piaget and usually take a pragmatic approach in that successful solution of probability problems has been taken as the criterion of probability understanding. The suggestive details that emerge from the Piagetian interview protocols have not been analyzed further when the more objective scoring procedures have been applied.

Possibly even more rewarding than pursuing some of these incidental observations would be consideration of alternative formulations of probability. The simple frequentist view of probability as the limit of a relative frequency is the dominant one, adhered to by Piaget and all other developmental investigators (including the innovative formulations of Fischbein and Brainerd), but it far from exhausts the field. Alternative conceptions of probability are possible, such as the logical subjectivist theories (see Kyburg & Smokler, 1964). At least one partially alternative approach is known to psychologists through their acquaintance with Bayesian statistics. More than 30 years ago Carnap (1950) was counseling the necessity for a dual conception of probability, logical as well as frequentist.

Our suspicion is that there are forms of reasoning by analogy that to some extent conform to nonfrequentist probability theories. The fit may be loose and the forms of reasoning intermediate in terms of present formalized theories, but the psychologist here as elsewhere is always in the position of bending normative logical and mathematical theories to his or her own uses. In spite of a paucity of empirical research we do not believe that our verdict will be reversed and that unselected late adolescents and adults will ever be shown to perform at a very high level with probability concepts formulated in frequentist terms. Yet with regard to making decisions under uncertainty, states of probability ignorance are not as handicapping as they *should be* in carrying out the transactions of everyday life. Forms of nonprobabilistic inferential reasoning might take up some of the slack and permit a logical rather than a frequentist approach to probability. The developmental psychologist is interested not only in identifying what some of these shifty dodges and hybrid evasions might be that adults resort to now and again but also in tracking their origins back to childhood cognitive operations.

References

Brainerd, C. J. Working memory and the developmental analysis of probability judgment. *Psychological Review*, 1981, *88*, 463-502.

Carnap, R. *Logical foundations of probability* (1st ed.). Chicago: University of Chicago Press, 1950.

Chapman, R. H. The development of children's understanding of proportions. *Child Development,* 1975, *46*, 141-148.

Davies, C. M. Development of the probability concept in children. *Child Development,* 1965, *36*, 779-788.

Fischbein, E. *The intuitive sources of probabilistic thinking in children.* Dordrecht, Holland: Reidel, 1975.

Furth, H. G. A thinking laboratory adapted for deaf children (Final Report, Project No. 18-2044). Washington, D.C.: U.S. Office of Education, Bureau of Education for the Handicapped, December 1971.

Goldberg, S. Probability judgments by preschool children: Task conditions and performance. *Child Development*, 1966, *37*, 157-168.

Goodnow, J. Determinants of choice-distribution in two choice situations. *The American Journal of Psychology*, 1955, *68*, 106-116.

Hoemann, H. W., & Ross, B. M. Children's understanding of probability concepts. *Child Development*, 1971, *42*, 221-236.

Hyde, J. S. How large are cognitive gender differences? A meta-analyst using ω^2 and *d*. *American Psychologist*, 1981, *36*, 892-901.

Inhelder, B., & Piaget, J. *The growth of logical thinking from childhood to adolescence*. New York: Basic Books, 1958.

Kyburg, H. E., Jr., & Smokler, H. E. (Eds.). *Studies in subjective probability*. New York: Wiley, 1964.

Maccoby, E. E., & Jacklin, C. N. *The psychology of sex differences*. Stanford, California: Stanford University Press, 1974.

Matalon, B. Épistémologie et psychologie des probabilités. In F. Bresson & M. de Montmollin (Eds.), *Psychologie et épistémologie génétiques: thèmes Piagétiens*. Paris: Dunod, 1966.

Perner, J. Discrepant results in experimental studies of young children's understanding of probability. *Child Development*, 1979, *50*, 1121-1127. (a)

Perner, J. Young children's bets in probabilistic tasks involving disjoint and part-whole related events. *Archives de Psychologie*, 1979, *47*, 131-149. (b)

Piaget, J. Une expérience sur la psychologie du hasard chez l'enfant: le tirage au sort des couples. *Acta Psychologica*, 1950, *7*, 325-336.

Piaget, J. Intellectual evolution from adolescence to adulthood. *Human Development*, 1972, *15*, 1-12.

Piaget, J., & Inhelder, B. *The origin of the idea of chance in children*. New York: Norton, 1975. (Original French publication, 1951.)

Pire, G. Notion du hasard et développment intellectuel. *Enfance*, 1958, (Mar-Apr., No. 2), 131-143.

Ross, B. M. Probability concepts in deaf and hearing children. *Child Development*, 1966, *37*, 917-927.

Ross, B. M., & Hoemann, H. W. The attainment of formal operations: A comparison of probability concepts in deaf and hearing adolescents. *Genetic Psychology Monographs*, 1975, *91*, 61-119.

Ross, B. M., & Levy, N. Patterned prediction of chance events by children and adults. *Psychological Reports*, 1958, *4* (Monogr. Suppl. 2), 89-124.

Sullivan, F. V., & Ross, B. M. What is learned in probability learning. *Developmental Psychology*, 1969, *2*, 58-65.

Weir, M. W. Developmental changes in problem solving. *Psychological Review*, 1964, *71*, 473-490.

Weisz, J. R. Developmental change in perceived control: Recognizing noncontingency in the laboratory and perceiving it in the world. *Developmental Psychology*, 1980, *16*, 385-390.

Yost, P. A., Siegel, A. E., & Andrews, J. M. Nonverbal probability judgments by young children. *Child Development*, 1962, *33*, 769-780.

4. The Development of Quantity Concepts: Perceptual and Linguistic Factors

Linda S. Siegel

In this chapter I shall be concerned with the development of various quantity concepts and some of the factors which influence their development. Two aspects of early quantity concepts will be examined: (a) linguistic factors and (b) perceptual factors. The relationship between children's linguistic skills and their quantitative concepts will be considered in an attempt to separate cognitive processes from linguistic abilities. I shall also examine the perceptual and nonquantitative factors that influence the development of these concepts in order to understand the growth of number as a conceptual dimension.

Linguistic Factors and the Development of Quantity Concepts

By number concepts, we do not mean counting. Many children, even some as young as 18 months, can count by rote; that is, they can correctly say the number names in the proper sequence. (Research on this point is reviewed in some detail in Chapter 2 by Fuson, Richards, and Briars in this volume.) But this counting is not associated with a concept of quantity. It seems more like nonsense words that a child recites in a sequence. It is not uncommon to find children who can rote count but who cannot properly count a set of objects and arrive at the correct answer for the number of objects in the set. In one of our studies, we asked a 4-year-old to

This research was supported by Grant No. MA3773 from the Medical Research Council of Canada and Ontario Mental Health Foundation Grants 738-77/79 and 762-79/81.

count a set of nine pennies. He responded, "One, two, three, four hundred, seven, nine, fiveteen, eleventeen, thirty" and was quite pleased with his answer. The idea of number corresponding to a set size, the so-called cardination principle, was absent. Ask a 3- or 4-year-old to count his or her fingers. The child will find a different number each time he or she counts, sometimes counting the same finger twice or three times or missing a few. In Saxe's Chapter 5 in this volume, some rather similar behaviors are reported for the Oksapmin people of Papua New Guinea.

Therefore, children's language skills should be separated from their understanding of number and quantity. Unfortunately, in many studies, a child is asked questions like "Which is more?," "Are they the same number?," "Put them in order from the biggest to the littlest," "Give me five," when, in fact, there is considerable evidence that children below the age of 6 or 7 do not understand some or all of these words (Donaldson & Balfour, 1968; Griffiths, Shantz, & Sigel, 1967; Siegel & Goldstein, 1969).

Adults are often confused by a child's use of language which on the surface seems to indicate an understanding. A 2-year-old will say, while holding an empty glass in his or her hands, "I want more milk." The child is using *more* to mean *some*. A child may know that his or her mother is bigger than he or she is, but ask a child, "Who is bigger, mommy or daddy?," and the child will say "You're both big." Ask again, "But who is bigger?" "You're both big." *Big* and *little* have only absolute meanings; all things in the world are either big or little but the child cannot understand the relational meaning of the words.

An example of linguistic confusion is the child's failure to differentiate words related to number and length. In a study of this problem, Lawson, Baron, and Siegel (1974) showed 3- to 6-year-old children configurations of dots that varied in length and number and asked them, "Which row is longer or are they the same length?" and, "Which row has more or are they the same number?" Few children answered all the questions correctly. Some children answered every question as if they were asked about number; they interpreted questions about *both* length and number to mean number. Most of the rest of the children answered every question in terms of length; a longer length meant a bigger number, independently of what the number actually was.

Because of this language problem, I have studied the development of number concepts using nonverbal tasks (Siegel, 1971a, 1971b, 1972a, 1972b, 1973, 1974a, 1974b, 1978). These tasks are problem-solving situations that have in common that the child must solve them on the basis of a rule involving some aspect of quantity. Importantly, the understanding of words related to number and the production of language are not critical to the solution.

A Taxonomy of Quantity Concepts

I have developed a series of tasks in which quantity concepts are defined several ways according to a taxonomy given below. It is important to note that in the majority of these concepts we are not dealing strictly with number in that there are other dimensions, specifically brightness, density, and/or length, which are sometimes correlated with number and may serve as cues instead of number. Therefore, these tasks are more properly referred to as *quantity concepts*, rather than number concepts. Studies such as that of Greenberg (Note 1) will be necessary to determine the extent to which number is really the relevant dimension in these concepts.

Magnitude

The simplest quantity tasks involve understanding the concept of "larger or smaller than" without any particular reference to exact numerical size. We have called these tasks magnitude tasks (e.g., Siegel, 1972a, 1972b). There are five of them.

Area. In the magnitude area task the children are presented with two circles of different sizes and are required to choose the larger (smaller) one. The circles are selected from among nine different sizes. To solve this problem, the children have to be able to understand the concept of "larger (smaller) area." A typical stimulus appears in Fig. 4.1.

Length. (also called length cue—Siegel, 1978). In the length task, children are presented with two lines of different lengths. They are required to select the longer (shorter) line to be correct. The line lengths are selected from among nine possible lengths. In this task, the concept of "longer" (shorter) is being tested. A typical stimulus appears in Fig. 4.1.

Number. (also called no length cue—Siegel, 1978). In the number task, children are required to select the set with more (fewer) dots from among two sets whose size varies from among two to nine dots. The two lines of different numbers of dots

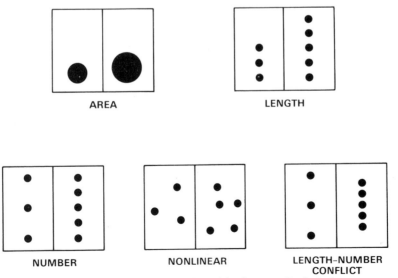

Fig. 4.1 Examples of stimuli used in the magnitude tasks.

are equivalent in length. In this task, the concept "more" ("fewer") is being tested. A typical stimulus appears in Fig. 4.1.

Nonlinear Magnitude. In this task, dots representing the numbers are arranged in a random pattern of approximately equal areas. The child is asked to select the larger (smaller) set size and there is no length cue to set size. A typical stimulus appears in Fig. 4.1.

Magnitude-Length-Number Conflict. The set of dots with the greater number of dots is shorter in length than the set with the smaller number of dots. Again, the child's task is to choose either the longer or smaller set size. A typical stimulus is shown in Fig. 4.1.

Oneness

There is, perhaps a quantity concept that appears to be simpler than any of those, in the preceding taxonomy, namely, the concept of "oneness." In this task, a set of size one is paired with all the other set sizes (e.g., two through nine) where the correct choice is either one, or for some children, the number besides one. While we have found that this is simpler than the above tasks (Siegel, 1972b), the problem is that one of the stimuli remains constant while the other varies. Hence, it may simply involve an oddity discrimination rather than a quantity concept because in all the other tasks both stimuli vary from trial to trial. As it stands now, the nature or the relationship of oneness to other quantity concepts is indeterminate.

Equivalence and Conservation

The above concepts are concerned with the perception of differences in quantity. Those that follow deal with the child's understanding of numerical equivalence. All of them have been designed to measure the understanding of "same number."

One-to-One Correspondence. (also called equivalence-length cue). In this task, the child is required to match sets of equal numerical size. The child has to select, from among two sets, the set that has the same number of dots as a standard set. The sizes of the correct sets and the incorrect alternative vary from two to nine dots. The length of the sets are the same. A typical stimulus appears in Fig. 4.2.

Equivalence-No Length Cue. The sample and the alternatives are all equal in length, irrespective of the number of dots in the set. There is no length cue to number, but the sets vary in density. A typical stimulus appears in Fig. 4.2.

Equivalence-Number-Length Conflict: Density. The correct alternative (identical in number) is a different length than the sample. The incorrect alternative is the same density as the sample. A typical stimulus appears in Fig. 4.2.

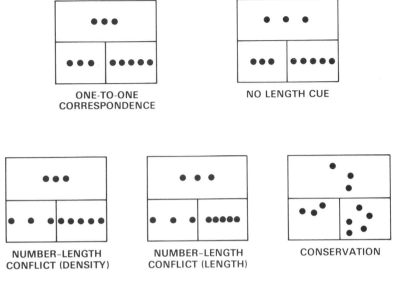

Fig. 4.2   Examples of stimuli used in the equivalence tasks.

Equivalence-Number-Length Conflict: Length. The correct alternative is a different length than the sample. The incorrect alternative is the same length as the sample. A typical stimulus is shown in Fig. 4.2.

Conservation. One aspect of the numerical reasoning is the understanding that number remains invariant in spite of spatial arrangement. This is the Piagetian concept of conservation (Piaget, 1965). I have designed a nonverbal conservation task to measure this concept. The child is required to select, from among two sets, the set that has the same number of dots as the standard on top of the card. The sizes of the correct sets and the incorrect alternative vary from two to nine dots. Unlike the one-to-one correspondence task, there are no spatial or density cues for number. A typical stimulus is shown in Fig. 4.2.

Summary

These tasks are some of the tests of quantitative knowledge I have used with young children. They are all nonverbal tasks in the sense that they do not rely on the child's understanding of particular quantitative terminology. The children may be given verbal instructions, usually to select the correct choice to receive a reward, but because they receive feedback about the correctness of their responses, understanding of the verbal instructions is not really necessary. The verbal instructions do not contain *any words* related to quantity. As the stimuli are different on each trial, problem solution is not a matter of stimulus-response association but of rule learning. I have used these tasks to study the relationship between language and thought in young children.

The Relationship between Language and Thought in the Child

The relationship of language to early conceptual development is central to many theories (Blank, 1974; Macnamara, 1972; Nelson, 1974). According to some approaches, language plays little, if any, role in the development and structure of the thought. Among these is the Piagetian position (e.g., Inhelder & Piaget, 1964; Pascual-Leone & Smith, 1969; Sinclair-de Zwart, 1969) that the development of cognitive structures occurs independently of language. According to this position, language is not a necessary condition for the emergence of operational thought, although both language and thought may depend on the development of the same underlying mechanisms of symbolic functioning. Similar views have been expressed by Furth (1966, 1971), Lenneberg (1967), Macnamara (1972), and Olson (1970).

Alternatively, according to other approaches, language is a cornerstone of cognitive development. Vygotsky (1962), for example, postulated an initial independence of language and thought, then the convergence when the child is approximately 2 years old. From then on, thought processes were said to be largely dependent on the child's mastery of language. Bruner (1964) also has assigned a critical role to language in cognitive development.

The relationship of cognition to language has been explored in a number of studies. In these studies, the order in which concepts and language associated with them are acquired have been studied. The assumption of such studies is: *If concepts precede the relevant language, then one can conclude that the concepts probably provide a basis for the acquisition of the related language or that language does not play a necessary role in the acquisition of the concepts.*

Quantitative and logical concepts provide an interesting case study of the language-thought relationship because nonlinguistic techniques exist to assess the concepts. In the area of quantity concepts, for example, Beilin and Kagan (1969) found that children's performance on a task involving the discrimination of one from two objects was superior to their ability to produce the correct plurals of nouns, possessives, and verbs. Koff and Luria (Note 2) found that children were able to learn the concepts of middle size before they could comprehend and produce comparatives expressing the relationship between objects of different sizes. For the development of logical concepts, Pascual-Leone and Smith (1969) found that children's ability to convey information about class membership was determined by the logical structure of the task, not by the language available to them. Similarly, Jones (1972) found that general verbal ability and the use of tentative statements were not related to the ability to solve certain logical problems. Weil (Note 3) found that the development of time concepts preceded the ability to understand the past progressive tense and terms such as "before" and "after." However, Bruner (1964) found that failure to transpose a 3 × 3 matrix was related to certain inconsistencies in the child's use of relational language, and Scholnick and Adams (1973) found that the ability to reverse a classification matrix was not a necessary prerequisite of the ability to comprehend the passive grammatical structure, which presumably involves a reversal of the active forms.

I shall now describe several studies designed to assess the relationship between young children's quantity concepts and their understanding of certain words related to quantity. An important departure from previous studies was that language and related concept abilities were tested on the same set of stimuli, thereby increasing the probability that these tasks were measuring related structures.

Study 1: Concept versus Language

This experiment was designed to assess the sequence of the development of elementary quantity concepts and the understanding of language about quantity.[1] The concept of relative quantity difference was measured by Siegel's (1971a, 1971b) magnitude length task (described earlier in this chapter). In this task, the child is required to select which of two sets has the greater or, for counterbalancing, fewer number of objects. The number of objects in each set varies from trial to trial so that the response is not merely to a single stimulus but is assumed to be mediated by a concept of relative size. In the corresponding language task, the child's understanding of the words "big" and "little" is tested with the same stimuli. These particular words, while not the most grammatically appropriate ones, were chosen because preschool children have difficulty in comprehending "more" and "less" (Donaldson & Balfour, 1968; Griffiths, Shantz, & Sigel, 1967; Siegel & Goldstein, 1969). "Bigger" and "littler" are also difficult (Koff & Luria, Note 2) for young children. The understanding of numerical equivalence was determined by one-to-one correspondence task (Siegel, 1971a, 1971b) described earlier in this chapter, in which the child is required to discriminate sets of objects which are numerically equal. In the corresponding language task, the child's understanding of "same number" was tested with the identical set of stimuli.

Method

Subjects. The subjects were 102 children enrolled in half-day nursery schools in Hamilton, Ontario. There were 45 3-year-olds, 21 boys and 24 girls, and 57 4-year-olds, 29 boys and 28 girls.

Design. Each child performed four tasks: magnitude-concept, magnitude-language, equivalence-concept, and equivalence-language. The tasks were administered to each child in one of eight orders, which varied the order of magnitude or equivalence (first or second) and concept or language within each of these (first or second).

Concept Tasks. The two concept tasks, described below, were complex problem-solving tasks. Both these concept tasks were tested with a Behavioral Controls 400-SR programmed learning apparatus. The response alternatives appeared under a

---

[1] This study has been briefly described in Siegel (1978).

clear plastic press panel, and the children responded by pressing the panel of their choice. The position of the correct alternative varied randomly from trial to trial. Correct responses were rewarded with tokens, which could be exchanged for a small toy at the end of a session. A noncorrection procedure was used. The only instruction that the child received was that selection of the correct alternative would result in some "play money" that could be exchanged for a toy. No relational terminology was used in the instructions. The criterion was nine out of ten consecutive correct responses. If criterion was not reached in 50 trials, the task was terminated.

Magnitude-Concept Task. There were 50 stimuli. Each stimulus consisted of two sets of dots of unequal number arranged in a horizontal line, each set containing from one to nine dots. The particular numbers in each stimulus varied from trial to trial; the combinations were selected randomly. Approximately one-half of the children were reinforced for selecting the stimulus with the larger number of dots and the remainder were reinforced for selecting the stimulus with the smaller number of dots.

Equivalence-Concept Task. The 50 sets of stimuli for this task each consisted of a sample and four alternatives. Only one of the alternatives was identical in number to the sample. Both the sample and the alternatives had between one and nine dots.

Language Tasks. Both language tasks used stimuli identical to their corresponding concept task. These stimuli were presented to the child on 5 inch × 7 inch index cards. For each stimulus, the children were asked about the word in question. They were not given any feedback about the correctness of their response, but they were told several times during the task that they were doing very well.

Magnitude-Language Task. The stimuli for this task were identical to those in the magnitude concept task, except that there were only 25 trials, chosen randomly from the set of 50. For each stimulus, the child was asked to select the "big" or, for counterbalancing "little" set.

Equivalence-Language Task. The stimuli for this task were identical to the equivalence concept task except that there were only 25 trials, chosen randomly from the set of 50. For each stimulus the child was asked to select the group of dots that had the "same number" as the sample.

Results

The criterion for passing the magnitude and equivalence concept tasks was nine out of ten consecutive correct responses. If a child did not reach criterion in 50 trials, he or she was considered to have failed the task. A score of 15 or more correct out of 25 for the equivalence language task (four choice) and 18 or more out of 25 (2 choice) for the magnitude language task, was required for a passing score. For the magnitude task 44% of the 3-year-olds and 30% of the 4-year-olds passed the concept task and failed the language comprehension task. The percentages for the equivalence task were as follows: 3-year-olds, 9% and 4-year-olds, 14%. Clearly, the concepts of quantitative equality and difference, as measured in the present study, developed before understanding of the relational terminology, specifically the words, "big," "little," and "same."

The concept of differences in magnitude may be a necessary condition for understanding the relational terms "big" and "little" when applied to the same stimuli. The same is true of the concept of numerical equality and the word "same" when same refers to numerical identity. These findings are clear from the larger percentage of children in the pass-concept, fail-language cells and the small numbers (in two cases, 0) of subjects in the pass-language, fail-concept cells. Thus, if a child failed the concept task, there was no chance of success in the equivalence-language test and a very small chance in the magnitude-language test. Only three of the 102 children showed a reversal of this trend in that their language developed before the corresponding concept, in these cases, the magnitude concept. While all of these children failed the magnitude-concept task, they consistently selected the wrong alternative on almost every trial, rather than responding randomly. In all cases, they were reinforced for the selection of the smaller group, yet consistently selected the bigger one. This pattern of responding, which was not noted in any other subjects, appears to indicate the presence of a concept rather than complete confusion about the difference between the stimuli.

A significantly higher percentage of the 4-year-olds passed the language task when it was administered after the concept task than when it was administered prior to the concept task (81.25% vs. 56.00%, $Z = 2.07$, $p < .04$, two tailed). Since in this case, the success on language task was greater after learning the concept than before it, learning the concept appeared to facilitate solution of the language task. Since there were no cases in which concept acquisition was facilitated by having the language task first, this is indirect evidence that language-thought effects are unidirectional. I shall return to this point later.

The concept tasks in this study were learning tasks with feedback provided for correct responses, since this seemed to be the most reasonable way to assess concepts nonverbally in the young child. But it could be argued that the children did not possess the magnitude and equivalence concepts when they started but acquired them in the course of the discrimination learning. There are two kinds of evidence that argue against this interpretation. First, the children who passed the concept task did so in relatively few trials. The mean number of trials to attain criterion for those who succeeded were: 3-year-olds, magnitude, 8.57; 3-year-olds, equivalence, 7.15; 4-year-olds, magnitude, 5.04; 4-year-olds, equivalence, 6.96. Therefore, if concept acquisition is involved, it is quite rapid. Second, the probabilities of correct responding in the precriterion trials for those who succeeded do not change from trial to trial. The precriterion data do not suggest gradual acquisition and these data may be evidence of all-or-none learning (see Brainerd & Howe, 1979, 1980, for additional evidence on this point). As for the possibility of differential motivation in the language and concept tasks, because of the presence of reinforcement in the latter, if this were the case, certain differences between orders of task administration would be expected. The shift from reward to nonreward should have produced a decrement when the language task was administered after the concept task. In fact, there were no order effects, except in one group in which the concept-first, language-second group performed better than the group which had the tasks in the reverse order, *opposite* to the above prediction.

On the basis of these results, it seems quite clear that, for the preschool child, concepts of numerical equality and inequality are learned before the relevant relational terminology. These type of concepts exist independently of, and prior to, language, at least the language investigated in this study.

Study 2: Does Language Training Facilitate Concept Acquisition?

Study 2 was designed to examine the degree to which a relevant word facilitates concept acquisition.[1] The role of language in concept development was assessed by manipulating the presence or absence of a specific verbal cue about the nature of the solution. Also, the child's production of terminology related to quantity was examined, and the relationship of linguistic skills to the performance on the concept tasks was assessed. The role of language was assessed in Study 2 by varying certain aspects of the operation of linguistic factors within the concept learning task. To the extent that language-thought independence exists and if cognitive operations develop before the appropriate language, then concept acquisition, at least early in development, should not be facilitated by language.

Evidence of the role of linguistic control of cognitive operations in children under 6 years of age is equivocal. Some studies have found little effect of subject generated or externally given verbal cues (e.g., Conrad, 1971; Flavell, 1970; Olson, 1970; Osler & Madden, 1973; Reese, 1962; White, 1965), while other studies, such as those of Blank and Bridger (1964) and Kendler and Kendler (1962), have found that verbal cues facilitated the acquisition of certain concepts. One of the purposes of Study 2 was to determine the degree to which verbal labels could facilitate the acquisition of quantity concepts. The basic technique was to administer the problems described previously to groups of 3- and 4-year-old children with instructions that spelled out the solutions, depending on which was appropriate to the task, as the "big," "little," or "same number" alternative (cue condition). Control groups (no cue condition) performed the identical task without the verbal cue. If these concepts exist prior to the relevant language, then, at least in the early stages of concept development, the verbal cue should not facilitate solution. However, if the verbal cue can influence the problem solving, then this may be a case of language facilitating thought.

A related question about the relationship between language and thought concerns the degree to which a child can generate language about quantity in relation to the stimuli used in these problems and whether this language production is related to problem solution. To the extent that a discrepancy between language and concepts exists, then language production and concept attainment may occur before language production. That is, if thought occurs prior to language, then children should be able to solve the problem before they can produce quantity language in relation to these stimuli. The child's ability to describe stimuli with meaningful language about the quantitative relationships was examined in an attempt to determine the extent to which language production is related to the ability to solve these problems.

Another purpose of this experiment was to investigate H. H. Clark's (1970) three postulated stages in the acquisition of relational terminology. In the first stage, children use this terminology in the nominal sense. A relational word or adjective is used to denote membership in some global class, but comparative properties are absent. Children at this stage might say of two unequal groups, "They are both the big one." In the second stage, both polar terms of some dimension are interpreted as referring to the most extended, or positive, end of the dimension, for example, both "more" and "less" are interpreted as meaning "more" (e.g., Donaldson & Balfour, 1968; Donaldson & Wales, 1970; Klatzky, Clark, & Macken, 1973; Palermo, 1973). In the final stage, children can use these words correctly.

Method

Subjects. The subjects were white middle-class children from nursery schools and day care centers in Hamilton and Burlington, Ontario. For the magnitude tasks, there were 180 preschool children (60 3-year-olds, 30 boys and 30 girls; 120 4-year-olds, 57 boys and 63 girls). For the equivalence tasks, the subjects were 80 preschool children, 24 3-year-olds (13 boys, 11 girls), and 56 4-year-olds (28 boys, 28 girls).

Tasks and Design. Both the magnitude and equivalence tasks were discrimination-learning tasks similar to those of Study 1. Instead of the programmed learning apparatus, the stimuli were presented to the child on 5 inch X 7 inch index cards. An individual child was only administered one task, magnitude or equivalence, and was randomly assigned to one of the conditions within each task.

Magnitude. For each of the three magnitude tasks, 40 stimuli were used, each with two vertical rows of dots. The particular numbers used on each stimulus were selected randomly from all the possible combinations of the numbers 2-9. For each task, stimuli were presented in a predetermined random order. A representative stimulus from each magnitude task is shown in Fig. 4.1 (length, number, and length-number conflict).

A representative stimulus for each equivalence task is shown in Fig. 4.2 [one-to-one correspondence, conservation, no length cue, number-length conflict (density), number-length conflict (length)].

The subjects were assigned to one of four independent groups. These were the absence or presence of the verbal cue (cue versus no cue) and, within each of these groups, one half of the subjects were reinforced for choosing the more numerous set (labeled "big" for the cue condition) and one-half for the set with fewer objects (labeled "little" for the cue condition). The instructions for each condition were as follows:

1. Cue. "Here is a picture. Here is another picture. (The experimenter pointed to each one in turn.) If you pick the big (little) picture, you will get some play money. When you have enough play money, you can buy these toys."
2. No Cue. "Here is a picture. Here is another picture. (The experimenter pointed to each one in turn.) If you pick the correct picture, you will get some play money. When you have enough play money, you can buy one of these toys."

Correct responses were reinforced with a coin. For the first five trials, if the child did not select the correct one, the experimenter told the child that his or her choice was wrong and then pointed to the correct one and told the child it was the correct one. Each child was administered 40 trials.

Results

Magnitude Task Analyses. The mean number of errors for the 40 trials of each task is shown in Fig. 4.3. A mixed model analysis of variance for condition (cue versus no cue), type of cue/concept (big versus little), and task was performed. For the 3-year-olds, there were no differences as a function of condition or type of cue/concept. There was a significant effect of tasks $[F(2, 112) = 7.64, p < .005]$. The length task was significantly easier than the other two (Duncan's multiple range test, $p < .05$). For the 4-year-olds, there were significant effects of condition $[F(1, 116) = 46.49, p < .001]$ and type of cue/concept $[F(1, 116) = 22.44, p < .001]$, and a significant interaction between these two variables $[F(1, 116) = 10.11, p < .005]$. There were no differences in error rates for the "big" and "little" concepts in the no cue condition, but there were in the cue condition. There was also a significant effect of task $[F(2, 232) = 7.96, p < .001]$. The length task was the easiest, the number task more difficult, and the number-length conflict task the most difficult (Duncan's multiple range test, $p < .05$).

Equivalence Task Analysis. The mean number of errors for each age group is shown in Fig. 4.3. Mixed-model analyses of variance for condition (cue versus no cue), and tasks were performed separately for each age group. For the 3-year-olds, there were no effects of tasks or condition. The majority of the 3-year-olds were performing at, or near, chance (20 errors). For the 4-year-olds, there were significant effects of cue $[F(1, 54) = 8.17, p < .005]$ and task $[F(3, 162) = 4.41, p < .01]$ and no interaction. The number-length conflict (length) task was significantly more difficult than the other three (Duncan's multiple range test, $p < .05$). For either the magnitude or the equivalence tasks, there were no order effects of differences between the performances of boys and girls.

Language Analysis. The subjects' responses to the language production task were scored for the presence or absence of correct quantity response by two inde-

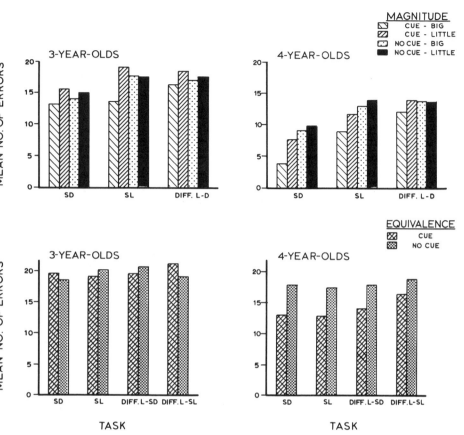

Fig. 4.3 Mean number of errors for 40 trials of each task in Study 2. (From L. S. Siegel and C. J. Brainerd, *Alternatives to Piaget: Critical essays on the theory.* New York: Academic Press, 1978, Fig. 3.4, p. 52. Reproduced by permission.)

pendent raters. Examples of appropriate responses were, "The big one," "The one with more dots (magnitude)," or "They both have the same number (equivalence)." Inappropriate responses were such statements as, "I wanted to," "I like that one," "The ones that have two," or "This has four and this has seven." Failures to respond were also included in this category. The relationship between success and failure on each task and production of quantity language was calculated by the McNemar test. For the 3-year-olds, successful performance on two of the magnitude tasks (length and number-length conflict task) occurred prior to the ability to produce the appropriate quantity language. Significant numbers of children passed the concept tasks and failed the language production tasks. The same was true for the 4-year-olds on the magnitude-length task and the equivalence-length cue and number-length conflict tasks. For the other tasks, concept solution did not precede quantity language production.

The language samples from the magnitude tasks were analyzed to determine the nominal or relational qualities of the child's descriptions of the stimuli. Analysis of the linguistic descriptions of the equivalence stimuli showed that if quantity language was used, it was relational. For the magnitude task, the children's responses were classified in one of three categories: nominal [e.g., "The big (little) one," "It's too big," "They are both big (little)"], relational [e.g., "The big picture has more dots than that one," "This is more bigger," "This has more (less) dots"], and other (including no response). For the 3-year-olds, 15% of the responses were nominal and 3% were relational. There was no significant difference in error rates between the children who used nominal or relational responses except for one task, the length task in the cue "little" condition. In this task, the relational responders made significantly fewer errors than the nominal ones. In addition, a number of children in this study showed a response pattern that is consistent with the inter-mediate stage proposed by Clark (1970) in which children use a single word to denote both ends of a polar dimension, for example, "more" is understood to mean both "more" and "fewer." This pattern consisted of selecting the wrong alter-native on most of the trials (at least 35 out of 40). Of the 3-year-olds, 6 out of 30 children who were administered the "little" tasks did this on at least one of them. No 3-year-old did this in the "big" tasks. Nine 4-year-olds showed the same pattern in the "little" conditions and four did in the "big" condition. Their verbalizations in the language production task were, for the most part, correct. For example, in the "little" groups, the children stated that they were selecting the littler stimulus, although, in fact, they were selecting the more numerous one. Therefore, they used the antonym to refer to the concept. Since most of the confusions occurred in the "little" conditions, and "little" was interpreted as meaning "big," this pattern could be a result of the child's assigning one term, usually the positive one, to both ends of the dimensions.

To determine whether or not there were tendencies to refer to the positive, as opposed to the negative end, of the dimension, responses in the language production task were classified as positive (e.g., big, more, taller), negative (e.g., little, less, short), mixed (use of both types of terminology), or irrelevant or no response. These data are shown in Table 4.1. Clearly, for both the 3- and 4-year-olds, in the "big" conditions (both cue and no cue), there were significantly more references to the positive end of the dimension. Even in the "little" conditions, there were more responses to the positive end of the dimension, although the differences were not significant.

Discussion

For the younger children, *a verbal cue did not facilitate the learning of numeri-cal similarity or difference.* For the older children, it did. These data suggest that in the early stages of quantity concept formation, language and thought function inde-pendently and that language has no facilitative effect on thought. Problem solution occurred prior to language production for some of the tasks, for others they were not related. In the case of the 4-year-olds, the facilitating effects of a cue can be considered evidence for verbal mediation. In this case, the argument for the indepen-dence of language and thought cannot be made, and it would appear that the older

Table 4.1 Asymmetry of Language Production in Magnitude Tasks: Study 2

Task	Proportion of responses[a]		
	Positive	Negative	Mixed
3-year-olds			
Cue-big*	.27	.02	.04
No cue-big**	.09	0	0
Cue-little	.09	.09	.09
No cue-little	.07	.02	.02
4-year-olds			
Cue-big*	.42	.05	.09
No cue-big**	.32	.04	.08
Cue-little	.21	.14	.16
No cue-little	.14	.09	.10

[a] Significance of difference between positive and negative:
*$p < .001$.
**$p < .03$.

children sometimes used language to help them to solve the problem. However, even in the older age group, there were many children who could arrive at the correct solution but not describe how they did so. It should be noted that one of the stimuli was available during the production task, so that memory failure was not a significant factor in poor performance.

As children mature, they are more likely to use comparative rather than nominal terminology. Occasionally, another use of language occurred that was suggestive of an intermediate level of responding. In these cases, the child used the same word to refer to opposite ends of a dimension and combined this word with a different adjective or modifying phrase to refer to each extremity. For example, the children said such things as, "This is big and this is a little bit big," "This has a little bit lotsa dots and this has lotsa lotsa dots," "These are wider in and these are wider out," "Those are farther together and they're almost together," "It's too long and it's not too long," and "This is long and this is a bit long" (pointing to the short of the two stimuli). This usage may account for the errors in labeling opposite ends of the same dimension with the same word. If children get confused and forget the modifier, the type of errors that Clark (1970) and Donaldson and Wales (1970) described could result quite easily.

While there is clear evidence for asymmetry in the acquisition of positive and negative relational terminology, the same asymmetry is not apparent in the acquisition of the concepts. There were no differences between the acquisition of the "big" and "little" concepts in the no cue condition, but "big" facilitated concept attainment more than "little" did in the cue condition. In Study 1, the "big" and "little" concepts were of equal difficulty. The asymmetries appear to be more related to language acquisition than to acquisition of the concepts, again suggesting independence of language and thought.

The order to task difficulty is consistent with earlier results (Siegel, 1974a, 1974b) suggesting that the child gradually learns to separate and coordinate the dimensions of length and number. The number-length conflict task, in which length and number are negatively correlated was especially difficult. One of the children stated the problem with this task: "This one is bigger (pointing to the more numerous, more dense set) but this one is two so it's smaller." Another child said, "It's big because if you get mixed up you know it's big." It is apparently the relationship of these two dimensions that creates the difficulty with the under-standing of number.

The development of children's perceptual and cognitive skills has been proposed as the basis for their early language acquisition (Bever, 1970; E. V. Clark, 1974; Slobin, 1973). This study suggests that conceptual development, in this case the ability to recognize numerical equality and inequality, occurs prior to the child's acquisition of relational terminology and is necessary, but not sufficient, for this acquisition. In addition, these data partially support the view that relative cog-nitive complexity determines the order in which language will be acquired. The magnitude concept presents a simpler, more basic quantity concept than equiva-lence (for a further discussion of this point see Brainerd, 1973; Siegel, 1974). Clearly, the magnitude concept was the easier. Understanding of the words "big" and "little" preceded the understanding of same number, which shows that words for the more complex concepts are learned later than words for the simpler ones.

The results of these studies strongly suggest that language and thought function independently in the young child and, as the child develops, concepts and language tend to become more related. The implications of these findings for the assessment of cognitive operations in the young child are quite clear; concepts emerge on a nonverbal, probably perceptual level, before language has any relationship to them. Therefore, to the extent that the results from these experiments are generalizable to other concepts, measurements of cognitive skills which rely on the understand-ing of language or the production of linguistic responses will underestimate the cognitive abilities of the young child. These studies demonstrate that children can process information about relative and absolute size in a meaningful way and assimi-late new instances of these concepts, yet not necessarily be able to respond to or produce language about quantity.

Study 3: Visual versus Verbal Functions

While we have found discrepancies between young children's ability to solve conceptual problems and to produce language about those concepts, an alternate explanation has been offered for this discrepancy. Blank (1974) has proposed that young children are more likely to use language in a situation in which visual cues are not present. She cites, as evidence, the fact that she taught a simple visual form discrimination problem to 3-year-old children. She then asked them to tell her "which one had the candy." When the stimuli were present, the children often failed to explain the reason for their choice. But when the objects were removed, most of the children could explain their responses.

I attempted to test Blank's hypothesis by requiring 3- and 4-year-old children to learn the magnitude discrimination problem described earlier. They had to select a set with the larger number of dots. Once they had learned the problem, they were asked, "Which one got the candy?" under one of two conditions. In the stimulus present condition, one of the stimuli from the task was present. In the no stimulus condition, the children did not see a stimulus from the task when asked the question. A third condition, stimulus first, was added in which the children were shown one of the stimuli before they started the concept learning task, and asked to "Tell me about this" and were encouraged to verbalize about the stimuli.

The purpose of the study was to test two hypotheses: (a) that a visual cue will retard language production; and (b) that language experience will facilitate concept learning. There were 32 3-year-olds and 32 4-year-olds in each of the three groups. The children were asked, "Tell me which one has the candy," at the end of the task. The percentage of children giving quantity responses in their answer is shown in Table 4.2. A quantity answer was defined as any answer that contained a specific number or a word denoting absolute size or a relational concept, for example, "The big one," "Two and nine," "Many more there," "Lots more there," "This is a big one," and "This is over the one and this is the big one."

For the 3-year-olds, there were no significant differences between the three groups $[\chi^2(2) = 11.29, p < .1]$. However, children who saw the card before they started the test were significantly more likely to give a quantity response than either the Stimulus Present or the No Stimulus group $[\chi^2(1) = 5.10\ p < .025, 3.65, .05 > p < .10$, respectively]. For the 4-year-olds, there were no significant differences among the three groups.

Therefore, Blank's hypothesis about visual interference with language production was not confirmed with this particular task. However, some prior exposure to the stimulus and having been encouraged to talk about it did facilitate the use of a quantity explanation at the end of the task, at least in the case of the 3-year-olds. This prior exposure may have called their attention to language and may have encouraged them to use language in the solution of the tasks.

One of the conclusions of this study is that the relevant language does not appear to be used spontaneously. Another is that there is no evidence that visual functions are dominant and compete with with verbalizations. Blank hypothesized that language emerges first in the situations dealing with the memory for absent

Table 4.2 Percentage of Children in Each Condition (Study 3) Who Produced a Quantity Response[a]

	Stimulus present	No stimulus	Stimulus first
3-year-olds	37.5	31.3	76.5
4-year-olds	52.4	62.5	66.7

[a] These percentages are calculated only for the children who passed the task.

but previously seen events or concepts does not seem to be true for this situation. This was not the case in the data from this study. Language occurs only if children this age are encouraged to verbalize, which again suggests an independence of language and thought in the young child.

Study 4: Training of Cognitive and Language Abilities

One way of investigating the relationship between language and thought is to examine the relative effects of training in these areas. If language training facilitates the acquisition of concepts, then the possibility exists that language may play a significant role in a thought of a young child. However, if training on concepts is more effective, then language may not have a primary role. The degree to which language or concept training generalizes to other concepts may provide information about the role of language in thought.

I have investigated these relationships with the magnitude concepts we have discussed earlier. Three- and 4-year-old children were tested for their understanding of two of the magnitude concepts, length and number. In each case, the child was required to select the larger set size. A concept or language training with either length or number concepts was then instituted.

Concept Training

The concept training procedure involved 40 trials of presentation of stimuli similar to the ones used in the concept task. One-half of the children were trained on the Length task, and half were trained on the Number task. They were reinforced for a correct response with a correction procedure. Wrong responses were corrected.

Language Training. The language training consisted of presentation of the same stimuli as in the concept task with 40 trials of feedback about the correctness or incorrectness of the child's response. The child was instructed to select the "big one." The children received the language training with either the length or number stimuli.

Pretest. Each child was administered a pretest of four tasks, Length-Concept, Length-Language, Number-Concept, and Number-Language. Four counterbalanced orders were used. After the children had been trained, they received a posttest of all four tasks.

The focus of this study was whether concept or language training would facilitate the learning and to what extent training would generalize to the other task on which the child had not been trained. These results are shown in Table 4.3. As can be seen, the concept and the language training were about equally successful when the posttest involved the same task. However, language training did not generalize to the other tasks, whereas the concept training did in about one-third of the cases. Therefore, it appears that the concept training is more successful when it comes to generalization. While the language training was successful for a particular task, it hardly generalized to other tasks, although most of the children were reasonably successful in the language training task.

Two trends have emerged thus far. First, language does not facilitate thought in the case of more complex concepts, but it may with simpler concepts. Second, language exerts more influence on cognition as children get older. In younger children, there appears to be an independence of language and thought, but language may serve a facilitative function with some concepts as children get older.

Study 5: Cognitive Development of Children with Impaired Language Development

Another way of investigating the language-thought relationship is to study children with language problems. We studied a group of preschool children who were language impaired, that is, they had normal nonverbal cognitive skills as measured by standardized tests, but their language development was delayed (Siegel, Lees, Allan, & Bolton, 1981). The aim of the study was to discover how they would perform on these cognitive tests. If they solved these tasks in a manner identical to normal children, then we could conclude that their significantly below average language abilities do not appear to influence their cognitive development. If, on the other hand, their performance was below average, then language might play a role in cognitive development, at least in relation to the particular concepts that we studied.

The subjects of this study were preschool children, aged 3-5 with impaired language development and a comparison group of children with normal language development, who were matched with language-impaired children on the bases of age, sex, and social class. The children in the language-impaired group had normal nonverbal intelligence scores (Leiter) and significantly below average scores on standardized tests of language comprehension and expression (Reynell). Their hearing was in the normal range, and they had no neurological or psychological problems that were assessed to be the primary reason for the language impairment.

Table 4.3 Proportion of Children Who Failed the Pretest and Passed the Posttest in Each Condition (Study 4)

	Posttest	
Training	Concept task	Language task
Language training on the identical task	.33	.47
Concept training on the identical task	.44	.27
Language training on a different task	0	.09
Concept training on a different task	.35	.33

The language-delayed and normal children were given the tasks area, length, number, and one-to-one correspondence and have been described previously. We added several others (see Fig. 4.4):

Seriation. In this task, the child was shown lines of four different lengths, arranged in a random order with the bottoms even. The child had to select the second largest. In order to achieve a correct solution, a child had to be able to seriate, that is, to order the lines by size.

The tasks also included three tasks which were nonverbal alternatives to certain spatial concepts in the Piagetian system (Piaget & Inhelder, 1956). These tasks were as follows:

Spatial Ordering. In this task, the child was required to match sets of 3-4 dots of different colors which were in the same spatial order. The child had to select from two sets of dots, the correct response being the set in which the order of the colors of the dots matched the standard.

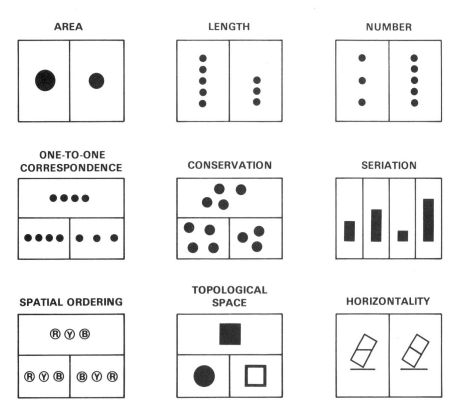

Fig. 4.4 Examples of the stimuli used in Study 5.

Topological Space. In this task, the child had to select between two alternatives the shape in which the topological features matched those of the standard. The incorrect alternative matched the standard in Euclidean features. In the example in Fig. 4.4, the circle matches the square topologically in that they are both closed. The incorrect alternative is a square, which has the same Euclidean features as the standard but a different topological feature (open).

Horizontality. In this task, the child was required to recognize that water level remains parallel to the surface in spite of the tilt of the container. The child had to select between two alternatives, one in which the water level was parallel to the surface and the other in which it was parallel to the bottom of the container. A stimulus from each of these tasks is illustrated in Fig. 4.4.

As can be seen in Table 4.4, there were no differences between the language-impaired and normal language children on the three magnitude tasks (area, length, and number). The judgment of relative quantity was, therefore, not significantly different in these groups. The language-impaired group had difficulty with the more complex concepts (one-to-one correspondence, conservation, seriation, spatial order, and topological space). Therefore, the understanding of these more complex concepts may require language for their solution. One concept, horizontally, did not show any difference between the groups because so few children in either group passed.

The language-impaired children had no difficulty with the simpler concepts of larger or more. It may be that these concepts involve global wholistic judgments and do not involve the use of language.

Table 4.4 Percentages of the Impaired Language and Normal Children Passing the Tasks Used in Study 5

	Language impaired	Normal language[a]
Magnitude concepts		
Area	62	69[b]
Length	50	65[b]
Number	62	73[b]
Concrete operations		
One to one correspondence	8	42**
Conservation	4	23[b]
Seriation	0	42
Spatial concepts		
Spatial order	8	42**
Horizontality	12	8[b]
Topological space	8	46*

[a] $n = 26$ in each group.
[b] Not significant.
* $p < .01$, two tailed.
** $p < .001$, two tailed.

On the other hand, the language impaired children's difficulty with the more complex concepts may reflect the role of language in these cognitive operations. They had difficulty with concepts such as one-to-one correspondence, conservation, spatial ordering, and seriation, which may involve some type of sequential processing. Language may be important in these situations because it helps in the storage of information and/or place marking in a sequence.

Therefore, it appears from the results of this study that the relationship of language and thought depends on task complexity. Based on the performance of the language impaired subjects, language may play a role in more complex tasks but does not appear to play a major role in simpler tasks.

Study 6: The Abstraction of the Concept of Number[2]

These demonstrations of the complex relationships between language and thought in young children lead to the inevitable conclusion that nonverbal methods are the appropriate means to study the development of quantity concepts in the young child. Using nonverbal methods, I have studied the emergence of the understanding of the concept of numerical equivalence, a fundamental cardination concept. The purpose of this study was to examine the children's emerging concepts of number, independent of their language skills.

It has been found in previous studies involving verbal methods that the child easily confuses a variety of dimensions with number. One of the most common of these is length. Children often have trouble differentiating number as a dimension independent of length (e.g., Baron, Lawson, & Siegel, 1975; Brainerd, 1977; Gelman, 1972; Lawson, Baron, & Siegel, 1974; Piaget, 1965; Pufall & Shaw, 1972; Siegel, 1974a). Children have difficulty recognizing that two sets are numerically equivalent if they have different spatial arrangements (Siegel, 1973). Children also have difficulty recognizing that two sets are numerically equivalent if they have different matching set with the correct numeral or judging the relative size of two sets if the arrangement of objects in a set is not linear (Siegel, 1972, 1974b). If a set is heterogeneous—that is, it is composed of sets of nonidentical objects—it is more difficult for children to judge the number in that set or to associate the correct numeral with it than if the set is composed of identical items (Siegel, 1973, 1974b), although Gelman and Tucker (1975) have found that heterogeneity does not interfere with the judgment of small set sizes. On the basis of these studies it appears that the child often has difficulty in extracting number as a dimension.

This study was designed to determine the manner in which children learn to abstract number from dimensions irrelevant to number. Specifically, the manner in which this abstraction process interacts with the child's perception of numerosity and with nonnumerical stimulus dimensions was examined. We chose the dimensions

---

[2]The author wishes to thank Fred Meek who assisted in the data collection and analysis of this study.

of color, form, size (area), and heterogeneity, all of which may vary along with number in sets that require numerosity judgments.

In studies, the child's concept of number depends on the absolute size of the set; that is, the child learns about the smaller numbers (set sizes 1-5) before he or she learns about the larger ones (set sizes 6-9). (For an extensive review of the literature see Gelman, 1972.) Therefore, we examined the hypothesis that the abstraction of number as a relevant dimension might depend on the absolute size of the set. It was expected that number might be more easily perceived as a relevant dimension with smaller set sizes than with larger set sizes. We also tested the hypothesis that the ability to recognize the numerical inequality of sets with identical items would depend on the absolute size difference between the sets. That is, if two sets were, for example, perceptually similar but 4-7 items different in numerical size, they would be more likely to be judged as not the same number as two sets perceptually similar but only 1-3 items different in size.

Thus, the ability to recognize the numerical equivalence or inequivalence of sets was expected to depend on two factors: (a) perceptual ones involving the perceptual similarity within and between sets; and (b) cardinality of the sets, both in terms of the absolute cardinal number in the sets and the absolute size of the difference between sets.

The results showed that the two processes of (a) abstracting number as a dimension; and (b) understanding of cardinality appear sequentially. Because we used totally nonverbal methods, the issue of linguistic confusion and understanding of relational terminology is not relevant.

Subjects. The subjects were 84 4-, 5-, and 6-year-old children, 28 children (14 boys and 14 girls) at each of the three age levels. They were chosen randomly from classes in various preschools and elementary schools in Hamilton, Ontario.

Procedure. The tasks involved learning the principle of numerical equivalence. The child was required to learn to match two numerically equivalent sets, using a series of stimulus configurations with a sample and four alternatives, only one of which matched the sample in numerical size (Fig. 4.5).

These were administered on a teaching machine apparatus. The children were instructed to select the one that had the same number as the "top one" (sample), and they received feedback about the correctness or incorrectness of each response. The feedback was both verbal ("Yes, that's right," or, "Not that one," etc.) and tangible, a small play coin, if the answer was correct. The first five trials were correction trials on which the machine did not advance unless a correct response was made. These forced-choice trials insured that the children understood there was a correct response. The individual tasks were:

1. Equivalence: The sample and all the alternatives were homogeneous sets of circles which were equivalent and arranged in a linear array. The numerical size of the sample and alternatives were chosen randomly from the set of 1-9. A typical stimulus from this task is illustrated in Fig. 4.5.

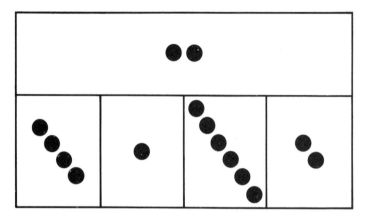

Fig. 4.5 An example of the stimuli for the equivalence task (Study 6).

The following six tasks were constructed so that the child could match the sample and the alternatives on either the dimension of number (correct) or some other dimension, specifically, shape, color, and size (incorrect). The correct choice was identical in numerical size, but was a different shape, color or size (depending on the task) from the sample. The alternative that was identical in shape, color or size, but not number, to the sample was called the *conflict alternative*. It matched with the sample on some dimension other than number. This allowed us to test the degree to which each dimension was confounded with number. The conflicting alternative was either close (1-3 items different) or not close (4-7 items different) to the sample in numerical size.

2. Shape (4-7): The sample and the correct alternative were identical in number but different shapes (e.g., circles and squares). A total of 10 different shapes were used. One alternative, 4-7 items different from the sample, was the same shape as the sample but, obviously, different in numerosity from the sample. The two remaining alternatives were sets composed of shapes that were the same as the sample, but different in number. A representative stimulus is illustrated in Fig. 4.6.

3. Shape (1-3): This task was the same as shape (4-7), but the sample and the conflicting alternative differed by 1-3 items.

4. Color (4-7): The sample and the correct alternative were identical in number, but different in color. A total of 10 different colors were used. One alternative, 4-7 items different from the sample, was the same color as the sample but different in numerosity. The two remaining alternatives were the same color as the correct alternative but different in number.

5. Color (1-3): This task was the same as color conflict (4-7), but the sample and the conflict alternative differed by 1-3 items.

6. Size (4-7): The sample and the correct alternative were different in size (area) but identical in number. A total of 10 sizes were used. For half the trials, the conflict alternative was a set of circles smaller in area than the correct one and for the other half of the trials, it was larger. The numerical size of the conflicting

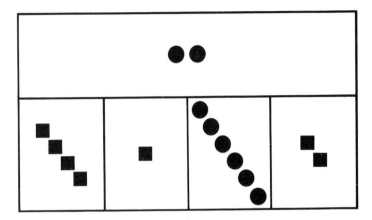

Fig. 4.6 An example of one of the stimuli for the shape (4-7) task. The conflict alternative has six dots.

alternative was 4-7 items different from the sample.
7. Size (1-3): This task was the same as size 4-7, but the size of the conflict alternative was 1-3 items different from the sample.

Two tasks called heterogeneous-shape and heterogeneous-shape/color, were included in the sets which were completely heterogeneous. A representative stimulus from the heterogeneous-shape task is shown in Fig. 4.7. Each set was composed of different items. These tasks were as follows:

8. Heterogeneous-shape: The sets were heterogeneous for shape.
9. Heterogeneous-shape/color: The sets were heterogeneous for both shape and color.

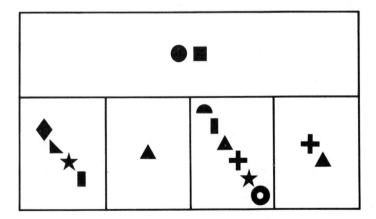

Fig. 4.7   An example of one of the stimuli from the heterogeneous shape task.

If the child has difficulty abstracting number as a dimension, we would expect two major findings. First, the simple equivalence tasks in which number was not in conflict with other dimensions should be the easiest. The tasks that had number in conflict with other dimensions should be especially difficult for the younger children. Second, the conflicting alternative (the set that was identical to the sample in some dimension other than number) should be chosen instead of the numerically correct but perceptually different one, especially by the younger children.

Results

The mean number of errors in 20 trials for each task and each age are shown in Table 4.5. A mixed model analysis of variance for the within subject variable of task and the between subjects variables of age and order was performed. There were significant effects of age [$F(2, 72) = 36.95, p < .001$], and task [$F(8, 576) = 20.57, p < .001$] and a significant Age × Task interaction [$F(16, 576) = 3.02, p < .001$].

The equivalence task, which did not have a dimension in conflict with number, was the easiest. The other tasks, which required the dimension of number to be differentiated from another dimension (size, shape, or color) or those involving heterogeneous sets, were more difficult for the 4-year-olds. Only some of the tasks requiring number to be selected from other dimensions were more difficult for the 5-year-olds. The 6-year-olds achieved relatively high levels of performance on all tasks. The 4-year-olds performed at almost as high a level as the 5- and 6-year-olds on the equivalence task, but on the tasks that required them to separate number from another dimension, they made many errors. In shape (4-7) and shape (1-3), they chose the correct alternative only one-third of the time. The 6-year-olds were correct 75%-80% of the time on these two tasks.

There were significant developmental changes in the children's ability to match perceptually dissimilar sets on the basis of number.

Perceptual: Nonnumerical Strategies. Six of the tasks had what was called a conflicting alternative which were different in cardinal number, but identical in shape, color, or size (depending on the task) to the sample. The correct answer was identical in cardinal number but different in size, shape, or color from the sample. The hypothesis was that younger children would be more likely to select the

Table 4.5 Mean Number of Errors in 20 Trials

Age	Task: Equiv- alence	Size 4-7	Size 1-3	Color 4-7	Color 1-3	Shape 4-7	Shape 1-3	Hetero- geneous shape	Heterogeneous shape and color
4	7.5	9.2	10.4	9.6	10.6	13.7	12.6	11.3	11.5
5	4.5	5.5	6.2	5.1	4.9	9.2	7.0	6.0	7.2
6	2.1	1.7	3.0	2.4	3.2	3.6	4.6	2.8	3.5

conflicting alternative than the older children. The percentage of errors that were choices of the conflicting alternative are shown in Table 4.6 for each age and task. These are contingent percentages (i.e., the number of conflict errors divided by the total number of errors) of all the children in this study were much less likely to choose the conflicting alternative than the younger children. There was a significant tendency for the younger children to select the conflicting alternative, even though they were never reinforced for it. Although this strategy was unproductive in obtaining the reward, it was quite prevalent. (The dimension of number was reinforced, but the younger children did not seem to be able to ignore the irrelevant dimension and pay attention to number.) The presence of other dimensions interfered. They had evidenced an understanding of number in their performance on the simple equivalence task, so that they possessed the capacity to perceive number. Thus, the problem seems to be one of abstracting number in the face of irrelevant information. The older children, especially the 6-year-olds, were making different types of errors, estimation errors, which I shall describe in detail below.

Estimation: Numerical Strategies. I also examined the hypothesis that the process of recognizing that two sets are equivalent in number occurs later than the process of abstracting number. Certain features of these data substantiate the hypothesis. The older children were more likely than the younger children to make errors based on the absolute or relative numerical size of the set. Essentially, they were not as likely to be distracted by the irrelevant dimensions but were more likely to choose an incorrect answer (a) in the trials with the higher cardinal numbers; and (b) close in cardinal number and close in numerical size to the correct one. Their responses were controlled much more by numerical size.

To illustrate the above trends, let us look at the relative percentage of errors made by each group as a function of the cardinal number of the correct answer. Table 4.7 shows the percentages of errors made in the trials in which the correct answer was 6-9. Again, these are contingent percentages. As can be seen, the 4-year-olds were equally likely to make errors if the set size was 1-5 or 6-9 on most tasks. However, the 6-year-olds made many more of their errors on the trials with the larger cardinal number sets. In one task, over 90% of the errors were on the trials with the large number sets. The 5-year-olds are typically at an intermediate level. Many of their errors were in the trials with the higher set sizes. There is clearly a developmental trend in the increased likelihood that an error will be made in the higher set sizes for the older children. This trend was tested statistically by χ^2 tests on the frequencies of errors in each set size category as a function of age.

Table 4.6 Mean Percentages of Errors That Were Choices of the Conflict Alternative[a]

Age	Size 4-7	Size 1-3	Color 4-7	Color 1-3	Shape 4-7	Color 1-3
4	34.82	55.86	23.71	73.86	48.36	66.36
5	19.04	58.43	8.93	66.75	16.00	51.29
6	3.10	47.50	0.00	56.50	7.50	40.25

[a] These are contingent probabilities.

Table 4.7 Percentage of Errors as a Function of Cardinal Number (6-9) of Correct
Alternative

Task	Age		
	4	5	6
Equivalence	49.72	70.59	75.15
Size 4-7	56.18	65.88	78.11
Size 1-3	56.29	72.18	66.11
Color 4-7	62.77	76.78	91.70
Color 1-3	68.53	85.39	88.34
Shape 4-7	54.20	57.58	57.18
Shape 1-3	63.51	78.48	81.15
Heterogeneous shape	50.32	66.82	71.48
Heterogeneous shape and color	64.50	73.94	87.77

The data for these tasks, as a function of age and set size in which error occurred, are shown in Table 4.8. Children who made no errors or an equal number of errors in each category have been eliminated from the analysis. In many of the tasks, there was a significant association between error rate and age. The older children made a greater proportion of their errors on the large set sizes, indicating that their errors were due to an inaccurate assessment of cardinal number, since cardinal number is harder to assess accurately with large set sizes. Thus, the younger children were making errors by selecting an incorrect stimulus dimension for matching, while the older children were making errors by selecting an incorrect alternative in the larger numerical set size comparisons.

Developmental Differences in Strategies. The findings described thus far suggest the sequential emergence of two processes relating to the child's understanding of cardinal number: (a) the abstraction of the dimension of number; and (b) the ability to match sets on the basis of cardinal number in spite of the presence of irrelevant dimensions. To assess the presence of these strategies, we examined the tendency to choose an incorrect alternative close in numerical size to the correct one (cardinal number strategy). Close in numerical size was defined as selecting a set size one item different from the sample. Children were defined as having the cardinal number strategy if they chose an alternative that was one different from the correct one more frequently than they chose the conflict alternative. Children were defined as having the perceptual strategy if they chose the conflict alternative more frequently than an alternative close in numerical size to the correct one. The number of children employing each strategy is shown in Table 4.8. Children who made no errors, or who made an equal number of each type of error, were eliminated from the analysis. As can be seen from the data in Table 4.8, there is a significant association between age and strategy in all the tasks except one size (1-3). This may result from the fact that the dimension of size is logically related to number while color and shape are not. The older children are more likely to use a cardinal number strategy, and the younger ones are more likely to use a perceptual

Table 4.8 Frequency of Errors as a Function of Set Size and Age[a]

	Equivalence			Size (4-7)			Size (1-3)	
	1-5	6-9		1-5	6-9		1-5	6-9
Age			Age			Age		
4	14	7	4	8	13	4	11	15
5	2	16	5	4	8	5	2	21
6	4	15	6	1	13	6	3	15
	$\chi^2 = 15.50, p < .001$			$\chi^2 = 4.28, p < .20$			$\chi^2 = 8.29, p < .02$	

	Color (4-7)			Color (1-3)			Shape (4-7)	
	1-5	6-9		1-5	6-9		1-5	6-9
Age			Age			Age		
4	8	15	4	7	20	4	14	12
5	1	21	5	2	23	5	8	17
6	1	25	6	1	23	6	4	15
	$\chi^2 = 12.05, p < .01$			$\chi^2 = 6.13, p < .05$			$\chi^2 = 5.50, p < .01$	

	Shape (1-3)			Heterogeneous (shape)			Heterogeneous shape and color	
	1-5	6-9		1-5	6-9		1-5	6-9
Age			Age			Age		
4	4	16	4	15	10	4	5	20
5	1	20	5	7	17	5	2	20
6	1	20	6	2	13	6	0	25
	$\chi^2 = 3.60, p < .20$			$\chi^2 = 9.85, p < .01$			$\chi^2 = 5.71, p < .10$	

[a] The entries in the cells represent the number of children who made a greater percentage of errors in each set size category.

one. Even in the simple equivalence task, the 6-year-olds, if they made errors, selected an alternative that was one different in numerical size from the sample 81.0% of the time, while the 4- and 5-year-olds did so only 48.7% and 38.7% of the time, respectively.

Relative Numerical Size of the Sets. Recognizing that two sets are different in cardinal number, obviously depends on the relative size of the sets. Sets very different in number are clearly easier to recognize as having different numerosity. Therefore, we included tasks in which the conflict alternative was close in numerical size (1-3 different) or more different in numerical size (4-7) from the correct answer. We expected that the 4-7 tasks would be easier than the 1-3 tasks. In fact, there was no significant difference in error rates between these two tasks, as can be seen Table 4.5. However, inspection of the data in Table 4.6 reveals that there was a significantly greater tendency in all age groups to choose the conflict alternative if it was close in size to the sample. The joint combination of perceptual identity and numerical similarity (but not identity) was a very powerful determinant of error responses. The oldest children made very few errors which involved the irrelevant dimension if it was not close in numerical size to the sample.

The younger children clearly had difficulty with the dimension of cardinal number in situations in which there were irrelevant dimensions present. Was this difficulty merely a problem of the perceptual salience of the other dimensions as opposed to number? That is, were the children merely selecting a more salient dimension and responding to it? Here is where the learning paradigm is useful and why the use of nonverbal techniques are important. If the children responded to a different dimension and chose a set identical in shape but not in number to the sample, they did not receive reinforcement. Therefore, even if they started off attending to the irrelevant dimension, this response was not reinforced. Even in this case, they made many errors (many of the younger children the percentage of errors was as high as 80%-90%). Therefore, the irrelevance of other dimensions to number was difficult to learn for the younger children. The majority of these children could all do a simple equivalence task, so they did have the ability to solve a number problem. However, their failure to understand number as a dimension and their attention to dimensions other than number interfered with their performance. The difficulty of understanding number as a dimension was not just a result of contrasting number with a particular dimension. Abstracting number was difficult with the dimension of shape, size, color, and even heterogeneous sets.

It could be argued that the children were attacking these problems as oddity ones. An examination of Fig. 4.6 shows that the conflict alternative is different in shape from the others. Again, the use of the learning paradigm is helpful. Even if the children chose this oddity strategy (in this case the wrong strategy), it was not reinforced, so they should have little reason to continue it.

Even if the child can count and understand simple equivalence, number is abstracted gradually as a dimension. Only after this process has occurred does cardinal number become important. The younger children's responses are controlled by perceptual equivalence, while the older ones by numerosity.

Conclusion

In summary, we have described two sequential processes in the young child's abstraction of number. First, the child must recognize number as an independent dimension; then the child must learn that cardinal number means exact numerical correspondence.

We have presented a series of studies illustrating a variety of linguistic and perceptual factors which influence the young child's acquisition of a variety of quantity concepts. In general, there is an increase with age in the degree to which language plays a role in the child's understanding of quantity. Perceptual, nonquantitative factors play a significant role early in development and appear to precede the use of language. As the child develops, there is a movement away from a perceptual matching strategy to a conceptual, numerically based one. However, counting, whether internal or audible is probably tied to language, and the child's estimation errors are probably a result of a failure to employ language skillfully, or perhaps at all, in the task.

There is evidence that language was playing a role in the more complex tasks in this study. When perceptual solutions fail, that is where sequence iteration information is important, language may become a significant component of the tasks.

In summary, we have demonstrated the predominance of perceptual nonlinguistic operations in early quantity concepts and the increasing role of language in the solution of tasks involving elementary notions of quantity.

Reference Notes

1. Greenberg, N. A. *Young children's perceptual judgments of nonredundant cardinal number equivalence.* Unpublished doctoral dissertation. University of Western Ontario, London, Ontario, 1981.
2. Koff, E., & Luria, Z. *Concept and language: The comparative relation.* Paper presented at the SRCD meeting, Philadelphia, 1973.
3. Weil, J. *The relationship between time conceptualizations and time language in young children.* Unpublished doctoral dissertation, The Graduate Center, City University of New York, 1970.

References

Baron, J., Lawson, G., & Siegel, L. S. Effects of training and set size on children's judgments of number and length. *Developmental Psychology,* 1975, *11*, 583-588.

Beilin, H., & Kagan, J. Pluralization rules and the conceptualization of number. *Developmental Psychology,* 1969, *7*, 692-706.

Bever, T. G. The cognitive basis for linguistic structures. In J. R. Hayes (Ed.), *Cognition and the development of language.* New York: Wiley, 1970.

Blank, M. Cognitive functions of language in the preschool years. *Development Psychology,* 1974, *10*, 229-245.

Blank, M., & Bridger, W. H. Cross-modal transfer in nursery school children. *Journal of Comparative and Physiological Psychology,* 1964, *58*, 277-282.

Brainerd, C. J. Mathematical and behavioral foundations of number. *Journal of General Psychology Monograph,* 1973, *88*, 221-281.

Brainerd, C. J. The effects of spatial cues on children's cardinal number judgments. *Developmental Psychology,* 1977, *13*, 425-430.

Brainerd, C. J., & Howe, M. L. An attentional analyses of small cardinal number concepts in five year olds. *Canadian Journal of Behavioural Science,* 1979, *11*, 112-123.

Brainerd, C. J., & Howe, M. L. Developmental invariance in a mathematical model of associative learning. *Child Development,* 1980, *51*, 349-363.

Bruner, J. S. The course of cognitive growth. *American Psychologist,* 1964, *19*, 1-15.

Clark, E. V. Some aspects of the conceptual basis for first language acquisition. In R. L. Schiefelbusch & L. L. Lloyd (Eds.), *Language perspective−Acquisition, retardation and intervention.* Baltimore, Maryland: University Park Press, 1974.

Clark, H. H. The primitive nature of children's relational concepts. In J. R. Hayes (Ed.), *Cognition and the development of language.* New York: Wiley, 1970.

Conrad, R. The chronology of the development of covert speech in children. *Developmental Psychology,* 1971, *5*, 298-405.

Donaldson, M., & Balfour, G. Less is more: A study of language comprehension in children. *British Journal of Psychology,* 1968, *59*, 461-471.

Donaldson, M., & Wales, R. J. On the acquisition of some relational terms. In J. R. Hayes (Ed.), *Cognition and the development of language.* New York: Wiley, 1970.

Flavell, J. H. Developmental studies of mediated memory. *Advances in Child Development and Behavior,* 1970, *5*, 181-211.

Furth, H. G. *Thinking without language.* New York: Free Press, 1966.

Furth, H. G. Linguistic deficiency and thinking: Research with deaf subjects, 1964-1969. *Psychological Bulletin,* 1971, *76*, 58-72.

Gelman, R. The nature and developments of early number concepts. In H. W. Reese (Ed.), *Advances in child development and behavior* (Vol. 7). New York: Academic Press, 1972, pp. 115-167.

Gelman, R., & Tucker, M. F. Further investigations of the young child's conception of number. *Child Development,* 1975, *46*, 167-175.

Griffiths, J. A., Shantz, C. U., & Sigel, I. E. A methodological problem in conservation studies: The use of relational terms. *Child Development,* 1967, *38*, 841-848.

Inhelder, B., & Piaget, J. *The early growth of logic in the child.* New York: Harper & Row, 1964.

Jones, P. A. Formal operational reasoning and the use of tentative statements. *Cognitive Psychology,* 1972, *3*, 467-471.

Kendler, H. H., & Kendler, T. S. Vertical and horizontal processes in problem solving. *Psychological Review,* 1962, *69*, 1-16.

Klatzky, R. L., Clark, E. V., & Macken, M. Asymmetries in the acquisition of polar adjectives: Linguistic or conceptual? *Journal of Experimental Child Psychology,* 1973, *16*, 32-46.

Lawson, G., Baron, J., & Siegel, L. S. The role of number and length cues in children's quantitative judgments. *Child Development,* 1974, *45*, 731-736.

Lenneberg, E. H. *Biological foundations of language.* New York: Wiley, 1967.

Macnamara, J. Cognitive basis of language learning in infants. *Psychological Review,* 1972, *79*, 1-13.

Nelson, D. Concept, word, and sentence: Interrelations in acquisition and development. *Psychological Review,* 1974, *81*, 267-285.

Olson, D. R. Language and thought: Aspects of a cognitive theory of semantics. *Psychological Review,* 1970, *77*, 257-273.

Osler, S. F., & Madden, J. The verbal label: Mediator or classifier? *Journal of Experimental Child Psychology,* 1973, *16*, 303-317.

Palermo, D. S. More about less: A study of language comprehension. *Journal of Verbal Learning and Verbal Behavior,* 1973, *12*, 211-221.

Pascual-Leone, J., & Smith, J. The encoding and decoding of symbols by children: A new experimental paradigm and a neo-Piagetian model. *Journal of Experimental Child Psychology,* 1969, *8*, 328-355.

Piaget, J. *The child's conception of number.* New York: Norton, 1965.

Piaget, J., & Inhelder, B. *The early growth of logic in the child.* New York: Harper & Row, 1956.

Pufall, P. B., & Shaw, R. E. Precocious thoughts on number: The long and short of it. *Developmental Psychology,* 1972, *7,* 62-69.

Reese, H. W. Verbal mediation as a function of age level. *Psychological Bulletin,* 1962, *59,* 502-509.

Scholnick, E. K., & Adams, M. J. Relationships between language and cognitive skills: Passive-voice comprehension, backward repetition, and matrix permutation. *Child Development,* 1973, *44,* 741-746.

Siegel, L. S. The sequence of development of certain number concepts in preschool children. *Developmental Psychology,* 1971, *5,* 357-361. (a)

Siegel, L. S. The development of certain number concepts. *Developmental Psychology,* 1971, *5,* 362-363. (b)

Siegel, L. S. The development of the concept of seriation. *Developmental Psychology,* 1972, *6,* 135-137. (a)

Siegel, L. S. The development of concepts of numerical magnitude. *Psychonomic Science,* 1972, *28,* 245-246. (b)

Siegel, L. S. The role of spatial arrangements and heterogeneity in the development of concepts of numerical equivalence. *Canadian Journal of Psychology,* 1973, *27,* 351-355.

Siegel, L. S. Heterogeneity and spatial factors as determinants of numeration ability. *Child Development,* 1974, *45,* 532-534. (a)

Siegel, L. S. The development of number concepts: Ordering and correspondence operations and the role of length cues. *Developmental Psychology,* 1974, *10,* 907-912. (b)

Siegel, L. S. The relationship of language and thought in the preoperational child: A reconsideration of nonverbal alternatives to Piagetian Tasks. In L. S. Siegel & C. J. Brainerd (Eds.), *Alternatives to Piaget: Critical essays on the theory.* New York: Academic Press, 1978.

Siegel, L. S., & Goldstein, A. G. Conservation of number in young children: Recency versus relational response strategies. *Developmental Psychology,* 1969, *1,* 128-130.

Siegel, L. S., Lees, A., Allan, L., & Bolton, B. Nonverbal assessment of Piagetian concepts in preschool children with impaired language development. *Educational Psychology,* 1981, *1,* 153-158.

Siegel, L. S., McCabe, A. E., Brand, J., & Matthews, J. Evidence for class inclusion in the preschool child: Linguistic factors and training effects. *Child Development,* 1978, *49,* 688-693.

Sinclair-de Zwart, H. Developmental psycholinguistics. In D. Elkind & J. H. Flavell (Eds.), *Studies in cognitive development.* New York: Oxford University Press, 1969.

Slobin, D. I. Cognitive prerequisites for the development of grammar. In C. A. Ferguson & D. I. Slobin (Eds.), *Studies of child language development.* New York: Holt, Rinehart, & Winston, 1973, pp. 175-208.

Vygotsky, L. S. *Thought and language.* Cambridge, Massachusetts: MIT Press, 1962.

White, S. H. Evidence for a hierarchical arrangement of learning processes. In *Advances in child development and behavior* (Vol. 2). New York: Academic Press, 1965.

5. Culture and the Development of Numerical Cognition: Studies among the Oksapmin of Papua New Guinea

Geoffrey B. Saxe

Psychologists concerned with the development of cognition have largely studied age-related changes in Western middle class children. Although some classic findings have been produced by this approach, it has its limitations. By studying development in only one society, we are blind to the way in which culture may influence cognitive development. It is only through the analysis of development in different cultural contexts that some perspective on the links between culture and cognitive development can be achieved. In this chapter, research concerned with the numerical concepts of a remote and recently contacted group in Papua New Guinea, the Oksapmin, is discussed. The Oksapmin people are just emerging from Stone Age conditions and hence present a radical contrast to the West in their patterns of social life as well as in their practices involving number concepts.

The research with the Oksapmin is presented in four sections. In the first section, some of the methodological preliminaries and problems inherent in cross-cultural research are discussed, a discussion that situates the Oksapmin research in the context of the general enterprise of cross-cultural cognitive studies. In the second section, the Oksapmin community is introduced. The focus is on the character of the Oksapmin body-part numeration system and the way in which it is employed in activities that involve number and measurement concepts. In the third section, research on developmental changes in numerical understanding in the Oksapmin community is summarized. The research is focused on both ontogenetic and socio-

This chapter was prepared while the author was supported by a grant from the National Institute of Education (G-78-0076 and G-80-0119) and a grant from the Indigenous Mathematics Project of Papua New Guinea. Appreciation is extended to Maryl Gearhart, Thomas Moylan, and Carl Saxe for comments on an earlier draft of this chapter.

historical changes in the way Oksapmin use their body-part numeration system to represent discontinous and continous quantities. In the fourth and final section, the findings with the Oksapmin are discussed as a contribution to our understanding of the interplay between culture and the individual's formation of numerical concepts.

Methodology and Cross-Cultural Number Research

The methodological problems inherent in cross-cultural cognitive research have received considerable discussion in the cross-cultural literature (see Berry & Dasen, 1974; Glick, 1975; Laboratory of Comparative Human Cognition, 1979). The crux of these problems is a tension between two different methodological goals. One goal is to maintain a consistent definition of cognition or "cognitive abilities" across cultural settings and, accordingly, a consistent operational definition of what stands for evidence that subjects do or do not possess these abilities. The other goal is to obtain rich descriptions of the unique and special forms of cognition within particular cultural settings. If one strives for standard operational definitions across settings, the consequence is often that the special characteristics of cognition in particular settings are ignored. But, if one strives to capture cognitive functioning as it occurs in context, comparability of observations across settings is often sacrificed. In the Oksapmin research, a developmental perspective is adopted, which, in part, circumvents the tension between these two methodological concerns.

A central tenet of the developmental approach is that cognitive phenomena should be understood as processes undergoing transformation, transformations that are produced as subjects attempt to gain better control and understanding of their interactions with their environments (cf. Piaget 1963, 1970; Vygotsky 1962, 1978; Werner 1957; Werner & Kaplan, 1963). Moreover, the process of transformation has a universal direction. It is toward the elaboration of systems of knowing which are progressively more comprehensive and powerful. From this perspective, the major task is to understand the principles that regulate these transformations, and it is this definition of the research task that leads to a strategy that accommodates both of the methodological concerns presented above. The strategy is to produce an ethnography of cognitive activities within a particular cultural setting and, at the same time, construct procedures that would reveal developmental transformations in these activities. The virtue of this approach is that it does not involve direct comparisons of cognition across social contexts, and, as a consequence, the standardization of procedures is related to indigenous concepts. Therefore, the standardization process does not directly interfere with the analysis of special forms of cognition that are unique to particular cultural groups. However, since the standardization is produced in order to illuminate general principles of developmental change, the findings are not limited to a single context, but rather can be used to inform our understanding of the general process of cognitive development.

The Oksapmin Community

The Oksapmin people live in a remote highlands area of the West Sepik province of Papua New Guinea. There are no roads to the area, and the only means of access is by single engine aircraft and travel by foot. There are between 6000 and 8000 speakers of the Oksapmin language, who live in small hamlets scattered through two valleys. This is a subsistence economy: people use slash-and-burn methods to cultivate taro and sweet potato, hunt for small game with bow and arrow, and keep pigs. (See Fig. 5.1.)

Western contact was first established with the Oksapmin by the Australian 1938-1940 Hagen-Sepik patrol, although it was not until the 1950s that the Oksapmin were contacted by additional patrols. A government patrol post and a mission station were established in the Oksapmin area in the early 1960s. By the late 1960s, a recruitment program was begun in which Oksapmin men were offered the opportunity to leave the area for two-year periods to work on copra and tea plantations and earn currency. In the early 1970s, the first government school was established in the Oksapmin area.

The standard Oksapmin numeration system differs markedly from the Western system, as do the systems of other Papua New Guinea groups (see Lancy, 1978). To count as Oksapmins do, one begins with the thumb on one hand and enumerates 27 places around the upper periphery of the body, ending on the little finger of

Fig. 5.1 A common scene on a major path in an Oksapmin valley.

the opposite hand. If one needs to count further, one can continue back up to the wrist of the second hand and progress back upward on the body (see Fig. 5.2). People use the system in everyday activities. For example, aside from using the system to count (pigs, currency, etc.), people also use it to denote the ordinal position of an element in a series of elements (the ordinal position of a hamlet in a series of hamlets on a path), or in basic measurement operations (as a means of measuring and representing the length of string bags, a common cultural artifact). In traditional life there is virtually no context in which Oksapmin use the system to do arithmetical computations. Now, however, with the introduction of currency and formal schooling, the need to use the system for computation is becoming a practical necessity for some individuals.

Studies on Numerical Cognition among the Oksapmin

In the studies described below, the developmental approach was translated into a research program through an analysis of two forms of cognitive developmental change, namely, cognitive developmental change in ontogenesis and in ongoing social history. In each case, the design and analysis are closely linked to an analysis of the sociohistorical context of Oksapmin life. For example, the analysis of ontogenetic change is focused on the way in which Oksapmin children come to incorporate the body numeration system into their own problem-solving activities involving discontinuous and continuous quantities. The analysis of historical change is is focused on the way traditional forms of numeration are changing to more powerful systems and the factors in the lives of the Oksapmin people which are moti-

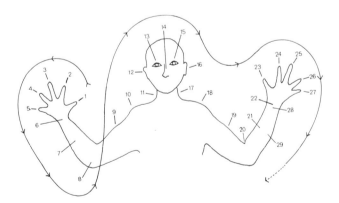

Fig. 5.2 The conventional sequence of body parts used by the Oksapmin. In order of occurrence: (1) tip⌃na, (2) tipnarip, (3) bumrip, (4) h⌃tdip, (5) h⌃th⌃ta, (6) dopa, (7) besa, (8) kir, (9) tow⌃t, (10) kata, (11) gwer, (12) nata, (13) kina, (14) aruma, (15) tan-kina (16) tan-nata, (17) tan-gwer, (18) tan-kata, (19) tan-tow⌃t, (20) tan-kir, (21) tan-besa, (22) tan-dopa, (23) tan-tip⌃na, (24) tan-tipnarip, (25) tan-bumrip, (26) tan-h⌃tdip, (27) tan-h⌃th⌃ta.

vating these changes. Though the studies are described individually, the separation between ontogenetic and sociohistorical change is merely for analytic purposes. It should be clear in the course of this section that the ontogenetic and sociohistorical changes discussed represent a dynamic system in which one serves as a necessary basis for the other.

There are a number of procedural similarities that each of the studies share. In each study, an Oksapmin informant administered the interview tasks in the indigenous language, and all interview procedures were standardized through either a back-translation method (see Saxe, 1981) or with the aid of Thomas Moylan, a linguistic anthropologist, who has considerable proficiency with the Oksapmin language. When age was used as a variable in any of the studies, it was determined either on the basis of missionary records of visual comparison of children of known ages with children of unknown ages. In general, age group contrasts are cautiously interpreted. Based on their recorded age, individuals are classified as a member of one of two age groups with a separation between age groups of one or two years. Those children who were identified as in that one- to two-year "limbo" period are excluded from age group analyses.

Ontogenetic Changes in Oksapmins' Use of Body Parts as a Notational System for Quantitative Relations

Before discussing the studies, it will be helpful to put the Oksapmin research in perspective by discussing some general features of numeration systems and some findings with Western children. The activity of numeration, whether it be with body parts or Western number words, involves establishing a one-to-one correspondence between two sets of elements. One set, the "standard," is a conventionally defined list of symbols that is always used in counting. It is a historical form of knowledge produced in the social history of a cultural group. The second set, the "variable," is a target array that varies from one count to another. The aim in counting is to establish a one-to-one correspondence between the sets such that the standard serves to denote a progressive summation of correspondences with the variable set. Thus, to count five objects, an individual establishes five correspondences between the standard set ("one, two, three, four, and five") and the variable set (the five objects). The fifth member of the standard set ("five") then serves as a notation for the summation of the five correspondence relations. When this summation is used to refer to the set of correspondences, it is known as the cardinal value of a set; when it is used to refer to a summation of the positions of the correspondences in the enumeration, it is referred to as the ordinal value of a set. If the variable set consists of a continous quantity, the subject must first consider it as units or discrete parts. Correspondences that the subject establishes between the standard set and the discrete parts are then progressively summed in the act of counting just as they are with a discrete set of elements.

Any formulation of cognitive development must account for how social forms of representation that are initially external to the child become the child's own and interwoven with its own cognitive functioning. One way in which this internalization might occur—and the working hypothesis for the Oksapmin research—is that children first acquire some part of their cultural group's standard set of number terms in the context of playful activites (e.g., in social interaction with adults or more capable peers). To the extent that children use these terms to solve numerical problems, children's use of the terms is regulated by the adult. The adult's conventionally defined system becomes a vehicle of number representation for the child through a further constructive process: The child attempts to understand the organization of its own enumerative activities. With progress in this understanding, the child would be increasingly capable of using number terms to solve numerical problems without the aid of the adult.

To date, there has been no research on the origins of number representation in children's social interactions with adults (see Wertsch, 1979, for an analysis of other forms of problem solving in adult-child interaction). However, various researchers have observed a developmental progression among Western children that is consistent with the formulation presented above concerning the shift from "premediational" to "mediational" uses of number terms. For example, children at the age of 3 or 4, when asked to compare two sets numerically, often count the sets, but do not base their comparisons on counting (see Russac, 1978; Saxe, 1977). Similarly, other researchers have noted that children may count a collection but not use the last numeral to refer to the summation of the set (Gelman & Gallistel, 1978; Schaeffer, Eggleston & Scott, 1974). If this process of change from a phase in which number terms are used in a "premediational" fashion to a phase in which they are used in a "mediational" fashion can be shown to be a general one, it would represent a way in which historical forms of knowledge become interwoven with the construction of concepts and problem-solving strategies during ontogenesis. It was this formulation that served as the organizing hypothesis for the studies on ontogenetic change described below.

Oksapmins' Use of the Body to Represent Discontinous Quantities. In order to determine whether Oksapmin children experienced a similar transition from a "premediational" (or rote) to a "mediational" (or problem-solving) phase in their use of counting as Western children as well as the characteristics of this transition, two methods were used (see Saxe, 1981). First, tasks from previous research in the United States (cf. Saxe, 1977; 1979) were adapted to give Oksapmin children the opportunity to demonstrate how they used counting both to compare and to reproduce sets. Second, tasks were created to determine whether there were confusions that arose from the organization of the body counting system. In particular, if young children do not view the last numeral recited as a notation for a summation, they may simply identify numerical equivalence on the basis of physical or "perceptual" characteristics of body parts. To test this possibility, children were required to compare the values of body parts that differed in their physical similarity. For example, children were asked to compare numerically symmetrical as opposed to asymmetrical body parts, or to compare the value of body parts arrived at from the left thumb as opposed to the right thumb.

The results of the interviews on children's use of counting to compare and reproduce sets revealed a comparable trend to that found in the United States. Young

Oksapmin children counted, though often in response to a probe question, but typically did not base their comparisons of reproductions on the products of their counting, whereas older children did. There was an exception to this sequence. When set size was small (e.g., three elements), subjects often solved that tasks without verbal enumeration of the elements. Rather, they simply stated whether one set contained more in the case of the comparison tasks or put out the same number as that contained in the model in the case of the reproduction tasks. It was only after some probing that children counted on the small set size tasks, and sometimes they would count only one array, as if to demonstrate that they had put out the correct number. Whether the small set size judgments were mediated by a non-counting process (i.e., "subitizing") or whether children had used a silent counting process could not be determined.

The second type of method required children to compare directly the numerical values of body parts instead of deploying body parts to help solve a task. Numerical comparisons were presented in the context of two different stories. In one story, children were told that one day a man was counting sweet potatoes and they were shown the place to which the man counted on their own bodies (a sweeping gesture was made from childrens' right thumbs to a specified body part on the right side of their bodies). Children were then told that on another day the man was counting sweet potatoes and counted to a different place on his body (another sweeping gesture was made from childrens' right thumbs to a specified body part on the left side of the childrens' bodies). Children were then asked if the man counted to the same amount of sweet potatoes (pointing to the two body parts) or different amounts. If children responded different amounts, they were asked which was the bigger amount. Six pairs of body parts were indicated, three symmetrical pairs and three asymmetrical pairs. They were (a) right wrist (6)/left ear (16); (b) right ear (12)/left ear (16); (C) right elbow (8)/left wrist (22); (d) right shoulder (10)/left shoulder (18); (e) right side of neck (11)/left biceps (19); (f) right biceps (9)/left biceps (19).

In a second story, children were told that people in their own village count from the right to the left sides of their bodies (this was indicated with a circling gesture around the upper periphery of the child's body); however, in a village over the mountains, people count from the left to the right side of their bodies (again, this was indicated with a circling gesture). Children were then told a story about two men counting sweet potatoes, one from the child's hamlet and the other from a faraway hamlet over the mountains. The child was told that both men counted to the same body part, one beginning at the right thumb, the other beginning at the left thumb (this was again demonstrated with circling gestures from left to right and right to left). The child was then asked whether the two men counted to the same number of sweet potatoes or whether they counted to a different number of sweet potatoes. If children claimed that the men counted to different numbers, the children were asked who counted to the bigger number. This procedure was repeated for several body parts.

Children's responses to these stories both corroborate and supplement the findings from the comparison and reproduction tasks. Young Oksapmin children who knew the standard set of numerals nonetheless compared body parts with respect to their physical similarity rather than with respect to their values as summations. When comparing the values of symmetrical of asymmetrical body-part pairs that were reached from a common point of origin in the first story, the younger children incorrectly identified symmetrical body parts as equivalent in value, and when they correctly identified asymmetrical body parts as nonequivalent, they did not regularly identify which of the two represented the larger value. Older children produced accurate body part comparisons, regardless of the physical similarity of the body parts. A similar developmental trend was evident with the second story. Younger children tended to consider the same body part reached from two different points of origin (left and right thumbs) to represent the same value. In contrast, children in the older age group considered the value of a body part to be based upon its ordinal position in an enumeration. Thus, the findings from these tasks indicate that the spatial organization of the Oksapmin system leads children who are in a premediational phase to some particular types of conceptual confusions. During a premediational phase, these children do not dissociate physical characteristics of their standard set of body parts from the use of these body parts as signifiers for correspondence relations. The finding that Oksapmin children go through a premediational phase with discrete quantities suggested that a parallel process might occur with continuous quantities. The developmental process with continuous quantities might serve both to provide further corroboration for the transition as well as illuminate how the organization of the Oksapmin system might lead to conceptual developments that differ from those found in Western culture.

Oksapmins' Use of the Body to Represent Continuous Quantities. As noted earlier, the Oksapmin use their body system as a measurement instrument to evaluate continuous quantities (e.g., in the evaluation of the size of a common cultural artifact, the string bag). The purpose of the study dicussed below was to explore developmental changes in how Oksapmin use the body system to mediate these measurement operations.

The string bag serves many functions in the Oksapmin society (see Fig. 5.3). People carry a variety of things of importance in the bags. These include infants, vegetables, and personal effects. In addition, bags are used in ceremonial dancing. The bags are made by Oksapmin women and girls by rolling pith from the inner bark of a local tree into a string, and weaving the string with a variety of stitches into a bag. String bags are measured for their depth both while they are being made and after they are completed by men, women, and children. To measure a bag, an individual inserts and extends both arms in the bag and notes the point at which the outer rim meets a point on the arms. With the exception of the knuckles, the same body parts used in the numeration system are used as indicators of the depth of a bag. The depth of bags are referred to as the knuckles, the wrist (6), forearm (7), inner elbows (8), bicep (9), and shoulder (10).

In order to use a standard measure for length, a subject must understand several interrelated facts that are relevant to the study of Oksapmin use of their arms as standard measures. First, the subject must understand that the length of the standard measure is conserved over spatial displacements. Thus, if a standard measure (S) is

Fig. 5.3 An Oksapmin woman nursing an infant in a string bag and an Oksapmin man wearing a string bag.

used to measure the length of an object (L), the subject must consider the relations established between the objects of measurement and the standard measure as invariant. Second, a subject must regard the length relation as transitive. For example, if the standard measure, S, is longer than an object L_1 and shorter than an object L_2 then the relative lengths of L_1 and L_2 can be inferred. Third, the subject must understand that in order for the measurements produced with two or more standard measures ($S_1, S_2, \ldots$) to be directly comparable, the length of the units used on each standard measure must be equivalent to one another. It is of interest that one property of the Oksapmin body-part system is that units are not equivalent since peoples' bodies vary in size. In other words, there is no universal standard for length as there is in Western society.

To investigate developmental changes in Oksapmins' understanding and use of their arms as a standard measure, a set of four tasks was devised (see Saxe & Moylan, in press). Concepts of conservation were assessed in two ways. The first task was embedded in the context of measuring string bags, and in order to relate observed developmental changes to a known developmental sequence in the conservation of length (Piaget, 1960), a standard conservation of length task was also administered. In the "string bag" conservation task, individuals were required to measure a string bag with their arms. While their arms were in the string bag, the point at which the outer rim met the subject's arm was marked with a piece of charcoal. The string bag was then removed and placed in such a way that the point from the bottom of the string bag to its rim was misaligned with the length from the finger tips to the charcoal mark on the body. The subjects were then interviewed as to whether or not these two distances were equivalent. This task procedure paralleled the standard task (cf. Piaget, 1960) that consisted of two sticks of equivalent length; the sticks were aligned in parallel with their end points matching, and then one was displaced so that the end points were no longer in alignment.

Another task was designed to assess developmental changes in the ability to produce length comparisons between string bags using the standard body parts as the intermediate term. In this type of task, subjects were told a story about two women who made string bags. String bags were then presented one by one to subjects, who were asked to measure them with their arms. After each measurement, the bags were folded and put on either side of the subject. The subject was then asked which was the bigger bag and to explain his or her judgment.

A fourth task was devised to assess developmental changes in Oksapmins' understanding of the necessity of equivalent units when comparing measurements produced by the two standard measures. In this task, stories were used again. Subjects were told two stories, one about a little girl who was making a string bag for her father and the other about a big woman who was making a string bag for her little son. In each story, the maker (the woman or the girl) measures the string bag before giving it. When the recipient of the gift (the man or the boy) receives the string bag, he also measures it. As part of the story, the subjects were told the maker's measurement (forearm, inner elbow, or bicep). Subjects were then asked whether they thought the string bag came up to the same place on the recipient as it did on the donor of the bags of whether it came up to a different place. Regardless of the subjects' judgments, they were asked to explain their answers. In addition, if subjects stated that the bag would come up to a different place, they were questioned about which place on the body it would come to and to explain why.

The results of the interviews with both nonschooled and schooled populations support and supplement the findings on ontogenetic changes in subjects' use of the conventional body system to represent discontinous quantities. Not only did the findings again show an age-related change from the premediational to the mediational use of body parts, they also revealed some traits that are specific to the Oksapmin community.

The conservation data showed that although there was a developmental change in the frequency of correct responses for both tasks, only a little over one-third of the adult subjects passed the standard test (with sticks), whereas virtually all of them demonstrated an understanding of conservation when the task was embedded in the context of measuring string bags. This obviously suggests that when task contexts more closely mirror the practical activities of people (using the arms to measure string bags), tasks will be more sensitive to the more sophisticated levels of individuals' cognitive adaptations. It was also found that differences in performance across tasks no longer held with Oksapmin adolescents who had received five years of schooling.

Unlike subjects' performance on the conservation tasks, which showed clear developmental trends, subjects' performance on the comparison tasks showed that virtually all of the adults and school children solved these tasks, and that a majority of nonschooled children solved the tasks. The facility with which subjects solved this task further corroborates the thesis that when measurement operations are embedded in the context of practical activities, it is more likely that subjects will display more sophisticated forms of cognition. These data are also consistent with evidence which suggests that certain forms of transitive inference are basic abilities that are present in young children (e.g., Brainerd, 1979; Bryant & Trabasso, 1971; Siegel, 1971).

The equivalent units data are perhaps the most interesting because they show how the Oksapmin come to take into account some of the special characteristics of their indigenous system. For an individual to understand equivalent units in the indigenous system, he or she must consider two series of asymmetrical relations and correspondences between these relations. For example, a subject must consider that the length from the finger tips to the inner elbow of a big person corresponds to the length from the finger tips to a point above the inner elbow in a smaller person. In addition, a subject must understand the inverse relation between the length of an arm and the point that the rim of a string bag would reach on an arm. For example, the longer the arm, the lower the point on the arm (the body part) the rim will reach. Only by understanding the correspondences between arms and the inverse correspondence between arm length and the point on the arm that the string bag would reach could subjects achieve correct predictions on the equivalent units stories.

Subjects' responses to the stories revealed the expected ontogenetic trends. Children tended to believe that the recipient of the string bag would measure the bag to the same body part as the donor, whereas adults tended to believe that the recipient would measure the bag to a different place on the arms and correctly indicate the direction of discrepancy. Of particular interest was evidence for a "transitional" understanding. Some individuals would correctly assume that the string bag would arrive at a different place but not invert the relation between the point that the bag would come up to on the arm and the size of the person measuring the bag (the bigger the person, the lower the point that the rim would reach). For example, these individuals would claim that if the little girl measured a string bag to the elbow, when her father put it on it would go to the bicep because his arms were longer. These findings suggest a sequence from not considering correspondences between two series, to considering correspondences but not understanding inverse correspondences, to considering correspondences and understanding inverse correspondences.

In summary, the findings from the studies on discontinuous and continuous quantities generally show that there is a developmental transformation in the way in which Oksapmin use their body part system to mediate their problem solving, a transformation that is comparable to findings in Western societies on the development of numerical representation. Young Oksapmin children know the conventionally defined set of body parts, yet do not use them to mediate their probelm solving with either discontinuous or continuous quantities. The generality of the premediational phase across the Oksapmin and Western settings suggests that it serves an important function in the early development of number and measurement operations. Through incorporating a conventionally defined list of symbols and enumerative procedures into their own activities, children establish the preconditions for discovering the structure of their cultural group's system for numerical reference. The different conventional systems, however, interact with the cognitive development of the child in different ways. Not only do the different systems create different conceptual problems for children who are trying to understand the structure of the systems, they also ultimately lead children to different conceptual procedures for solving problems.

Thus far, the concern has been with the Oksapmin child's acquisition of a conventional system of representation without an examination of how conventional systems themselves develop in the social history of a cultural group. In the following section, the studies are concerned with profound changes in number symbolization that are emerging in Oksapmin culture and the mechanisms whereby these changes are occurring.

Sociohistorical Changes in Oksapmins' Use of Body Parts as a Notational System

The organizing hypothesis for the studies on sociohistorical change is that as new forms of social interactions emerge in a community, new cognitive problems arise. As individuals attempt to achieve solutions to these new types of problems, they construct novel forms of problem-solving strategies. Those strategies that can be generalized to new situations become conventional procedures and emerge as cognitive norms in community life.

This framework served as the organizing basis for an investigation of the way in which two new social institutions, the trade store and the community school, are leading Oksapmin individuals to construct new collective systems of representation for number. An inherent part of participation in either of these institutions is that arithmetic problems are posed in social interactions. Since arithmetic problems have no direct counterpart in traditional Oksapmin life, the Oksapmin must invent new ways of using their body part system to solve them.

The Trade Store: The Influence of Participation in Western-Style Economic Exchange on the Formation of Arithmetic Concepts. The introduction of Western-style currency was a new form of exchange for the Oksapmin. Traditionally, Oksapmin traded goods directly (e.g., bows for salt, axes for bows). Perhaps the only analog of currency in traditional life were shells traded from the coast. Shells were (and still are) considered valuable in and of themselves. They were used as a medium of exchange for some but not all local goods.

The history of currency in the Oksapmin community is short but complex. Three Western currencies have been used, but only the first and the third (the current kina) have left a lasting mark. The first currency was Australian shillings and pounds (20 shillings = 1 pound) and was brought by early missionaries and patrol officers to the region. Since 1966, currency has taken other forms. In 1966, the Australian dollar was instituted (100 cents = 1 dollar), and in 1975, when the country became independent, Papua New Guinea issued its own currency in the form of kina and toea (100 toea = 1 kina, 200 toea = one 2-kina note). Many Oksapmin people, particularly individuals older than about 30, translate kina and toea into pounds and shillings (the first currency system). On this basis, people call one 10-toea coin 1 shilling (a 20-toea coin is called 2 shillings) and one 2-kina note is called 1 pound. Many people count kina and toea as their pound and shilling equivalents.

Some Oksapmin people have adapted the indigenous numeration system in order to communicate about currency (cf. Moylan, Note 1), and this adaptation itself reflects a sociohistorical change in Oksapmins' approach to number representation. Oksapmin can now count considerably larger quantities than they could using the standard indigenous system. Using the adapted system, an individual counts shillings up to the inner elbow on the other side of the body (20) and calls it one round or one pound. If the individual needs to continue the count, he or she begins again at the thumb of the first hand and then verbally records each round. Similarly, an individual may count 2-kina notes and thus count forty kina (20 2-kina notes = 40 kina) as one round. The adapted system, then, is a hybrid. It employs the same conventionally defined system of body parts that are used in the traditional system [at least up to the elbow on the other side (20)], but it has incorporated the base principle of a Western currency system (i.e., the base 20 system of the early Australian currency). It is important to point out that Oksapmin use this system flexibly. There are many ways of expressing the same value either through combinations of the traditional and the adapted system or using only one system. Not suprisingly, the individuals who use the adapted system regularly are those who engage in frequent economic transactions involving currency. The studies that are now summarized were concerned with how these transactions provide contexts in which new arithmetical concepts evolve.

The institution that dominates economic exchange is the trade store. In recent years, Oksapmin men have been flown out of the region to work on tea and copra plantations. After two years, they return with currency (about 200 kina). Some of them invest in tins of fish and bags of rice and build trade stores in which they sell goods to the members of their hamlets.[1]

As an inherent part of the interactions that occur at the trade store, customer and owner pose arithmetic problems to one another. From the customer's perspective, the trade store owner sells goods for a specified price, and the customer must offer the currency that is required for the purchase. From the trade store owner's perspective, the customer has a certain amount of money, and the trade store owner must evaluate whether the customer has presented the appropriate amount and/or how much change the customer should receive. In fact, transactions such as those that occur in trade stores can be successfully negotiated in any number of ways, owner and customer contributing in different degrees to the completion of the exchange. For example, one possibility is that the trade store owner completes the entire transaction and selects the appropriate amount of currency from the customer. Another would be that the customer requests a commodity, overpays, and

---

[1] The first trade store was built in 1972, and now trade stores are widespread in Oksapmin region numbering about one hundred.

then receives change from the trade store owner. A third would be that the customer calculates the exact amount and determines the change. The style of transaction depends on, among other factors, the owner and customer's relative competencies at producing arithmetic calculations. Regardless, the trade store presents a social context for arithmetic computation, a context that is very new to Oksapmin life.

To determine how the use of currency in economic transactions is influencing arithmetic concepts, adults who had different levels of experience with the money economy were asked to solve problems involving currency transactions (see Saxe, in press). These included trade store owners, men who had returned from a period of work at a plantation, and groups of young and old adults who had little experience with economic exchange that involved currency. The problems presented involved the addition and subtraction of coins. In half of these problems, coins were actually presented to the subjects, and in the other half, the problems were merely presented by indicating appropriate body parts. In both cases, the problems mirrored typical problems that an individual might encounter in everyday life. For instance, in a typical addition problem, a subject was told, "You have 7 coins and are given 14 more. How many do you have altogether?" In a typical subtraction problem, an individual was told, "You have 16 coins and spend 7 at the trade store. How many do you have left?"

An analysis of subjects' strategies revealed some dramatic differences between the four groups. For the sake of brevity, only some of the strategies for the solutions of the problems without coins will be presented here. People who had little experience with economic exchange involving currency typically did not differentiate body parts from body parts as numerical symbols in solving arithmetic problems. The plantation goers and the trade store owners typically did make this differentiation. Thus, to subtract 9 coins from 16 coins, traditional people would often first enumerate the thumb (1) to the ear-on-the-other-side of the body (16)—the number of coins that they had. Then, they would enumerate the thumb (1) to the bicep (9) to indicate the number of coins "taken away." Finally, as their answer, they would state the names of the remaining body parts as they enumerated them; these included the shoulder (10), neck (11), ear (12), eye (13), nose (14), eye-on-other-side (15), and ear-on-other-side (16), or simply gesture at the body parts that remained. In contrast, people who had regular experience with economic exchange would differentiate between body parts as body parts and body parts as numerical symbols, enabling them to offer a specific representation for the remainder. For instance, to solve the same problem a typical strategy would be to enumerate the shoulder (10) to the ear-on-the-other-side (16), using the terms thumb (1), index finger (2), middle finger (3), . . . forearm (7). Thus, unlike the people who had little experience with economic exchange, these people would call one body part by the name of another body part to achieve a precise numerical representation ("forearm" or 7) for the product of the subtraction. Some individuals, particularly trade store owners, would achieve quite sophisticated uses of the body system to mediate arithmetic computations that went beyond the differentiation of the body system as a system for numerical representation. For example, consider a strategy that a number of trade store owners used that incorporated the base structure of the currency system into their body part computations. To subtract 9 coins from 16 coins, the individual would group the 16 coins into two parts on his body, putting 10 on one side up to his shoulder (shoulder = 10) and 6 on the other side up to his wrist (wrist = 6). The individual would then state that he spent 9 (bicep = 9), and indicate that the body parts from the bicep (9) down to the thumb (1) no longer were present. This left only the shoulder (10th) on the first side of the body. The individual would then add the shoulder (the remaining 10th on the first side) to the wrist (6) on the second side of the body, which results in the correct answer, forearm, or 7.

Between-group differences in arithmetic concepts were also clearly evident in addition problems. For example, to solve 14 + 7, traditional people would again not differentiate body parts from body parts as numerical symbols. Typically, they would enumerate the first 14 body parts [the thumb (1) to the nose (14)], and then, to add seven additional coins they would continue to enumerate additional body parts [eye-on-other-side (15), ear-on-other-side (16), . . .], and not know when to end their enumeration. In contrast, the trade store owners and plantation goers made this differentiation between body parts and body parts as numerical symbols, in that, similar to the subtraction problems, they called one series of body parts by the names of another series of body parts in order to effect a correct solution. To solve the same problem, a typical strategy would be first to enumerate the thumb (1) to the nose (14), and then, rather then calling the eye-on-the-other-side (15) its proper name, these people would call it the thumb (1). The ear-on-the-other-side (16) was, in turn, called the index finger (2), and this enumeration proceeded until the individual called the forearm-on-the-other-side (21) the forearm (7), the correct answer to the problem. It is of some interest to note that there were a number of variants of each strategy, some of which were probably transitional forms. For example, to solve the same problem, some individuals would establish spatial correspondences between two series of body part names in their addition procedure. Thus, the individual would point to the thumb (1) and the eye-on-the-other-side (15), and then point to the index finger (2) and the ear-on-the-other-side (16), and this would continue until the final pair was reached, the forearm (7) and the forearm-on-the-other-side (21).

The variations in arithmetical problem-solving strategies has a developmental parallel in Western culture. Various investigators have documented developmental changes in children's incrementing strategies as well as using their fingers in "counting on" procedures that bear a resemblence to the body strategies used by the Oksapmin people (e.g., Groen & Parkman, 1972; Groen & Resnick, 1977; Carpenter, Note 2; Fuson, Note 3; Steffe, Note 4). Not only do the Oksapmin data point to the universality of the subject's use of correspondences between two series to establish solutions to arithmetical problems, they also point to the dependence of this process on certain forms of social interaction.

The Community School. A very different institution from the trade store that has also been introduced with contact is the community school. At school, Oksapmin children participate in a wide range of activities—from formal school lessons to the building and maintanence of the school grounds. The teachers do not know the Oksapmin language nor the Oksapmin numeration system, and as in all community schools in Papua New Guinea, formal teaching is conducted in English.

Just as in the trade store, arithmetic problems are posed between individuals in the school setting. Teachers pose arithmetical problems to children as a part of school instruction, and children pose arithmetical problems to one another in the course of daily activities. Although there is formal instruction in how to solve arithmetic problems using Western conventions, it would be natural for children to create ways of using their existing knowledge about number—their indigenous counting system—to attempt to solve the Western-styled problems especially since English is not well understood in the lower grades. Two methods were used to explore this possibility. First, children in Grades 2, 4, and 6 were observed in their classrooms as they took an arithmetic test, and two coders noted whether or not individual children showed signs of pointing around their bodies as they took the test (see Fig. 5.4). Second, the same children were individually interviewed about their strategies for solving arithmetic problems (Saxe, Note 5).

Many children used the conventional body part system to help them solve the arithmetic problems during the test; however, the frequency with which children used their bodies to solve the tasks differed over grade level. While a majority of the children in Grade 2 used their bodies, by Grade 6, only 10% used their bodies. To discover the body part strategies children employed, children were interviewed individually about a variety of arithmetic problems. In addition, a group of nonschooled

Fig. 5.4 Oksapmin school children taking an arithmetic test in class. The two children at the left are using the indigenous system.

adolescents was interviewed to determine, if the schooled children had invented sophisticated body part strategies, whether these inventions were attributable to the school experience.

In the initial interview, children were presented with four arithmetic problems, one by one (5 - 3, 3 + 5, 14 + 7, and 16 - 7). The problems were presented in a story format involving the addition and subtraction of pigs. If children used an overt body-part counting strategy, the nature of the strategy was recorded, and if they did not, they were asked to explain how they arrived at their answer. They were also asked whether or not they could use their bodies to help them solve the problems. If children were successful at solving these problems with body strategies, they were given additional, more difficult problems that went beyond the standard 27 body parts (41 - 6, 34 + 12, etc.).

A wide range of body strategies was used to solve the problems, and, as was the case in the study on the influence of currency, some of the strategies involved a differentiated use of body parts as symbols for number, and others did not. Similar to the adults who had little experience with exchange involving currency, Grade 2 children iterated body parts while trying to solve the problems, and did not call one body part by the name of another body part in their solutions. In contrast, Grade 4 and Grade 6 children tended to use strategies that resembled those of the adults who had experience with currency. The exception to this parallelism was in the way in which the children solved the second series of problems. With these more difficult problems, children had to know how to count in English, and it was only at Grade 6 that children regularly used an adequate body strategy to solve these problems. For instance, to add 34 + 12, children would start with the larger of the two numbers, 34. Children would then count the thumb (1) in English as "35," the index finger (2) as "36," the middle finger (3) as "37," and so on until they reached the ear (12), which was called "46," the correct answer. Grade 6 children tended to use a similar procedure for subtraction problems. For example, to subtract 41 - 6, children would again start with the larger of the two numbers, 41. Children would then count the wrist (6) in English as "41," the little finger (5) as "40," the ring finger (4) as "39," and so on on until they reached the thumb (1), which was called "35."

Summary. The studies discussed in this section have been concerned with how the trade store and the community school are influencing the way in which the Oksapmin people are structuring arithmetic concepts. The focus on these new social institutions was important for different reason. The trade store, though a product of outside contact, has arisen by the work of Oksapmin people themselves and is not a context within which arithmetic is taught to people by teachers. Instead, arithmetical reasoning is being spontaneously invented by people participating in the institution, both owners and buyers. In contrast, the community school has been introduced directly from the outside. Teachers do not speak the language, nor do they know the indigenous numeration system. Their mission is to teach children Western-style arithmetic. What is striking is that Oksapmin people are constructing new ways of using their traditional numeration system in order to cope more adequately with problems encountered in both social institutions.

Together, the findings imply that "primitive" forms of numerical thought change to more "abstract" forms as a result of adaptations to new types of problems, problems for which the primitive forms are ill-suited. Moreover, the problems arise in the course of social interactions, interactions that are linked to the social and historical conditions of development. The findings also suggest that the new adaptations in numerical thought are not a simple replacement of old forms with new ones; rather, the change is a product of subjects' construction of more specialized forms of symbolization out of the subject's existing ones.

Concluding Remarks

The research described in this chapter demonstrates the way in which developmental analysis can circumvent basic methodological problems in cross-cultural cognitive research. By organizing a research program to reveal cognitive changes that are a part of ongoing life, it is possible to at once approach a faithful description of cognition within a cultural context, and at the same time, produce findings that will illuminate our understanding of universal processes of cognitive developmental change.

The overriding theme of this chapter is that cognitive development is rooted in both the historical conditions of development and individuals' attempts to gain control over their interactions with their environments. Thus, in the case of ontogenetic change, Oksapmin children grow up in a historical period in which the body system is used as the symbolic vehicle for numerical representation. Early in development, this system becomes a part of children's enumerative activities as a result of social interactions with adults or more capable peers. However, this early use of the body system is "premediational" and is only used effectively in problem solving with the guidance by another. As children crack the code of this socially defined system, the system becomes a vehicle whereby they mediate their quantitative evaluations. Through this process, children at once render a historical achievement of culture their own, and at the same time, shift the bases of their quantitative problem solving. In the case of sociohistorical change, Oksapmin people are living in a period in which new social institutions are emerging. These institutions create new conditions for social interaction, an inherent aspect of which is that people pose arithmetic problems to one another. As a product of these interactions, Oksapmin people are elaborating new types of numerical thought which are intertwined with the concerns of social life. Thus, in both domains of developmental change, change results from the individual's construction of solutions to problems that arise in social life. As a consequence, we observe cognitive adaptations in ontogenesis and social history that are linked to the sociohistorical context of development.

Finally, though ontogenetic and sociohistorical aspects of development were separated for analytical purposes, they are inherently related. The studies reviewed each present a single view of the complex interactions between these processes. A perspective that emerges from these studies is the need to understand cognitive development in the context of a historical period which is itself changing. Indeed the studies imply that sociohistorical changes create new conditions for social interaction which, in turn, lead to the construction of new collective representations. The new generation then addresses sociohistorical conditions from a new knowledge base and constructs new sociohistorical adaptations. The advantage of cognitive studies in the Oksapmin community is that it presents a cultural context in which this complex of interactive relations is remarkably visible, a complex that is critical for any general treatment of the origins and development of human cognition.

Reference Notes

1. Moylan, T. Doctoral dissertation, City University of New York/Graduate Center, in preparation.
2. Carpenter, T. Presentation at Symposium on Children's Counting Types, University of Georgia, Athens, Georgia, 1981.
3. Fuson, K. Presentation at Symposium on Children's Counting Types, University of Georgia, Athens, Georgia, 1981.
4. Steffe, L. Presentation at Symposium on Children's Counting Types, University of Georgia, Athens, Georgia, 1981.
5. Saxe, G. B. *Social change and cognitive growth*. Paper presented at the 1981 Biennial Meetings of the Society for Research in Child Development, Boston, Massachusetts.

References

Berry, J. W., & Dasen, P. R. History and method in the cross-cultural study of cognition. In J. W. Berry & P. R. Dasen (Eds.), *Culture and cognition: Readings in cross-cultural psychology*. London: Methuen, 1974.

Brainerd, C. J., *The origins of the number concept*. New York: Praeger, 1979.

Bryant, P. E., & Trabasso, T. R. Transitive inferences and memory in young children. *Nature*, 1971, *232*, 456-458.

Gelman, R., & Gallistel, C. R. *The child's understanding of number*. Cambridge, Massachusetts: Harvard University Press, 1978.

Glick, J. Cognitive development in cross-cultural perspective. In T. D. Horowitz (Ed.), *Review of child development research*. Chicago: University of Chicago Press, 1975.

Groen, G. J., & Parkman, J. M. A chronometric analysis of simple addition. *Psychological Review*, 1972, *79* (4), 329-343.

Groen, G., & Resnick, L. B. Can preschool children invent addition algorithms? *Journal of Educational Psychology*, 1977, *79*, 645-652.

Laboratory of Comparative Human Cognition. What's cultural about cross-cultural cognitive psychology? *Annual Review of Psychology*, 1979, *30*, 145-172.

Lancy, D. Cognitive testing in the indigenous mathematics project. *Papua New Guinea Journal of Education*, 1978, *14*, 114-142.

Piaget, J. *The origins of intelligence in children*. New York: Norton, 1963.

Piaget, J. Piaget's theory. In P. H. Mussen (Ed.), *Carmichael's manual of child psychology*. New York: Wiley, 1970.

Piaget, J. *The child's conception of geometry*. New York: Basic Books, 1960.

Russac, R. G. The relation between two strategies of cardinal number: Correspondence and counting. *Child Development*, 1978, *49*, 728-735.

Saxe, G. B. A developmental analysis of notational counting. *Child Development*, 1977, *48*, 1512-1520.

Saxe, G. B. Developmental relations between notational counting and number conservation. *Child Development*, 1979, *50*, 180-187.

Saxe, G. B. Body parts as numerals: A developmental analysis of numeration among remote Oksapmin village populations in Papua New Guinea. *Child Development*, 1981, *52*, 306-316.

Saxe, G. B. Developing forms of arithmetic thought among the Oksapmin of Papua New Guinea. *Developmental Psychology*, in press.

Saxe, G. B., & Moylan, T. The development of measurement operations among the Oksapmin of Papua New Guinea. *Child Development*, in press.

Schaeffer, B., Eggleston, V. H., & Scott, J. L. Number development in young children. *Cognitive Psychology*, 1974, *6*, 357-379.

Siegel, L. S. The sequence of development of certain number concepts in preschool children. *Developmental Psychology*, 1971, *5*, 357-361.

Vygotsky, L. S. *Thought and language*. Cambridge, Massachusetts: MIT Press, 1962.

Vygotsky, L. S. In M. Cole, V. John-Steiner, S. Scribner, & E. Souberman (Eds.), *Mind in society*. Cambridge, Massachusetts: Harvard University Press, 1978.

Werner, H. *The comparative psychology of mental development*. New York: International Universities Press, 1957.

Werner, H., & Kaplan, B. *Symbol formation*. New York: Wiley, 1963.

Wertsch, J. V. From social interaction to higher psychological processes: A clarification and application of Vygotsky's theory. *Human Development*, 1979, *22*, 1-22.

6. Children's Concept Learning as Rule-Sampling Systems with Markovian Properties

Charles J. Brainerd

One of the principal routes to generality in any science is the formulation and testing of mathematical models of the events that one studies. Mathematical models offer investigators a number of technical advantages in the treatment and reporting of data, with the most obvious ones being elegance, precision, and predictive power. In addition, however, the vigorous application of mathematical models to well-defined data spaces often produces more than mere technical advantages. Models that have especially simple and comprehensible forms may precipitate advances in theoretical understanding by focusing our attention on abstract communalities between seemingly disparate phenomena. The classic example of this effect in psychology is the remarkable degree of theoretical unification that was achieved in Bush and Mosteller's (1955) application of linear difference equations to conditioning paradigms. More recently, the impetus for many hypotheses about the mechanics of adult memory has come from simple stochastic models (see Greeno, 1974; Greeno, James, DaPolito, & Polson, 1978). The distinction between short-term and long-term storage, for example, was motivated in large measure by the application of finite Markov chains to paired-associate data (e.g., Atkinson & Crothers, 1964; Greeno, 1967).

My concern in this chapter is to explore an elementary, three-state model of children's concept learning. The model is derived from a rule-sampling theory of

Preparation of this paper and the research reported herein were supported by Grant No. A0668 from the Natural Sciences and Engineering Research Council. Portions of the manuscript were written while I was on leave at the Institute of Child Development, University of Minnesota, and I am grateful to the Institute for its support. Computer funds were provided by a grant from the Faculty of Social Science, University of Western Ontario.

how children learn concepts in training experiments. This theory, which is a continuation of some earlier analyses of conservation learning (Brainerd, 1978a, 1979a, 1979b), is based on some rather simple assumptions. Despite their simplicity, the assumptions imply a reasonably powerful stochastic model. The model can be used to evaluate both the statements of the theory about concept learning and its interpretations of related phenomena with precision and economy.

The chapter proceeds as follows. In the first section, three general issues are considered. First, some problems that arise with traditional approaches to explaining children's concept learning are briefly reviewed. Second, a rule-sampling theory is outlined. The main premise of the theory is that the learning of a broad range of logical, physical, spatial, and mathematical concepts can be conceptualized as abstract rule-sampling systems. More particularly, it is argued that during the course of a concept-learning experiment: (a) children hold rules that they use to generate responses to concept-test items; (b) each rule belongs to one and only one of three mutually exclusive and exhaustive sets; and (c) learning consists of discrete, all-or-none transitions from one rule state to another. Third, a mathematical model that is implied by these proposals is discussed. Here, interest centers on how one goes about converting qualitative statements about learning into numerical statements about the free parameters of the model.

The second section is concerned with five questions that have been the subjects of much attention in previous research, namely, learning on errors, stage skipping, information-processing efficiency, the learning-development relationship, and transfer of concept learning to untrained concepts. It is shown that these questions can be analyzed within the framework developed in the first section and that such analyses lead to numerical predictions about the parameters of the model. Some of these predictions seem counterintuitive when judged by the current climate of theoretical opinion and, for that reason, are well worth investigating. For example, the analysis of the learning-development relationship causes one to expect that concept learning will be inversely related to pretraining knowledge under certain conditions. Cognitive-developmental theory makes the opposite prediction (cf. Brainerd, 1977a). Concerning transfer, the analysis causes one to expect that training affects subjects' rule states for untrained concepts but does not help them to learn these concepts in subsequent training experiments. Again, cognitive-developmental theory predicts the opposite result.

A series of concept-learning experiments is reported in the last section. The data of these experiments are used to address a number of technical questions that arise whenever quantitative models are applied to learning data (e.g., parameter estimation, hypothesis testing, goodness of fit). However, the main emphasis is on evaluating the numerical predictions discussed in the second section.

Concept Learning as Rule Sampling

Theoretical Traditions in Children's Concept Learning

Since the appearance of two landmark studies by Smedslund (1959) and Wohl-will (1959), an impressive amount of data has accumulated on children's learning of concepts that are nominally associated with Piaget's concrete-operational and formal-operational stages. The preponderance of this work, of course, has been concerned with conservation. However, learning experiments have been reported for concepts such as class inclusion (e.g., Kuhn, 1972; Youniss, 1971), seriation (e.g., Coxford, 1964; Bingham-Newman & Hooper, 1974), transitivity (e.g., Brainerd, 1973a, 1974a), identity (e.g., Hamel & Riksen, 1973; Litrownik, Franzini, Livingston, & Harvey, 1978), classification (e.g., McLaughlin & Brinley, 1973; Parker, Sperr, & Rieff, 1972), isolation of variables (e.g., Case, 1974; Siegler, Liebert, & Liebert, 1973), proportionality (e.g., Brainerd, 1971; Brainerd & Allen, 1971b), perspective taking (e.g., Burns & Brainerd, 1979; Iannotti, 1978), ordinal and cardinal number (e.g., Brainerd, 1974b; Brainerd & Howe, 1979), and even subjective morality (e.g., Arbuthnot, 1975; Jensen & Larm, 1970). Reviews of various segments of this literature are available (e.g., Beilin, 1971, 1978; Brainerd, 1973b, 1977a, 1978b; Brainerd & Allen, 1971a; Glaser & Resnick, 1972; Strauss, 1972).

Research on children's concept learning, thought quite productive empirically, suffers from something of a theoretical vacuum. The main problem is that 20 years of experimentation has left little doubt that Piagetian theory is incapable of explaining the laboratory learning of its own concepts (Brainerd 1978b; Siegel & Hodkin, in press). The principal claims about learning expounded in the theory are, first, that it is chiefly confined to children who already possess measurable knowledge of the to-be-trained concept and, second, that it is only produced by training procedures which incorporate processes operating in everyday cognitive development. On the former point, Piaget (1970a) states that "teaching children concepts that they have not acquired in their spontaneous development . . . is completely useless" (p. 30). On the latter point, Inhelder, Sinclair, and Bovet (1974) state that, "We started with the idea that under certain conditions an acceleration of cognitive development would be possible, but that this could only occur if training resembled the kind of situations in which progress takes place outside the experimental set-up" (p. 24). These statements have not received much empirical support.

The first claim is contradicted by at least three facts. First, amount of concept learning has not been found to covary with amount of pretraining knowledge (Brainerd, 1977a, 1979a; Thomas, 1980). Second, learning routinely occurs in children who show no evidence of the to-be-trained concept on pretests (Brainerd, 1977a, 1978b). Third, preschool children, who are far below the age range for concrete and formal operations, are known to learn concepts such as class inclusion, ordinal number, cardinal number, conservation, transitivity, and perspective taking in the laboratory (Brainerd, 1977a; Siegel & Hodkin, in press). The second claim is contradicted by the fact that procedures which have little or nothing to do with "spontaneous development" produce tolerably good concept learning (Siegel & Hodkin, in press). Interestingly, these procedures normally produce more substantial evidence of learning than an alternative procedure (active self-discovery) that embodies Piagetian laws of spontaneous development (Brainerd, 1978b).

Generally speaking, investigators have attempted to fill the vacuum left by Piagetian theory by borrowing explanations from other theoretical traditions, usually from some well-known learning theory. The theories that have been so employed include perceptual differentiation (e.g., E. J. Gibson, 1969; Smothergill, 1979), cognitive dissonance (e.g., Murray, 1972, 1979), attentional theories of discrimination learning (e.g., Boersma & Wilton, 1974; Gelman, 1969), operant theory (e.g., Bucher & Schneider, 1973), and social learning theory (e.g., Rosenthal & Zimmerman, 1978; Zimmerman & Rosenthal, 1974). Unfortunately, this theory-adaptation strategy has three weaknesses that limit its usefulness as a method of formulating explanations of children's concept learning: (a) potential irrelevance; (b) concept specificity; and (c) process specificity.

The first limitation is that it is not immediately clear why theoretical constructs designed to explain the results of attitude change experiments with adults (dissonance), or the results of discrimination learning experiments with infrahumans (attention), and so forth should also explain the results of concept-learning experiments with children. [For a related discussion, see J. J. Gibson's (1976) critique of information-processing interpretations of infant perception.] This is especially true of theories that deal with elementary forms of learning (e.g., attentional theory and operant theory). Concerning (b), a given theory is usually adapted to the learning of one target concept, normally conservation, and the question of whether it applies to other concepts is left moot. In many cases, it is difficult even to imagine how the theory could be extended to concepts other than the target. This statement applies, for example, to attentional and dissonance explanations of conservation learning. Concerning (c), the theory-adaptation strategy commits an investigator to the view that some mode of experience specified by the theory (observation of skilled models, being instrumentally conditioned, experiencing dissonance, learning to extract perceptual invariants, learning to attend selectively, etc.) is the path whereby children normally acquire the target concept. However, the literature establishes beyond reasonable doubt that logical, physical, spatial, and mathematical concepts can be trained by a plethora of apparently unrelated experiences (Beilin, 1971, 1978). For example, we know that perspective-taking concepts can be trained by such disparate methods as acting in skits (Chandler, 1973), engaging in fantasy play (Burns & Brainerd, 1979; Scheffman, 1980), and receiving response-contingent feedback (Cox, 1977). In short, the data provide unmistakable signals that the road to understanding children's concept learning does not lie in some specific training experience or in some class of closely related experiences.

Rule-Sampling Systems and Concept Learning

Conceptual Responses as Rule-Governed Behavior. If the goal is to devise an acceptable theory of children's concept learning, common sense suggests that conceptual behavior itself—not attitudes, aggression, bar pressing, sensory discrimination, etc.—should be our point of departure. Consider the structure of the typical concept-learning experiment. First, we administer a series of items for the to-be-trained concept as pretests. Next, we administer a series of training trials. Further concept-test items may or may not appear as part of these trials. Finally, more concept-test items are administered as posttests. If items are given during training and errors and successes are the performance measures, we have two measures of learning, namely, the rate of improvement during training and the level of posttest performance (relative to control subjects). If no items are given during training, only the second measure is available.

To explain the results of such experiments, we need to describe a mechanism whereby the frequency of correct responses increases on concept-test items. This, in turn, requires a description of some processes that children could use to generate responses to these items. On this point, there seems to be some consensus that such responses can be viewed as instances of rule-governed behavior. That is, children can be thought of as holding rules (strategies, algorithms, hypotheses, etc.) that they use to generate their responses (cf. Brainerd, 1979a, 1979b; Siegler, 1979, in press). Although several facts converge on this conclusion, there are two principal lines of evidence. The first and older source is children's explanations of their responses. The wealth of explanation protocols reported in Piaget's many normative studies and in similar studies conducted outside Geneva show three things that are relevant to the present discussion. First, when children are asked to explain a response, their replies usually consist of citing a rule of some sort. On an animism test, for example, a child who says that automobiles are alive and refrigerators are not may explain these responses by stating that "only things that move are alive" (Piaget, 1929). The principle "movement equals life" is obviously an algorithm that allows the subject to decide whether or not an object is alive. Second, children who give different responses cite different rules. To continue the animism example, a child who says that neither refrigerators nor automobiles are alive may explain these responses by stating that "only things that move by themselves are alive" (Piaget, 1929). Third, only one rule is typically cited to justify any given response. For example, children who give correct responses on number conservation items tend to rely on one of the following rules: qualitative identity, quantitative identity, inversion, compensation, and addition-subtraction. However, when they are asked to explain several responses, they normally cite a single rule repetitively (Brainerd & Brainerd, 1972), though several other rules may be available in their repertoires.

The second and more recent source of evidence is nonverbal rule assessment. Siegler and his associates (e.g., Siegler, 1976, 1979, in press; Siegler & Richards, 1979; Siegler & Vago, 1978) have adapted Levine's (1966) probe-trial methodology to the task of diagnosing the rules that children use on concept tests. To date, this technique has been applied to concepts such as proportionality, speed, conservation, the fulcrum principle, and time. Generally speaking, it has been found that: (a) virtually all children are diagnosed as holding rules that are relevant to a focal concept test, where a "relevant rule" is one that produces a consistent pattern of choice responses on the test; (b) children who give different responses on a concept test are diagnosed as holding different rules; and (c) individual children are diagnosed as holding only one of the rules being assessed. Note that these are the same three findings that can be culled from explanation data.

At first glance, these data on rule usage might not seem to provide much leverage on the problem of how to devise a general explanation of children's concept learning. If children's responses to concept-test items are rule based, then it is not unreasonable to view concept learning as a process whereby children surrender old rules in favor of new rules—that is, to view it as a rule-sampling system of some sort. However, the rules that one observes for individual concept tests, whether in explanation data or in nonverbal rule-assessment data, are quite different. The rules used on animism items, for example, are not anything like the rules used on proportionality items. This disparity would seem to pose serious obstacles to a general theory based on the idea that concept learning consists of rule sampling. Fortunately, however, rules share some abstract properties on which a theory that is not wedded to particular rules or concepts can be erected.

Rule-Sampling Description of Concept Learning

The abstract properties in question are the probabilities with which different rules produce correct responses on their respective concept tests. Logically, we can partition all the rules that children might conceivably use on any test into just three equivalence sets: W, a set of wrong rules whose members produce incorrect responses with probability one; V a set of valid rules whose members produce correct responses with probability one; and P, a set of partially valid rules whose members produce correct responses with probability $0 < p < 1$. The p values taken on by rules in P may differ. The only requirement for membership in P is that p should be greater than zero and less than one.

From the standpoint of the probability of a correct response on a concept test item, these equivalence sets exhaust the universe of possible rules, and they are also mutually exclusive. Evidently, we can apply this scheme to any concept test whatsoever. Moreover, since the scheme is exhaustive for any conceivable concept test, we do not have to know *anything* about specific rules on any given test to apply it. The broad applicability of the scheme and the fact that we do not have to know anything about specific rules allows us to avoid the problem that different rules are used on different concept tests.

Before considering a formal description of concept learning in terms of the three equivalence sets, let us remind ourselves of some relevant normative facts. Generally speaking, the concepts that have been most often studied in concept-learning experiments with children share the following stereotyped pattern of development. Below a certain age, which usually corresponds to the preschool and early elementary school years, the probability of a correct response on items that measure target concepts is effectively zero. Above a certain age, which usually corresponds to the late elementary school and early adolescent years, the probability of a correct response on the same items is effectively one. In between, the probability of a correct response is greater than zero but less than one. If these responses are viewed as rule governed, it is apparent that there is a correlation between age and the use of rules from different equivalence sets.

In what remains of this section, a stochastic description of concept learning is given. The description, which is based on the notion that learning consists of sampling rules in response to feedback, is developed with reference to a paradigmatic experiment concerned with a hypothetical concept C. To begin with, we have a pool of test items that measure C. We select j items from the pool and administer them before training as a pretest. Subjects who show some predetermined level of pretest performance (e.g., those who do not make correct responses on all the items) continue to the training phase. During the training phase, subjects receive a sequence of trials designed to improve their performance on C items. Each trial consists of the administration of an item from the pool, followed by the subject's response, followed by feedback as to the correctness of the response. The term "feedback" is a general word that covers a variety of informative inputs—for example, simple correction, observation of a skilled model, discussion with peers, statement of a verbal rule, or perceptual demonstration of a rule. Training continues until the subject has met some criterion of success or until some fixed number of trials has been reached. Finally, i more items are selected from the pool and administered as posttests. The general problem is to describe the psychological events that occur during the training trials.

It is assumed that subjects occupy exactly one of three states on any training trial—namely, State W, State P, or State V—and that learning involves all-or-none transitions between states. Occupying any one of these states simply means that the subject is using a rule from that equivalence set. Subjects may start in State W, State P, or State V on Trial 1. Learning proceeds as follows for subjects who start in State W. On Trial 1, an incorrect response occurs with probability one. After feedback is received, the subject may retain the current W rule, with probability $1 - a$, or the subject may sample a new rule from either P or V, with probability a. If sampling occurs, then either a V rule is selected, with probability b, or a P rule is selected, with probability $1 - b$. If a V rule is selected, the process enters State V and the subject makes correct responses on all subsequent items. If a P rule is selected, the process enters State P and the subject either makes a correct response on Trial 2, with probability p, or makes an incorrect response with probability $1 - p$. These statements also apply to any subsequent pair of trials n and $n + 1$ for which the subject was in State W on Trial n.

Consider some subject who starts in State W and enters State P following the nth training trial. The subject now holds a partially valid rule. Suppose that the subject's response on Trial $n + 1$ is correct (with probability p). After feedback, the subject may either retain the current P rule, with probability $1 - e$, or sample a new rule with probability e. In the former case, correct responses and errors occur on Trial $n + 2$ with probabilities p and $1 - p$, respectively. In the latter case, either a V rule is sampled, with probability f, or another P rule is sampled with probability $1 - f$. If a V rule is sampled, the process enters State V and only correct responses occur on subsequent trials. If a P rule is sampled, correct responses and errors occur on Trial $n + 2$ with probabilities p' and $1 - p'$, respectively. For simplicity, let $c = ef$ and $g =$

$(1 - e)p + e(1 - f)p'$. The parameter c gives the probability of sampling a V rule after any correct response generated by a P rule.

Suppose that the same subject who entered State P following feedback on Trial n after starting in State W makes an error on Trial $n + 1$. After feedback on Trial $n + 1$, the subject may either retain the current P rule, with probability $1 - k$, or sample a new rule with probability k. In the former case, correct responses and errors occur on Trial $n + 2$ with probabilities p and $1 - p$, respectively. In the latter case, either a V rule is sampled, with probability f, or another P rule is sampled, with probability $1 - f$. If a V rule is sampled, the process enters State V, and only correct responses occur on subsequent trials. If a P rule is sampled, correct responses and errors occur on Trial $n + 2$ with probabilities p'' and $1 - p''$, respectively. Let $d = kf$ and $h = (1 - k)p + k(1 - f)p''$. The parameter d gives the probability of sampling a V rule after any error in State P.

Up to this point, the learning process has been described for subjects who hold a W rule on Trial 1. It only remains to describe the process for subjects who hold a P rule or a V rule on Trial 1. The latter subjects make correct responses on Trial 1 and all subsequent trials. Rule sampling does not occur in these subjects; they continue to hold whatever V rule they began with. Subjects who start in State P make correct responses and errors on Trial 1 with probabilities p and $1 - p$, respectively. In the latter case, learning proceeds in the same manner as for subjects who entered State P on Trial n after starting in State W and made an error on Trial $n + 1$. In the former case, learning proceeds in the same manner as for subjects who entered State P on Trial n after starting in State W and made a correct response on Trial $n + 1$. Since subjects can only be in State W, P, or V on Trial 1, this completes the rule-sampling description of learning.

Markov Model and Numerical Predictions

These statements imply a three-state Markov process. Like any Markov model, the process is completely specified by its starting vector, transition matrix, and response vector:

$$P[V(1), P_E(1), P_C(1), W(1)]$$
$$= [t, (1 - t)(1 - s)(1 - p), (1 - t)(1 - s)p, (1 - t)s],$$

	$V(n+1)$	$P_E(n+1)$	$P_C(n+1)$	$W(n+1)$		P(Correct)
$V(n)$	1	0	0	0		1
$P_E(n)$	d	$(1 - d)(1 - g)$	$(1 - d)g$	0	, and	0
$P_C(n)$	c	$(1 - c)(1 - h)$	$(1 - c)h$	0		1
$W_C(n)$	a	$a(1 - b)(1 - p)$	$a(1 - b)p$	$1 - a$		0

, (1)

where P_E and P_C are substates of State P, denoting trials on which errors and correct responses, respectively, occur.

Before Eq. (1) can be applied to data, several elaborations are necessary. In particular, ways must be found to estimate its parameters, to assess goodness of fit, and to test hypotheses about the numerical values of its parameters. Although these elaborations are not difficult, they are tedious. Consequently, they have been relegated to a short statistical appendix at the end of the chapter. The only point to be made here is that Eq. (1) turns out to be exceptionally tractable and easy to apply.

Setting aside the technical details of the mathematical machinery for the moment, let us suppose that Eq. (1) has been shown to give a statistically satisfactory account of the data of some concept-learning experiment—that is, the data seem to approximate a three-state, all-or-none process closely. In such circumstances, interest centers on *testing hypotheses about the observed numerical values of the parameters of Eq. (1).* In the case of any one experiment, there will normally be several questions that we wish to pose about how the rule-sampling process works. Since the theory implies a well-defined model, a very efficient procedure is available for addressing such questions: Covert them to predictions about the numerical values of the parameters of the model and determine whether the observed values of the parameters conform to predictions. The fact that substantive questions about learning can be translated into numerical predictions about the parameters of Eq. (1) is the reason that principal interest attaches to testing hypotheses about its parameters in applications to data. I now consider some illustrative questions which can be investigated in this manner.

Some Questions about Concept Learning

Five questions are examined below to illustrate how Eq. (1) can be exploited: (a) learning on errors; (b) stage skipping; (c) efficiency of information processing; (d) the learning-development relationship; and (e) transfer of training. These particular points have been chosen because each is of some historical significance. It is obvious that there are other important questions about concept learning that could be translated into numerical statements about Eq. (1).

Learning on Errors

A common idea about concept development is that it depends on committing errors. In instructional psychology, for example, advocates of so-called mastery learning claim that the best learning in classroom situations takes place when children are allowed to make mistakes and then discover that they were wrong: "if we want learning to be permanent and solid enough to permit cognitive development throughout the child's life, we must let the child go from one stage after another of being 'wrong' rather than expect him to reason logically . . ." (Kamii, 1973, p. 225). Another illustration of this basic idea may be found in writers who believe that cognitive conflict is essential to learning. For example, Murray (1972) reported that his experiments on conservation learning were motivated by the assumption that "the young child's ability to give conservation judgments . . . would improve after he had been subjected to the contrary arguments and viewpoints of other children" (p. 1).

Clearly, feedback of this sort is "contrary" only to the extent that the young child is making erroneous judgments.

A third illustration comes from writers who maintain that correct responses are dead weight in a learning experiment. Specifically, it has been sometimes been proposed that, regardless of the training method being used, feedback does not improve conceptual performance on those training trials on which correct responses occur (Brainerd, 1979a, 1979b).

How can the rule-sampling theory and its mathematical realization be brought to bear on the learning-on-errors hypothesis? First, the theory states that learning consists of state changes, which are consequences of rule sampling. Rule sampling may occur on three types of trials, namely, W trials (with probability a), P_E trials (with probability k), and P_C trials (with probability e). Since W and P_E trials are, by definition, trials on which errors occur, we expect that the relevant parameters will both be greater than zero. However, a more important pair of predictions deals with the relationship between the two intermediate-state learning parameters, e and k. Strong support for the learning-on-errors hypothesis would consist of showing that $e = 0$, while d was greater than zero. Since P_C trials are the only types of trials on which correct responses are observed before entry into State V, this result would suggest that rules are never sampled after correct responses. Weaker support for the hypothesis would consist of showing that $e < k$. This result would suggest that, although rule sampling sometimes occurs after a correct response, it is more likely to occur after an error. Since $c = ef$ and $d = kf$, the hypothesis that $e = 0$ can be tested by determining if $c = 0$, and the hypothesis that $e < k$ can be tested by determining if $c < d$.

Stage Skipping

Another common belief about concept development is that children's knowledge of concepts consists of sets of discrete states that are ordered in time. In Piagetian theory and in the writings of neo-Piagetian theorists (e.g., Kohlberg, 1968), these knowledge states are called stages. Now, the notion of "stage" has a complex and obscure eschatology (e.g., see the papers in Brainerd, 1978c, 1979c), which I do not propose to examine here. Despite the ineffability of "stage" in cognitive-developmental theory, the basic idea, that conceptual knowledge consists of discrete levels, is simple enough. In the present theory, this idea is embodied in the assumption that children use rules to generate responses to concept-test items and the assumption that learning consists of sampling rules. The former assumption also enters into information-processing analyses of concept development (e.g., Simon, 1962).

When conceptual knowledge is viewed as transitions through sequences of discrete stages, it becomes important to ask whether, in general, each stage is necessary. Must children go through all the stages in a sequence, or can they skip some? The standard position of cognitive-developmental theory, of course, is that stage skipping does not occur (e.g., Inhelder, 1956; Piaget, 1960; Vanden Daele, 1969). This hypothesis is grounded in the familiar assumption that a stage has its own set of cognitive structures and that these structures presuppose those of the immediately preceding stage: "As regards intellectual operations, it is clear . . . that the initial sensorimotor structures are integrated into the structures of concrete operations and the latter into formal structures" (Piaget, 1960, p. 13). Or, more simply: "no stage can be skipped . . ." (Kamii, 1973, p. 226). These statements translate into numerical predictions as follows.

The rule-sampling theory incorporates the notion of discrete stages of knowledge in the form of discrete rule states. It permits five types of transitions between these states, namely, W to V (with probability ab), W to P_E [with probability $a(1 - b)(1 - p)$], W to P_C [with probability $a(1 - b)p$], P_E to V (with probability d), and P_C to V (with probability c). Note that the first transition is *two* state and, hence, it violates the no-skipping rule. Therefore, the parameter b provides a direct measure of state-skipping propensity for any given experiment. Strong evidence for the no-skipping hypothesis would be $b = 0$. Weaker support would be $b < 1 - b$. Either $b = 1 - b$ or $b > 1 - b$ would constitute evidence against the hypothesis.

Information-Processing Efficiency

A ubiquitous fact about learning is that it develops. Adults will learn almost anything more rapidly than children will. Why? A familiar answer is that children are inefficient information processors. That is, they are less likely to alter their current state of knowledge or behavior as a consequence of feedback than adults are. According to this view, an important goal of the developmental analysis of learning is to identify skills whose acquisition permits more efficient processing of information. The developmental analysis of discrimination learning, for example, has suggested several skills that may mediate age changes in this area: selective attention (e.g., Fisher & Zeaman, 1973); perceptual differentiation (e.g., Tighe & Tighe, 1972); verbal labeling (e.g., Kendler & Kendler, 1962); and hypothesis testing (e.g., Phillips & Levine, 1975). Likewise, the developmental analysis of verbal learning has suggested that the acquisition of memorization strategies such as rehearsal, elaboration, or clustering may mediate age changes in memory (e.g., Pressley, 1980).

In this theory, the subjects' task in a concept-learning experiment is to locate a rule that will generate correct responses with probability one, and this is said to be accomplished via rule sampling. If subjects always processed information perfectly, we would expect that they should sample a new rule whenever feedback indicates that their current rule is not a V rule—that is, an error should produce rule sampling with probability one. There are two types of trials that are relevant to this prediction, namely, W trials (on which sampling occurs with probability a) and P_E trials (on which sampling occurs with probability k). Thus, the parameters a and k provide quantitative measures of information processing efficiency. The closer the observed value of each is to one, the more efficiently information was processed in the experiment for which they were estimated.

The parameter a measures processing efficiency in State W, whereas k measures processing efficiency in State P. It may be that the efficiency rates of these states are different. Therefore, we would like to test the hypothesis that $a = k$. This poses a technical difficulty. Although the parameter a can be estimated for the data of any given experiment (see the Appendix), k cannot be estimated. The parameter d in Eq. (1) can be estimated (see the Appendix). But since $d = kf$, the finding $d < 1$, unlike the finding $a < 1$, does not tell us anything definite about information processing. The value of d is affected by both the sampling probability of V rules (i.e., f) and by the probability of initiating rule sampling following an error in State P (i.e., k). Fortunately, it is possible to obtain some quantitative evidence bearing on State P efficiency by considering the parameters g and p.

For any pair of consecutive trials in State P, g is the probability of a correct response on Trial $n + 1$ given an error on Trial n. If processing efficiency is perfect in State P (i.e., $k = 1$), then we expect that $g > p$. The rationale runs as follows. The parameter p gives the *average* probability of a correct response for P rules. However, this value is smaller for some P rules than others. (Recall that the defining characteristic of a P rule is that it generates correct responses with a probability *somewhere* between zero and one.) The rules used on P_E trials will obviously tend to have correct response probability values somewhat lower than the average value p, and conversely for the rules used on P_C trials. But if subjects always resample after a P_E trial, the value of g must be at least as large as p, with the exact value depending on whether the subject samples with or without replacement. Suppose that sampling is with replacement (i.e., the current P rule is returned to the set of P rules before another P rule is sampled). Under this assumption, the correct response probability of new P rules must be the same as the average value for the set as a whole (i.e., $g = p$). If sampling is without replacement (i.e., the current P rule is not returned to the set before another P rule is sampled), it follows that the correct response probability of new P rules will be somewhat higher than the average value for the set as a whole (i.e., $g > p$).

Thus, the relative magnitudes of g and p provide some useful hints about the efficiency of the rule-sampling process in State P. If $g > p$, it seems reasonable to conclude that subjects normally sample a new rule after an error. But if $g < p$, it seems reasonable to conclude that they often retain a rule for at least one more trial following an error.

The Learning-Development Relationship

One of the oldest and most contentious issues in the study of children's concept learning concerns whether or not children's ability to learn depends on their pretraining levels of cognitive development. The significance of this issue stems from the fact that it is related to one's assumptions about what sorts of constraints development imposes on learning. Theorists who believe that developmental constraints are weak and general (e.g., Bandura & McDonald, 1963; Rosenthal & Zimmerman, 1978) have usually maintained that learning and pretraining level of cognitive development are not closely related. Theorists who believe that developmental constraints on learning are both tight and concept specific take the opposite view. Of course, Piaget is the most influential representative of the second position. He claims, first, that "learning is no more than a sector of cognitive development" (Piaget, 1970b, p. 714) and, second, that concept learning will "vary very significantly as a function of the initial cognitive levels of the children" (Piaget, 1970b, p. 715).

Although several experiments have been reported in which these predictions were examined, the relationship between concept learning and cognitive development remains murky. The main difficulty is that most extant studies suffer from an elementary methodological flaw. In these studies, the learning-development relationship has been estimated via the relationship between pre- and posttest performance on concept-test items. The underlying assumption is that although "level of cognitive development" cannot be directly measured, because it is a theoretical construct, children's pretest performance is monotonically related to their cognitive levels. Subjects are stratefied in terms of their levels of performance on the target concept before and after training, and the pre-post performance levels are correlated. A positive correlation has usually been observed; the posttest rank ordering preserves the pretest rank ordering. This correlation has been interpreted as supporting the hypothesis that development imposes strong constraints on concept learning, but it is actually irrelevant to the hypothesis.

The problem is that pre-post correlations are contaminated by the reliability of the tests (Brainerd, 1977a; Thomas, 1980). As long as the items being administered are reliable, these correlations should be positive. They will be positive even if the true relationship between pretraining performance and learning is zero or negative. Since the subjects' posttest performance is a function both of what they learned during training *and* of what they knew before they were trained, it is necessary to correct posttest performance for pretraining knowledge to produce an unbiased estimate of the relationship between learning and pretraining knowledge. When these corrections are made, previous studies seem to show that the two variables are not highly correlated (Brainerd, 1977a; Thomas, 1980).

The learning-development question can be investigated with the machinery of the rule-sampling theory. Subjects are at one of three performance levels when training begins, namely, W, P, or V. Subjects in State V do not make errors, and so learning is restricted to subjects who start in either W or P. Therefore, the hypothesis that level of pretraining performance is related to learning becomes a statement about differential learning rates for W and P subjects. If the hypothesis is correct, P subjects should learn more rapidly than W subjects. If we recall at this point that learning refers to *interstate transitions*, this means that the probability of making an interstate transition when the process is in P (i.e., a P-to-V transition) is greater than the probability of making an interstate transition when the process is in W (i.e., W to V or W to P). Since parameters corresponding to these probabilities are available in the transition matrix of Eq. (1) and can be independently estimated (see the Appendix), it appears that the learning-development question can be addressed by examining their numerical values.

The relevant parameters in Eq. (1), then, are the interstate transition parameters. There are two such parameters for State W, a and b, and two more for State P, c and d. The parameters a and d are of primary concern because they refer to identical events in the two states. a gives the probability of making an interstate transition on *any* trial in State W, whereas d gives the probability of making an interstate transition on any error trial in State P. Only errors occur in State W, and, consequently, these parameters give the probability of an interstate transition following an error trial in their respective states. Under the hypothesis just discussed, we obviously expect that $a < d$. But it is logically possible that either $a = d$ or $a > d$. Both of the latter results appear counterintuitive. In addition to the aforementioned claims of cognitive-developmental theorists, most other theories of cognitive learning seem to imply that subjects would find it easier to learn a concept if they knew something about it than if they knew nothing about it (Brainerd, 1973b, 1979a).

The other two interstate transition parameters, b and c, are not of interest here for reasons suggested above. b measures something other than the probability of leaving State W. It measures the probability of going to V without passing through P on trials when the process leaves W. In other words, b is conditional on the process leaving W *in the first place*, but it is the probability of leaving W that we are interested in. Concerning c, it refers to trials which are not comparable to W trials because the subject's response is correct. We saw earlier that there are reasons for supposing that rule sampling in State P is less likely to occur following correct responses than following errors, and we would not be surprised to find that $c = 0$. Hence, the finding that $a \geq c$ would not be particularly interesting or informative. Such a result would only be of interest if it were found that $d = c$, which does not seem probable.

Transfer of Training

The study of transfer has received much attention in concept-learning experiments with children. The reasons for this emphasis are chiefly historical. When experimentation began, it was commonly assumed that Piagetian theory predicted no learning effects. Although it has subsequently become clear that this assumption was an oversimplification, it has also become clear that Piaget and his co-workers define "learning" in a rather special way. They do not accept training-induced improvements in performance as evidence that concept learning has occurred unless it can be shown that these improvements are extremely general. For example, Inhelder and Sinclair (1969) describe their methods of measuring conservation learning as follows:

> The posttests should comprise all the items of the pretest . . . . At least one item should pertain to a structure in a different field but of the same level as the structure that was the object of the learning sessions . . . . They should comprise at least one item pertaining to the same structure but touching a different problem (for example, conservation of weight-transitivity of weight) . . . . (p. 5)

Since the Genevan definition of learning emphasizes generality, transfer tests have been ubiquitous. The two types that have been most thoroughly studied are near transfer and far transfer. Tests of the former sort consist of items that measure the *same* concept learned during training but in a slightly different format. For example, suppose that the subjects in some experiment were trained on length conservation and that the training materials were pieces of colored string. Suppose that these subjects were administered posttest items for length conservation in which new materials were used (e.g., pieces of dowling stock or Müller-Lyer illusions). These stimulus alterations count as near transfer tests. Slight permutations of the wording of questions asked during and after training also count as near transfer tests. Far transfer tests consist of items which measure a concept that is different than but related to the one learned during training. In our illustrative experiment, post-test items concerned with any conservation concept other than length would be far transfer tests. Similarly, if transitivity of length were the object of training, posttest items for transitivity of weight or transitivity of number would be far transfer tests.

The available literature shows that near and far transfer are routinely observed and that near transfer effects are larger than far transfer effects. The rule-sampling theory provides an explanation of these two results. Consider a hypothetical experiment concerned with some concept C. On the assumption that training continues to a strict acquisition criterion, the subjects hold V rules for C at the end of training. If transfer tests are then administered, it would seem that a subject's performance should depend on at least two factors: Is the V rule that the subject holds applicable to the transfer items—that is, can it be used to generate correct responses to these items? If the current V rule *is* applicable, does the subject recognize that it is? It seems obvious that the answers to these questions will depend in large measure on the similarity of training and transfer items. The probability that the answer to both questions is "yes" should increase as a function of similarity. As long as training and transfer items resemble each other in major respects, as they do on both near and far transfer tests, then the performance of trained subjects on transfer items should be better than the performance of untrained controls. As long as the amount of re-semblance varies for different types of transfer items, as it does for near and far items, transfer should be more pronounced for items that are more similar to training items.

An interesting feature of this explanation of transfer is that it generates some rather surprising predictions about transfer experiments in which subjects are trained on two consecutive and related sets of items. It leads to the expectation that transfer is an all-or-none phenomenon and, more specifically, to the expectation that transfer effects are confined to the parameters in the starting vector of Eq. (1). To see how these predictions follow, let us return to the illustrative experiment in the preceding paragraph. After subjects have been trained to criterion on C items, suppose that they are trained to criterion on a set of items that differ from C items in one or more ways. This different set of items may either be concerned with the same concept (near transfer) or with a different but related concept (far transfer). At the end of the first series of training trials, subjects hold V rules for the first set of items. From the standpoint of the second set of items, these subjects may be divided into three groups: (a) subjects whose V rules are applicable to the second set (i.e., will produce correct responses with probability greater than zero) *and* who recognize that they are applicable; (b) subjects whose V rules are applicable to the second set but who fail to recognize this fact; and (c) subjects whose V rules are not applicable to the second set of items. Subjects in Group (a) will show higher levels of performance at the outset of training on the second set of items than previously untrained controls. Subjects in Groups (b) and (c) will not show higher levels of performance than controls at the outset. Finally, the proportions of subjects falling in these three groups will depend on the type of items in the second set. Presumably, the proportion of subjects in Group (a) should be larger for more similar items (near transfer) than for less similar items (far transfer).

These statements are easily converted to numerical predictions about Eq. (1). First, note that the implications are for the starting vector. If, as a result of initial training, the proportion of subjects in Group (a) is larger than it is for untrained controls, then the proportion of subjects who start in states V and/or P will be greater than it is for controls—or, conversely, the proportion of subjects who start in State W will be smaller than for controls. In short, positive transfer means that the parameter t should be larger and the parameter s should be smaller for pretrained subjects than for controls. Turning to near versus far transfer, it was mentioned that the proportion of subjects in Group (a) should depend on the similarity between training and transfer items. Given two groups of subjects who have received initial training on the same set of items, the proportion of Group (a) subjects should be greater for those whose second set of items more closely resembles the first set. This also translates into a statement about t and s: t should increase and s should decrease as the similarity between the first and second sets increases.

This analysis of transfer implies that such effects are all or none in nature. By this, I mean that if transfer effects do not materialize on Trial 1 of the second task (i.e., changes are not observed in the starting vector parameters), then they will not show up at all. This aspect of the analysis, like the earlier possibility that $a \geqslant b$, appears counterintuitive. Intuitively, it would seem that a large number of training trials on a set of closely related items should have more carry over to the transfer phase than simply determining the states in which subjects start on Trial 1. But the theory tells us that if learning consists of sampling rules in response to feedback, the rules that subjects hold from a previous task affect only their starting states on any subsequent task. This leads us to expect that the parameters in the transition matrix of Eq. (1)—particularly the learning parameters a, b, c, and d—will tend to have the same numerical values for pretrained subjects and untrained controls.

Some Experimental Evidence

I now report three experiments, one on the learning of class-inclusion concepts and two others on the learning of conservation concepts. The general aim of these experiments was to generate a large data base for purposes of illustrating how to explore numerical predictions such as those discussed in the preceding section. There were, in addition, some restricted aims on which the experiments differed. For example, a specific motivation of the class-inclusion experiment was to undertake a detailed analysis of goodness of fit. Although some quantitative evidence has been reported which suggests that class-inclusion learning may be a three-state Markov process (Brainerd, 1979b), the evidence came from a fixed-trials experiment whose data did not permit the parameters of Eq. (1) to be estimated. For conservation, on the other hand, reasonably comprehensive analyses of goodness of fit have already been reported (Brainerd, 1979a). The specific motivations for these experiments were to investigate questions other than goodness of fit (e.g., the locus of transfer effects).

General Method and Design

Since all three experiments relied on similar training methodologies and their subject samples were drawn from the same pool, it is convenient to discuss the procedural aspects of the experiments together. They are grouped under familiar headings.

Subjects. The subjects for all three experiments were drawn from a larger sample of chilren who were administered pretests for class inclusion, number conservation, and liquid quantity conservation. The larger sample consisted of 491 kindergarten and first grade children, which comprised the entire kindergarten and first grade enrollments of eight elementary schools located in middle class residential areas of two eastern Canadian cities (London and Toronto). On the basis of the pretests, 80 children were selected for Experiment 1 (class inclusion), 125 children were selected for Experiment 2 (number conservation), and 125 children were selected for Experiment 3 (quantity conservation). The selection criteria are described below. The mean ages of the subjects in the three experiments were 6 years 6 months (Experiment 1), 5 years 7 months (Experiment 2), and 5 years 7 months (Experiment 3).

Materials. The same sets of materials were used during the pretest and training phases of these experiments. They are described separately for the class inclusion and conservation experiments.

Experiment 1: Class Inclusion Training. Pictorial arrays based on stimuli administered by Brainerd and Kaszor (1974) were used to test class inclusion knowledge before training and to train the concept. A total of 50 arrays were available. Two familiar class of objects, both of which were members of a familiar superordinate class, appeared in each array. Examples of some of the superordinate and subordinate classes include: articles of clothing (shoes and coats), fruits (apples and oranges), vegetables (carrots and potatoes), animals (cow and horse), insects (fly and ant), flowers (tulip and rose), trees (maple and pine), birds (robin and chicken), and tools (hammer and saw). The total number of elements appearing in any one array (i.e., the sum of the two subordinate classes) ranged from 5 to 10. The total number of elements in each subordinate class ranged from 2 to 8. The number of elements in the two subordinate classes were equal in half the arrays and unequal in half the arrays.

Experiments 2 and 3: Conservation Training. The materials used to assess number conservation before training and to train the concept consisted of sets of toy-size objects. There were 11 sets in all: cups, chairs, drums, birds, automobiles, boats, fish, erasers, crayons, butterflys, and footballs. By pairing each set with every other set, a total of 66 unique comparisons involving differing sets were possible (7 fish and 7 birds, 8 fish and 8 cups, etc.). The number of items from a set used in any given number conservation item ranged from 5 to 10. The materials used to assess quantity conservation were sets of different-size glasses and containers of different-colored water. The glasses ranged from a height of 35 cm and a width of 2.5 cm to a height of 10 cm and a width of 7.5 cm. There were five containers of colored liquid, the colors being green, red, yellow, blue, and colorless. To assess quantity conservation, the glasses were presented in triads consisting of two same-size glasses and a third glass that was either shorter and wider or taller and thinner (see Brainerd, 1977b). By varying glass size and water color independently of each other, 60 unique combinations were possible.

Procedure. The procedure for all three experiments consisted of a series of pretests and a series of training trials. The pretest items were administered in a single session lasting approximately 15 minutes. The training trials were administered one day later in a session lasting approximately 15 minutes (Experiment 1) or approximately 30 minutes (Experiments 2 and 3).

Pretests. The pretests were the same for all subjects. A total of ten class inclusion items, nine number conservation items, and nine quantity conservation items were administered. For the class inclusion items, the pretests followed Brainerd and Kaszor (1974). Briefly, an array was first selected at random from the pool of 50. The subject was shown the array and asked to count all the items in the superordinate class and to count all the items in the two subordinate classes. After counting, two questions were posed. If the subordinate classes contained the *same* number of elements, the questions were: "Are there more As (superordinate class) than there are Bs (subordinate class)?" and "Are there less Bs than there are As?" If the subordinate classes contained the *different* numbers of things, the questions were: "Are there more Bs (*larger* subordinate class) than there are As (superordinate class)?" and "Are there less As than there are Bs?" These questions control for the tendency of children who do not understand the inclusion concept to respond in terms of the numerical relationship between the two subordinate classes (see Brainerd & Kaszor, 1974). After the two questions for the first array had been answered, four more arrays were randomly chosen and the procedure was repeated for each of them. The arrays were sampled without replacement (i.e., none was used more than once). Arrays used on the pretest were not used during training.

For the number conservation items, the pretests followed Brainerd and Brainerd (1972, deformation items). First, one of the possible set pairings was randomly selected, and two parallel rows containing the same number of elements were constructed. After the subject had agreed that the rows contained the same number of objects, one of them was either lengthened or shortened (randomly) and the following three questions were posed: "Are there more As (longer row) than there are Bs (shorter row)?," "Are there the same number of As as there are Bs?," and "Are there less Bs than there are As?" After the questions had been answered, two more set pairings were randomly selected and the procedure was repeated for each pairing. Across subjects, a lengthening transformation was used on half the pretest items and a shortening transformation was used on the other half. Set pairings were sampled with replacement.

For the quantity conservation items, the pretests also followed Brainerd and Brainerd (1972, deformation items). First, one of the possible combinations of triads and water colors was selected at random. At the outset, the two same-size glasses contained equal amounts of colored liquid and the different-size glass was empty. After the subject had agreed that there was the same amount to drink in the two same-size glasses, the contents of one of them was poured into the empty glass and the following three questions were posed: "Do these two glasses have the same amount to drink?," "Does this glass (indicating the one with the higher liquid level) have more to drink than the other one?," and "Does this glass (indicating the one with the lower liquid level) have less to drink than the other one?" After the questions had been answered, two more glass-liquid combinations were randomly selected and the procedure was repeated for each combination. Across subjects, half the pretest combinations involved pouring the liquid into a taller-thinner glass and half involved pouring the liquid into a shorter-wider glass. The pretest combinations were sampled without replacement.

The order in which the three types of pretests were administered to individual subjects was random. After completing the pretests, subjects were assigned to the three experiments as follows. First, subjects who passed all of the pretest items for both conservation and class inclusion were discarded. Second, subjects who failed at least one item on *both* the number conservation and quantity conservation pretests were assigned to either Experiment 2 or Experiment 3. This continued until a total of 125 children had been assigned to each experiment. Third, subjects who failed at least one item on the class inclusion pretest, regardless of their performance on the conservation pretests, were assigned to Experiment 1 until a total of 80 subjects had been reached. Subjects who did not satisfy the second criterion but who satisfied the third were immediately assigned to Experiment 1.

Training. One day after the pretests, a series of training trials concerned with class inclusion (Experiment 1) or conservation (Experiments 2 and 3) was administered. The training method was a judgment-contingent feedback procedure that is not unlike the feedback administered in concept identification experiments. Since this method has been described in earlier papers (e.g., Brainerd, 1972a, 1972b, 1974a, 1977b), it is only briefly summarized here.

In Experiment 1, the training trials consisted of a sequence of items that, except for the administration of feedback, was identical to the pretraining items. On Trial 1, an array was randomly selected and the subject was asked to count the number of elements in the superordinate class and in each subordinate class. The questions mentioned above (two per array) then were posed. After each answer, the subject received verbal feedback from the experimenter as to the correctness or incorrectness of the response. On each subsequent trial, a new array was selected (sampling was without replacement) and the feedback procedure was repeated. Training continued until the subject had given eight consecutive correct responses.

The training phase of Experiments 2 and 3 was more complicated. In Experiment 1, it consisted of a series of training trials on *number* conservation followed by a repetition of the nine-item pretest for *quantity* conservation. For Experiment 2, it was the reverse (i.e., quantity training, followed by a repetition of the number pretest with new set comparisons, followed by number training trials). The training procedure for number consisted of a series of items that were identical to the number pretest items except for the administration of feedback. On Trial 1, a pair of sets was randomly selected and two identical rows containing equal number of elements were constructed by the experimenter. After the subject had acknowledged equality, one row was either shortened (half the trials) or lengthened (half the trials), and the questions noted above (three per problem) were posed. After each answer, the experimenter provided verbal feedback about the correctness of the subject's response. On each subsequent trial, a new pair of sets was randomly selected (sampling was without replacement) and the feedback procedure was repeated. Training continued until the subject had given nine consecutive correct responses. The training trials for quantity conservation were identical except, of course, for the fact that items for which the subjects received feedback were concerned with quantity rather than number.

None of the arrays, set comparisons, or glass-liquid combinations used on the pretests was used during training. The apparatus used to present the stimulus materials on the training trials was a modified Wisconsin General Testing Apparatus. It was used in all three experiments, and it has been described in detail elsewhere (Brainerd, 1979a).

Results

Goodness of Fit. In reporting the results, emphasis will be placed on the numerical values of the parameters of Eq. (1) and on testing hypotheses about these values. Logically, however, such analyses make no sense unless one is confident that the data conform to the model. This is a question about goodness of fit. It asks whether the observed distributions of learning statistics such as those considered in the Appendix (see Eq. A12-A16) can be predicted, within statistically acceptable limits, by expressions for these statistics that are derived from Eq. (1).

The three experiments provided five sets of data for which goodness of fit was separately investigated: (a) the class inclusion acquisition data (Experiment 1); (b) the number conservation acquisition data of children who had not received previous training (Experiment 2); (c) the quantity conservation acquisition data of children who had already been trained on number conservation (Experiment 2); (d) the quantity conservation acquisition data of children who had not received previous training (Experiment 3); and (e) the number conservation acquisition data of children who had already been trained on quantity conservation (Experiment 3). For each set, the goodness-of-fit analysis proceeded as follows. First, the observed distributions of the five learning statistics discussed in the Appendix (errors before first correct, corrects before last error, errors after first correct, trial of last error, and the learning curve) were tabulated. Second, Eqs. (A3)-(A11) were used to find the maximum likelihood estimate of each of the eight parameters. Third, the parameter estimates were substituted in the theoretical expression for the sampling distribution of each statistic (Eqs. A12-A16), and the predicted distribution of the statistic was calculated. Fourth, a formal test of goodness of fit (Kolmogorov-Smirnov one-sample test) was computed to determine whether the observed distribution of each statistic departed significantly ($p < .05$) from the distribution predicted by Eq. (1).

These analyses showed that Eq. (1) gave a tolerably good account of all five sets of data. In the case of the four sets of conservation data, this result was expected because previous goodness-of-fit analyses have produced good agreement between such data and the predictions of a three-state Markov process (Brainerd, 1979a). However, detailed goodness-of-fit results have not previously been reported for class inclusion. As illustrations of the degree of correspondence between observation and prediction for the class inclusion data, the predicted and observed distributions of one statistic concerned with the first stage of learning (errors before first correct) and two statistics concerned with the second stage of learning are shown in Table 6.1. Interested readers can calculate the predicted distribution of each statistic for themselves by substituting the parameter estimates appearing in Table 6.2 in the appropriate expression in the Appendix.

Likelihood Ratios. The numerical estimates of the parameters are given in Table 6.2 for each set of data. As discussed in the Appendix, these parameters were estimated by the method of maximum likelihood. Although other procedures are available for estimating the parameters of a Markov model (e.g., the method of moments, the method of minimum χ^2), maximum likelihood is usually the procedure of choice, when it is applicable, because it has several advantages over other methods. The chief one is that maximum likelihood estimators are known to be *sufficient* estimators: If a sufficient estimator of some parameter exists, then the method of maximum likelihood will find it. Another advantage, one that is exploited here, is that a well-defined technology exists for testing statistical hypotheses about parameters which involves the computation of likelihood ratios.

The method for conducting likelihood-ratio tests of hypotheses about the parameters of Eq. (1) is outlined in the Appendix (see Eq. A17). More general discussions

Table 6.1 Observed and Predicted Distributions of Three Random Variables for the Class Inclusion Experiment

Random variable	k										
	0	1	2	3	4	5	6	7	8	9	10
Errors before first correct											
Observed	19	20	16	14	7	2	0	1	2	1	1
Predicted	19	18	17	11	7	4	3	2	1	1	0
Runs of errors after first correct											
Observed		17	19	8	4	4	0	1	1	0	0
Predicted		23	14	8	4	3	1	1	0	0	0
Runs of corrects before last error											
Observed		19	10	5	1	1	0	1	0	0	0
Predicted		19	9	5	2	1	1	0	0	0	0

Table 6.2 Maximum Likelihood Estimates of the Eight Parameters for the Five Data Sets

Experiment	t	s	p	a	b	c	d	g	h
					Parameter				
Experiment 1	0	.625	.367	.327	.658	0	.293	.191	.492
Experiment 2									
Number	0	.728	.427	.544	.676	0	.449	.241	.621
Quantity	.424	.427	.444	.474	.602	0	.299	.330	.541
Experiment 3									
Number	.550	.283	.459	.537	.692	0	.501	.290	.711
Quantity	0	.702	.463	.398	.655	0	.381	.306	.582

of likelihood-ratio testing in the context of learning models may be found in Greeno (1967), Levine and Burke (1972), and Theios, Leonard, and Brelsford (1977). Since the results reported below may not be comprehensible without some understanding of how likelihood ratios are computed, I briefly discuss the logic of likelihood-ratio tests and give two illustrations.

Equation (A2) is a likelihood function from which estimates of the parameters of Eq. (1) can be obtained by solving the system of Eqs. (A3)-(A11). Once estimates have been obtained for some set of data, we proceed to test hypotheses about the estimates such as those considered earlier. There are two general classes of hypotheses, within group and between group. The former are hypotheses concerned with parameter values for a *single* set of data. The latter are hypotheses concerned with parameter values for *two or more* sets of data.

Tests of within-group hypotheses are conducted as follows. First, the numerical value of L in Eq. (A2) is found when all eight parameters are free to vary. Next, Eqs. (A3)-(A11) are manipulated algebraically to find a restriction or restrictions on Eq. (A2) implied by the hypothesis that we are testing. Once an appropriate restriction has been identified, it is introduced into Eq. (A2), and a new value of L (call it L') is computed. When this value is in hand, the ratio L'/L is calculated. A theorem originally proved by Anderson and Goodman (1957) tells us that the statistic $-2\ln(L'/L)$ has a $\chi^2(n)$ distribution, where n is the number of restrictions on Eq. (A2) implied by the hypothesis under test. If a significant χ^2 value is obtained, we reject the hypothesis; otherwise, we accept it. The hypothesis that $c = 0$ is a within-group hypothesis of this sort. Manipulation of Eqs. (A3)-(A11) reveals that $c = 0$ implies that $\theta = 0$ in Eq. (A2). Therefore, we test $c = 0$ by computing a L' value under the restriction that $\theta = 0$. Since $\theta = 0$ is a single restriction, the test statistic $-2\ln(L'/L)$ is $\chi^2(1)$.

Tests of between-group hypotheses proceed as follows. First, the value of L in Eq. (A2) is found for *each* of the two (or more) sets of data being compared. Call these values L_1 and L_2. The joint likelihood $L_1 \times L_2$ then is calculated. Next, Eqs. (A3)-(A11) are manipulated to find a restriction or restrictions on the *joint* likelihood function implied by the hypothesis being tested. This restriction takes the form of an equivalence relationship between the two sets of data on one or more parameters. This restriction is introduced into Eq. (A2), and new values of L_1 and L_2 (call them L_1' and L_2') are obtained. After the joint likelihood $L_1' \times L_2'$ has been found, the test statistic $-2 \ln(L_1' \times L_2')/(L_1 \times L_2)$ is calculated. The Anderson-Goodman theorem tells us that the distribution of the statistic is $\chi^2(n)$, where n is the number of restrictions on Eq. (A2) imposed by the hypothesis, and that the hypothesis should be rejected if a significant χ^2 value is obtained. The hypothesis that the starting parameter t is the same for different sets of data, which is relevant to questions about transfer, is a between-group hypothesis. Manipulation of Eqs. (A3)-(A11) reveals that the assumption that t is same for two sets of data implies that the parameter π is the same for these data sets. Consequently, we find the joint likelihoods with and without this restriction on π. Since only one restriction has been imposed by the hypothesis, the test statistic $-2 \ln(L_1' \times L_2')/(L_1 \times L_2)$ is a χ^2 test with one degree of freedom.

Results of Parameter Tests. I now report results which bear on the questions about how children learn concepts in training experiments that were raised earlier. Tests of within-group hypotheses are reported first, and the between-group data are reported second. The significance level for all likelihood ratio tests was .05.

Four of the five topics considered earlier generate hypotheses about the within-group behavior of the parameters, namely, (a) learning on errors versus learning on corrects; (b) stage skipping; (c) efficiency of information processing; and (d) the learning-development relationship. Concerning (a) it will be recalled that the idea that children use rules to guide their responses strongly suggests that the effectiveness of feedback on any given trial will depend on the response that has just been made. Feedback confirms or disconfirms the current rule, accordingly as the response was correct or incorrect, and this leads one to expect that $c = 0$ or at least that $d > c$. The former result was obtained for all five sets of data. Interestingly, no significance tests were needed: Examination of the sixth column of Table 6.2 shows that the maximum likelihood estimate of c was always zero. It seems, therefore, that correct response trials were simply dead weight in these experiments.

Concerning (b), the no stage skipping rule of cognitive-developmental theory entails that jumping from W to V without going through P should be an uncommon event, that is, $b = 0$ or at least $b < 1 - b$. Neither of these predictions was confirmed. Inspection of the fifth row of Table 6.2 indicates that significance tests are not required to disconfirm either prediction. None of the observed values of b was even close to zero. All values were greater than ½, which shows that $b < 1 - b$ is also false. In fact, the values are sufficiently greater than ½ that the hypothesis that $b > 1 - b$ suggests itself. This hypothesis was tested with likelihood ratios for all the data sets. It was accepted in each case (i.e., the hypothesis that $b = $ ½ was rejected). Contrary to the no stage skipping rule, the subjects in these experiments were more likely to go directly from W to V than to go from W to P.

Concerning (c), we saw earlier that the efficiency with which children process information in a concept-learning experiment comes down to a question about the numerical values of the learning parameter a and the performance parameters p and *g*. If processing is perfect in State *W* (i.e., if children invariably sample a *P* or *V* rule following disconfirmatory feedback), then we expect that *a* = 1. If processing is perfect in State *P*, then we expect that *p* = *g*. Judging from the values appearing in the third, fourth, seventh, and eighth rows of Table 6.2, neither of these predictions hold for the present data. Likelihood-ratio tests of the hypothesis that *a* = 1 produced significant χ^2 statistics for all five data sets. Similarly, likelihood-ratio tests of the hypothesis that *p* = *g* produced significant χ^2 statistics. In other words, the hypothesis could not be accepted for any of the data sets. Under the rule-sampling interpretation, this result suggests that when subjects were in State *P* they often failed to sample a new rule when their current rule was inconsistent with feedback. Likewise, *a* < 1 suggests that the subjects often failed to initiate rule sampling in State *W*.

Concerning (d), the notion that children who know something about a concept are more likely to benefit from training than children who know nothing about it translates into the prediction that interstate transitions are more likely to occur when the process is in State *P* than when it is in State *W*. This, in turn, is a statement about the relative magnitudes of the learning parameters *a*, *c*, and *d*. The last two parameters should be larger than the first. Since the assumption that concept learning is a rule-sampling system provides grounds for supposing that *c* will be small, a prediction that has already been confirmed, we are primarily concerned with the relationship between *a* and *d*. Comparison of the values for these parameters that appear in each row of Table 6.2 reveals that, contrary to the relationship between learning and development envisioned by cognitive-developmental theorists, *a* < *d* cannot be accepted for these data; *a* was always larger than *d*. In some instances, the difference is large enough that one is prompted to investigate the converse of the cognitive-developmental hypothesis, *a* < *d*. Likelihood-ratio tests showed that this hypothesis could be accepted for all four sets of conservation data but not for the class inclusion data. The present subjects apparently were at least as likely to make an interstate transition (*W* to *P* to *W* to *V*) when they were in State *W* as when they were in State *P*.

Finally, the questions about transfer of training that were examined earlier imply between-group predictions about the parameter values obtained when children learn a concept with or without prior training on a related concept. Two sets of between-group comparisons were possible: a comparison of the quantity conservation data from Experiment 2 (prior training on number conservation) to the quantity conservation data of Experiment 3 (no prior training on conservation) and a comparison of the number conservation data from Experiment 2 (no prior training on conservation) to the number conservation data of Experiment 3 (prior training on quantity conservation). It will be recalled that there are at least three plausible, parametric explanations of positive transfer effects with such data (starting parameter differences only, learning parameter differences only, and both starting and learning parameter differences). For both comparisons, the analysis began with an *omnibus* between-group test rather than tests focusing on specific parameters. An omnibus likelihood-ratio test, which is analogous to the omnibus *F* test in analysis of variance, asks if there are *any differences at all* between the pairwise parameter values of two or more sets of data (see Brainerd, Howe, & Desrochers, 1980). Specifically, it is a likelihood-ratio test with eight degrees of freedom which evaluates the hypothesis that the values of each parameter are the same for the different data sets. If this hypothesis is rejected, we can then proceed to test pairwise hypotheses about specific parameters.

The omnibus test produced a null hypothesis rejection for both of the two sets of quantity data and the two sets of number data. If we inspect pairs of quantity parameters and pairs of number parameters in Table 6.2, it seems that the value of t is larger and the value of s is smaller for children who have been previously trained. Conversely, it does not appear that the four learning parameters are much larger for previously trained subjects, although there is a slight trend in this direction. To evaluate these possibilities, likelihood-ratio tests concerned with the hypothesis that a given parameter was the same for two sets of data were conducted for the parameters t, s, a, b, and d. Separate tests were conducted for the quantity and number data. For both comparisons, the hypothesis that t was larger for pretrained subjects and the hypothesis that s was smaller for pretrained subjects received statistical support. However, no support was obtained for the hypothesis that the learning parameters differed as a function of pretraining. Insofar as quantity and number conservation are concerned, the effects of previous training on a related concept apparently were confined to determining the subjects' starting states.

Some Interpretations

Throughout this chapter, my central purpose has been to draw attention to the fact that a simple mathematical model, under an equally simple cognitive interpretation, can help us articulate questions about how children learn concepts in training experiments. In view of the fact that this has traditionally been a contentious area of research with sharp divisions of theoretical opinion, such a neutral device for applying leverage to theoretical questions seems to have considerable utility, or at least so I believe. A secondary aim has been to transmit to other workers in this area the necessary mathematical machinery for applying the model to data. The experiments reported above were means of accomplishing these ends. They are not intended to provide definitive evidence on any of the issues discussed earlier on, and the reader is encouraged to avoid viewing them in this manner. Instead the intent of the experiments was to show how Eq. (1) can be exploited to answer theoretical questions. The specific questions posed earlier are merely illustrations (albeit ones that are presumably familiar to most students of children's concept learning) of the sorts of questions that investigators may wish to ask.

With these caveats in mind, the experiments did manage to produce three results that, by dint of their counterintuitiveness, merit some further discussion. First, there is the finding that $a \geqslant d$. Cognitive-developmental theory, other theories of cognitive learning, and our intuition all seem to tell us that knowing a little about a concept is an aid to learning (Brainerd, 1973a). It was not helpful in these experiments, however, and what is more, it was a significant disadvantage in the conservation experiments. The latter result is quite bothersome because of the apparent suggestion that a little knowledge is sometimes a bad thing. Although the observed relationship between a and d seems counterintuitive, it is important to note that it does not conflict with the rule-sampling theory. The theory permits any numerical relationship between a and d. Further, if it were *generally* observed in concept-learning experiments that $a > d$, the theory gives a possible explanation. Suppose, as the observed values of c indicate, that learning is largely confined to error trials. An important difference between State W and State P, therefore, is that all W trials provide opportunities for learning but only *some P* trials provide opportunities for learning. This difference could well affect the relative efficiency of learning in the two states. Specifically, feedback on P trials confirms the subjects' current rule, and this could conceivably make subjects unwilling to surrender such rules on error trials. More simply, confirmation of a P rule may reduce the effectiveness of subsequent disconfirmations. This extraneous influence is absent in State W.

Second, there is the finding that $b > 1 - b$. In addition to violating the rule prohibiting stage skipping, this result troubles our intuition because we expect that it should be easier to learn a little about a concept than to learn a lot. Evidently, the reverse is sometimes true. Once again, there is nothing in this fact that is inconsistent with the rule-sampling theory. Indeed, at least two plausible explanations can be devised. First, suppose that the average number of V rules that subjects have available is greater than the average number of P rules. Second, suppose that, regardless of the relative number of V and P rules, V rules have much larger sampling probabilities than P rules. In either case, children who hold a W rule would be more likely to select a V rule than a P rule when sampling first occurs.

Last, there is the finding that transfer of previous concept training affects children's starting states but does not affect the rate at which they learn a related concept. Since performance on Trial 1 is determined by the subjects' starting states while performance on subsequent trials is determined by starting states and learning rate, the implication is that previous training on a related concept does not transfer beyond Trial 1. When one considers that all the subjects in the two transfer experiments received at least 10 pretraining trials and several subjects received 20-30 pretraining trials, it is natural to assume that transfer effects would be more general. Despite the intuitive appeal of this assumption, we have previously seen that the specificity of transfer is interpretable within a rule-sampling framework. We saw, more particularly, that the result can be interpreted as showing that previous concept training affects the rules held at the outset of subsequent training but not the rule-sampling system operative during subsequent training.

Remark

In most sciences, progress consists of simultaneous movement in two directions. The first and more familiar direction is outward toward the study of new paradigms and the discovery of new empirical phenomena. The second and less familar direction is inward toward organization, systematization, integration, and, most important of all, explanation of what we think we know. Progress in the first direction is a necessary prerequisite for progress in the second direction: The data base must reach a fairly advanced state before organization, systematization, integration, and explanation become essential.

This means that investigators must decide when the data base in their particular area is sufficiently articulated to permit reasonable progress in the second direction. In the older areas of psychological research (e.g., psychophysics, animal conditioning, and human memory), this point was reached long ago. The implicit thesis of this chapter is that it has now been reached in the study of children's concept learning.

Appendix

Although the model in Eq. (1) is relatively simple, some mathematical developments are necessary to put it into shape for application to data. These developments are of three general sorts, namely, methods of parameter estimation, methods of evaluating goodness of fit, and methods of testing statistical hypotheses about the numerical values of the parameters of Eq. (1).

Parameter Estimation

The parameters of Eq. (1) refer to theoretical processes (using and sampling rules) that cannot be observed in concept-learning data. Consequently, its parameters cannot be directly estimated. However, it is possible to obtain unique estimates of all the parameters for a paradigmatic experiment of the sort described in the first section of the paper by using the so-called observable-process strategy (Levine & Burke, 1972). This strategy, which was introduced into the psychological literature by Greeno (Greeno, 1967, 1968), consists of three steps. First, a Markov process that involves only the observable data (i.e., errors and successes on the pretests and on the training trials) and that is implied by Eq. (1) is constructed. Second, a likelihood function is written for the observable process from which the maximum likelihood estimates of its parameters can be found for any set of data. Third, a set of functions is written that expresses the theoretical parameters in Eq. (1) as functions of the parameters of the observable process. This system of equations can then be used to obtain the necessary estimates of the theoretical parameters. One merely substitutes the estimates of the observable parameters in the equations and solves the system for each theoretical parameter in turn.

The observable process that is implied by Eq. (1) has the following starting vector, transition matrix, and response vector:

$$P[Q(1), I_Q(1), I_R(1), I_S(1), E_1(1)]$$
$$= [\pi, \theta, \phi, \lambda, 1 - \pi - \theta - \phi - \lambda],$$

	$Q(n+1)$	$R(n+1)$	$S(n+1)$	$E_2(2)$	$\ldots$	E_j		$P(\text{Correct})$	
$Q(n)$	1	0	0	0	$\ldots$	0		0	
$R(n)$	u	$(1-u)v$	$(1-u)(1-v)$	0	$\ldots$	0		0	
$S(n)$	0	z	$1-z$	0	$\ldots$	0		1	
$E_1(1)$	α_1	0	β_1	$(1-\alpha_1-\beta_1)\ldots$		0	and	0	(A1)
.	.	.	.		.			.	
.	.	.	.		.			.	
.	.	.	.		.			.	
$E_{j-1}(j-1)$	α_{j-1}	0	β_{j-1}	0	$\ldots$	$(1-\alpha_{j-1}-\beta_{j-1})$		0	

The states of the process are as follows. Q is the state on all training trials after the last error in protocols with one or more training-trial errors, the state on all training trials in protocols with no training-trial errors and no pretest errors, and the state on all training trials after Trail 1 in protocols with no training-trial errors but one or more pretest errors. R is the state on all training-trial errors after the first trial if (a) the first correct training-trial response has occurred; or (b) there were one or more correct responses on the pretest; or (c) both (a) and (b). S is the state on correct training-trial responses after Trial 1 if the last error has not yet occurred. E_i is the state on the ith training trial if (a) the response is an error; (b) the responses on the previous $i - 1$ training trials were all errors; and (c) there were no correct responses on the pretest. The substates I_Q, I_R, and I_S in the starting vector all refer to protocols in which there were both errors and correct responses on the pretest. I_Q is the state on Trial 1 for such protocols if there are no training-trial errors. I_R is the state on Trial 1 for such protocols if the response is an error. I_S is the state on Trial 1 for such protocols if the response is correct and if there is at least one error on some subsequent training trial.

Analysis of Eq. (A1) using techniques developed by Greeno (1968) shows that there are a total of ten free parameters, which I shall denote by the set $\pi, \theta, \phi, \lambda, \gamma, \rho, u, v, z, w$. The likelihood function that expresses the a posteriori probability of any set of data in terms of these parameters is

$$L = (\pi)^{N(Q)} (\theta)^{N(I_Q)} (\phi)^{N(I_R)} (\lambda)^{N(I_S)} (1 - \pi - \theta - \phi - \lambda)^{N(E_1)} (u)^{N(R,Q)}$$

$$\cdot (1 - u)^{N(R,R)+N(R,S)} (v)^{N(R,R)} (1 - v)^{N(R,S)} (z)^{N(S,R)} (1 - z)^{N(S,S)}$$

$$\cdot \left\{ \prod_{i=1}^{j} [(\alpha_i)^{N(E_i,Q)} (\beta_i)^{N(E_i,S)} (1 - \alpha_i - \beta_i)^{N(E_i,E_{i+1})}] \right\}. \tag{A2}$$

The terms α_i and β_i are complex functions of some of the other parameters in the set mentioned above. Their definitions are

$$\alpha_i = \frac{(w)^{i-1}(u - (1 - \gamma)\rho)}{\left[\dfrac{(w)^{i-1}(\gamma - (1 - u)v)}{(w - (1 - u)v)}\right] + \left[\dfrac{(1 - (\gamma - (1 - u)v))}{(w - (1 - u)v)}\right]((1 - u)v)^{i-1}} ,$$
(A3)

$$\beta_i = [(1 - u)(1 - v)]$$

$$\frac{\dfrac{[(w)^{i-1}(\gamma - (1 - u)v)(1 - (u - (1 - \gamma)\rho))]}{[\gamma - (1 - u)v]}}{\left[\dfrac{(w)^{i-1}(\gamma - (1 - u)v)}{(w - (1 - u)v)}\right] + \left[\dfrac{(1 - (\gamma - (1 - u)v))}{(w - (1 - u)v)}\right]((1 - u)v)^{i-1}}$$
(A4)

For any set of data, the maximum likelihood estimates of the ten parameters of the observable process can be found by using any standard optimization program (e.g., SEEK, SIMPLEX, STEPIT) to minimize either L or the negative natural log of L or some positive multiple of the negative natural log of L. It is most convenient to minimize twice the negative natural log of L because $-2 \ln L$ is a statistic that figures prominently in hypothesis testing (see below).

It only remains to exhibit a set of expressions that maps the ten parameters of the observable process onto the parameter space of the theoretical model in Eq. (1). Once estimates of the former parameters are in hand for some experiment, the maximum likelihood estimates of the latter parameters can be found by algebraic manipulation of this system of equations. The relevant expressions are

$$\pi = t + \frac{[(1 - t)(1 - s)(p)^{j+1}]}{[(c)/(1 - (1 - c)h)]} ,$$
(A5)

$$\theta = [(1 - t)(1 - s)pc(1 - (p)^j)]/[1 - (1 - c)h],$$
(A6)

$$\phi = (1 - t)(1 - s)(1 - (p)^j)(1 - p),$$
(A7)

$$\lambda = [(1 - t)(1 - s)(1 - (p)^j)p(1 - c)]/[1 - (1 - c)h],$$
(A8)

$$u = d + [(1 - d)gc]/[1 - (1 - c)h],$$
(A9)

$$v = [(1 - g)(1 - (1 - c)h)]/[(1 - g)(1 - (1 - c)h) + g(1 - c)(1 - h)],$$
(A10)

$$w = 1 - a,$$
(A11)

$$z = 1 - (1 - c)h,$$
(A12)

$$\rho = \frac{as\left\{b + (1-b)(1-e)\left[\dfrac{c}{(1-(1-c)h)}\right]\right\} + \dfrac{[(1-s-t)(1-p)(ch+(1-g)d)]}{[1 - (1-c)h]}}{as(1 - (1-b)e) + (1-s-t)(1-p)(g + (1-g)d)}$$
(A13)

$$\gamma = \frac{[s(1 - a + a(1 - b)e) + (1 - s - t)(1 - p)(1 - d)(1 - g)]}{[s + (1 - s - t)(1 - p)]}.$$ (A14)

Goodness of Fit

For a multistate model such as Eq. (1), it is desirable to evaluate the ability of the model to account for data generated by individual states of the process as well as the data of the process as a whole. I now consider some expressions for five relevant statistics of the data. The statistics that refer to individual states are errors before first success (State W), runs of errors after the first success (State P), and runs of successes before the last error (State P). The learning curve and trial number of the last error refer to the process as a whole.

Errors before First Success. Let C be a random variable that counts the number of errors that occur before the first correct training-trial response. The sampling distribution of C is

$$P(C = k) = t + (1 - t)(1 - s)p \qquad \text{for} \quad k = 0,$$ (A15a)

$$P(C = k) = (1 - t)sa(b + (1 - b)(1 - e)) \quad \text{for} \quad k = 1,$$ (A15b)

$$P(C = k) = [(1 - t)(1 - s)(1 - p), (1 - t)s] \times \begin{vmatrix} (1 - d)(1 - g) & 0 \\ a(1 - b)e & 1 - a \end{vmatrix}$$

$$\times \begin{vmatrix} 1 - (1 - d)(1 - g) & 0 \\ a(1 - b)(e) & a \end{vmatrix} \times \begin{vmatrix} 1 \\ 1 \end{vmatrix} \text{ for } k = 2, 3, \dots.$$ (A15c)

Although Eqs. (A15a) and (A15b) are in standard algebraic notation, Equation A15c is in matrix notation. That is, the first term is a row vector, the last term is a column vector, the other two terms are square matrices, and $\times$ denotes matrix multiplication rather than standard algebraic multiplication.

Runs of Errors After First Success. Let LR be a random variable that counts the length of each run of training trials in which the process is in State R. The sampling distribution of LR is

$$P(LR = k) = d + (1 - d)g \qquad \text{for} \quad k = 1,$$ (A16a)

$$P(LR = k) = [(1 - d)(1 - g)]^{k-1} [d + (1 - d)g] \quad \text{for} \quad k = 2, 3, \dots.$$ (A16b)

Runs of Successes Before the Last Error. Let LS be a random variable that counts the length of each run of training trials in which the process is in State S. The sampling distribution of LS is

$$P(LS = k) = 1 - (1 - c)h \qquad \text{for} \quad k = 1,$$ (A17a)

$$P(LS = k) = [(1 - c)h]^{k-1} [1 - (1 - c)h] \quad \text{for} \quad k = 2, 3, \dots.$$ (A17b)

Trial of Last Error. Let LE be a random variable that counts the trial number on which the last error occurs. The sampling distribution of LE is

$$P(LE = k) = t + (1 - t)(1 - s)p \qquad \text{for} \quad k = 0, \qquad \text{(A18a)}$$

$$P(LE = k) = sa(1 - t)(b + [(1 - b)(1 - e)c] \div [1 - (1 - c)h])$$
$$+ (1 - t)(1 - s)e(d + [(1 - d)gc]/[1 - (1 - c)h]) \quad \text{for} \quad k = 1, \qquad \text{(A18b)}$$

$$P(LE = k) = [(1 - t)(1 - s)(1 - p), (1 - t)s]^k \times \begin{vmatrix} (1 - d)g \\ a(1 - b)p \end{vmatrix}$$

$$\times [c/(1 - (1 - c)h] \times [1] + [(1 - t)(1 - s)(1 - p), (1 - t)s]^k$$

$$\times \begin{vmatrix} d \\ ab \end{vmatrix} \times [1] \quad \text{for} \quad k = 2, 3, \ldots. \qquad \text{(A18c)}$$

In Eq. (18c), the first and fourth terms are row vectors, the second and sixth terms are column vectors, the other three terms are scalars, and $\times$ denotes matrix multiplication.

Learning Curve. Let $X_1, X_2, X_3, \ldots$ be a sequence of binary random variables such that $X_k = 0$ if a correct response occurs on the kth training trial and $X_k = 1$ otherwise. The sampling distributions of these random variables are given by

$$P(X_1 = 0) = t + (1 - t)(1 - s)p, \qquad \text{(A19a)}$$

$$P(X_k = 0) = [t, (1 - t)(1 - s)(1 - p), (1 - t)(1 - s)p, (1 - t)s] \times M^{k-1} \times V. \quad \text{(A19b)}$$

Equation (A19b) is in matrix notation. The terms M and V are the transition matrix and the response vector, respectively, from Eq. (1).

Hypothesis Testing

Whenever the parameters of a Markov chain are estimated by the method of maximum likelihood, likelihood ratio tests can be used to evaluate hypotheses about the numerical values of parameters by relying on a theorem from Anderson and Goodman (1957). In the experiments reported in the last section of this paper, three types of hypotheses about the parameters of Eq. (1) are of interest: (a) hypotheses which state that certain parameters shall have fixed values (e.g., $c = 0$ or $h = \frac{1}{2}$); (b) hypotheses which state that the numerical values of certain parameters are equal (e.g., $p = g$); and (c) hypotheses which state that the numerical values of certain parameters shall be different under some conditions than under others (e.g., starting parameters shall have different values on transfer problems than on initial learning problems). In general, such hypotheses are tested as follows.

First, Eq. (A2) is used to find the likelihood of the data when all ten parameters are free to vary. Second, Eq. (A2) is used to estimate the likelihood of the data when the restrictions on parameter variation implied by the hypothesis being tested have been imposed on the expression. Call this new value L'. Finally, Anderson and

Goodman's (1957) theorem tells us that the test statistic $-2 \ln[\hat{L}'/\hat{L}]$ has an asymptotic χ^2 distribution with degrees of freedom equal to the number of independent restrictions that were imposed on Eq. (A2) to obtain $\hat{L}'$.

References

Anderson, T. W., & Goodman, L. A. Statistical inference about Markov chains. *Annals of Mathematical Statistics,* 1957, *28,* 89-110.

Arbuthnot, J. Modification of moral judgment through role playing. *Developmental Psychology,* 1975, *11,* 319-324.

Atkinson, R. C., & Crothers, E. J. A comparison of paired-associate learning models having different acquisition and retention axioms. *Journal of Mathematical Psychology,* 1964, *1,* 285-315.

Bandura, A., & McDonald, F. J. Influence of social reinforcement and the behavior of models in shaping children's moral judgments. *Journal of Abnormal and Social Psychology,* 1963, *67,* 274-281.

Beilin, H. The training and acquisition of logical operations. In M. F. Rosskopf, L. P. Steffe, & S. Taback (Eds.), *Piagetian cognitive-developmental research and mathematics education.* Washington, D.C.: National Council of Teachers of Education, 1971.

Beilin, H. Inducing conservation through training. In G. Steiner (Ed.), *Psychology of the twentieth century* (Vol. 7). Munich, West Germany: Kindler, 1978.

Bingham-Newman, A. M., & Hooper, F. H. Classification and seriation instruction and logical task performance in the preschool. *American Educational Research Journal,* 1974, *11,* 379-393.

Boersma, F. J., & Wilton, K. M. Eye movements and conservation acceleration. *Journal of Experimental Child Psychology,* 1974, *17,* 49-60.

Brainerd, C. J. The development of the proportionality scheme in children and adolescents. *Developmental Psychology,* 1971, *5,* 469-476.

Brainerd, C. J. Reinforcement and reversibility in quantity conservation acquisition. *Psychonomic Science,* 1972, *27,* 114-116. (a)

Brainerd, C. J. The age-stage issue in conservation acquisition. *Psychonomic Science,* 1972, *29,* 115-117. (b)

Brainerd, C. J. Order of acquisition of transitivity, conservation, and class inclusion of length and weight. *Developmental Psychology,* 1973, *8,* 105-116. (a)

Brainerd, C. J. Neo-Piagetian training experiments revisited: Is there any support for the cognitive-developmental stage hypothesis? *Cognition,* 1973, *2,* 349-370. (b)

Brainerd, C. J. Training and transfer of transitivity, conservation, and class inclusion. *Child Development,* 1974, *45,* 324-344. (a)

Brainerd, C. J. Inducing ordinal and cardinal representations of the first five natural numbers. *Journal of Experimental Child Psychology,* 1974, *18,* 52-534. (b)

Brainerd, C. J. Cognitive development and concept learning: An interpretative review. *Psychological Bulletin,* 1977, *84,* 919-939. (a)

Brainerd, C. J. Feedback, rule knowledge, and conservation learning. *Child Development,* 1977, *48,* 404-411. (b)

Brainerd, C. J. *A neo-Piagetian approach to concept learning.* Paper presented as part of the symposium "New Approaches to Concept Learning," Midwestern Psychological Association, Chicago, 1978. (a)

Brainerd, C. J. Learning research and Piagetian theory. In L. S. Siegel & C. J. Brainerd (Eds.), *Alternatives to Piaget: Critical essays on the theory.* New York: Academic Press, 1978. (b)

Brainerd, C. J. The stage question in cognitive-developmental theroy. *The Behavioral and Brain Sciences,* 1978, *1*, 173-213. (c)

Brainerd, C. J. Markovian interpretations of conservation learning. *Psychological Review,* 1979, *86*, 181-213. (a)

Brainerd, C. J. A neo-Piagetian model of children's concept learning. *Le Bulletin De Psychologie,* 1979, *32*, 509-521. (b)

Brainerd, C. J. Continuing commentary. *The Behavioral and Brain Sciences,* 1979, *2*, 137-154. (c)

Brainerd, C. J., & Allen, T. W. Experimental inductions of the conservation of "first-order" quantitative invariants. *Psychological Bulletin,* 1971, *75*, 128-144. (a)

Brainerd, C. J., & Allen, T. W. Training and generalization of density conservation. *Child Development,* 1971, *42*, 693-704. (b)

Brainerd, C. J., & Brainerd, S. H. Order of acquisition of number and liquid quantity conservation. *Child Development,* 1972, *43*, 1402-1405.

Brainerd, C. J., & Howe, M. L. An attentional analysis of small cardinal number concepts in five-year-olds. *Canadian Journal of Behavioural Science,* 1979, *11*, 112-123.

Brainerd, C. J., Howe, M. L., & Desrochers, A. Interpreting associative learning stages. *Journal of Experimental Psychology: Human Learning and Memory,* 1980, *6*, 754-765.

Brainerd, C. J., & Kaszor, P. An analysis of two proposed sources of children's class inclusion errors. *Developmental Psychology,* 1974, *10*, 633-643.

Bucher, B., & Schneider, R. E. Acquisition and generalization of conservation by pre-schoolers, using operant training. *Journal of Experimental Child Psychology,* 1973, *16*, 187-204.

Burns, S. M., & Brainerd, C. J. Effects of constructive and dramatic play on perspective taking in very young children. *Developmental Psychology,* 1979, *15*, 512-521.

Bush, R. R., & Mosteller, F. *Stochastic models for learning.* New York: Wiley, 1955.

Case, R. Structures and strictures: Some functional limitations on the course of cognitive growth. *Cognitive Psychology,* 1974, *6*, 544-573.

Chandler, M. J. Egocentrism and anti-social behavior: The assessment and training of social perspective-taking skills. *Developmental Psychology,* 1973, *8*, 326-332.

Cox, M. V. Perspective ability: The conditions of change. *Child Development,* 1977, *48*, 1724-1717.

Coxford, A. F. The effects of instruction on the age placement of children in Piaget's seriation experiments. *Arithmetic Teacher,* 1964, *10*, 4-9.

Fisher, M. A., & Zeaman, D. An attention-retention theory of retardate discrimination learning. In N. R. Ellis (Ed.), *International review of research in mental retardation* (Vol. 6). New York: Academic Press, 1973.

Gelman, R. Conservation acquisition: A problem of learning to attend to relevant attributes. *Journal of Experimental Child Psychology,* 1969, *7*, 167-187.

Gibson, E. J. *Principles of perceptual learning and development.* New York: Appleton-Century-Crofts, 1969.

Gibson, J. J. Commentary. In M. J. Mendelson & M. M. Haith, The relation between audition and vision in the human newborn. *Monographs of the Society for Research in Child Development,* 1976, *41* (4, Whole No. 167).

Glaser, R. E., & Resnick, L. B. Instructional Psychology, *Annual Review of Psychology,* 1972, *23,* 207-276.

Greeno, J. G. Paired-associate learning with short term retention: Mathematical analysis and data regarding identification of parameters. *Journal of Mathematical Psychology,* 1967, *4,* 430-472.

Greeno, J. G. Identifiability and statistical properties of two-stage learning with no successes in the initial stage. *Psychometrika,* 1968, *33,* 173-215.

Greeno, J. G. Representation of learning as discrete transition through a finite state space. In D. H. Krantz, R. C. Atkinson, R. D. Luce & P. Suppes (Eds.), *Contemporary developments in mathematical psychology,* Vol. 1: *Learning, memory, and thinking.* San Francisco: Freeman, 1974.

Greeno, J. G., James, C. T., DaPolito, F. J., & Polson, P. G. *Associative learning: A cognitive analysis.* Englewood Cliffs, New Jersey: Prentice-Hall, 1978.

Hamel, B. R., & Riksen, B. O. M. Identity, reversibility, verbal rule instruction, and conservation. *Developmental Psychology,* 1973, *9,* 66-72.

Iannotti, R. J. Effects of role-taking experiences on role taking, empathy, altruism and aggression. *Developmental Psychology,* 1978, *14,* 119-124.

Inhelder, B. Criteria of the stages of mental development. In J. M. Tanner & B. Inhelder (Eds.), *Discussions on child development* (Vol. 1). London: Tavistock, 1956.

Inhelder, B., & Sinclair, H. Learning cognitive structures. In P. H. Mussen, J. Langer, & M. Covington (Eds.), *Trends and issues in developmental psychology.* New York: Holt, Rinehart, & Winston, 1969.

Inhelder, B., Sinclair, H., & Bovet, M. *Learning and the development of cognition.* Cambridge, Massachusetts: Harvard University Press, 1974.

Jensen, L. C., & Larm, C. Effects of two training procedures on intentionality in moral judgment among children. *Developmental Psychology,* 1970, *2,* 310.

Kamii, C. Piaget's interactionism and the process of teaching young children. In M. Schwebel & J. Raph (Eds.), *Piaget in the classroom.* New York: Basic Books, 1973.

Kendler, H. H., & Kendler, T. S. Vertical and horizontal processes in problem solving. *Psychological Review,* 1962, *69,* 1-16.

Kohlberg, L. Stage and sequence: The cognitive-developmental approach to socialization. In D. Goslin (Ed.), *Handbook of socialization.* Chicago, Illinois: Rand McNally, 1968.

Kuhn D. Mechanisms of change in the development of cognitive structures. *Child Development,* 1972, *43,* 833-844.

Levine, M. Hypothesis behavior by humans during discrimination learning. *Journal of Experimental Psychology,* 1966, *71,* 331-338.

Levine, G., & Burke, C. J. *Mathematical model techniques for learning theories.* New York: Academic Press. 1972.

Litrownik, A. J., Franzini, L. R., Livingston, M. K., & Harvey, S. Developmental priority of identity conservation: Acceleration of identity and equivalence in normal and moderately retarded children. *Child Development,* 1978, *49,* 201-208.

McLaughlin, L. J., & Brinley, J. F. Age and observational learning of a multiple-classification task. *Developmental Psychology*, 1973, *9*, 9-15.

Murray, F. B. Acquisition of conservation through social interaction. *Developmental Psychology*, 1972, *6*, 1-6.

Murray, F. B. The conservation paradigm: The conservation of conservation research. In I. Sigel, R. Golnikoff, & D. Brodzinsky (Eds.), *New directions and applications of Piaget's theory*. Hillsdale, N.J.: Erlbaum, 1979.

Parker, R. K., Sperr, S. J., & Rieff, M. L. Multiple classification: A training approach. *Developmental Psychology*, 1972, *7*, 188-194.

Phillips, S., & Levine, M. Probing for hypotheses with adults and children: Blank trials and introtacts. *Journal of Experimental Psychology: General*, 1975, *104*, 327-354.

Piaget, J. *The child's conception of the world*. New York: Harcourt, Brace, 1929.

Piaget, J. The general problems of the psychobiological development of the child. In J. M. Tanner & B. Inhelder (Eds.), *Discussions on child development* (Vol. 4). London: Tavistock, 1960.

Piaget, J. A conversation with Jean Piaget. *Psychology Today*, December, 1970, 25-32. (a)

Piaget, J. Piaget's theory. In P. H. Mussen (Ed.), *Carmichael's manual of child psychology* (Vol. 1). New York: Wiley, 1970. (b)

Pressley, M. *Developmental shifts in children's production of elaborations*. Unpublished manuscript, University of Western Ontario, London, Ontario, 1980.

Rosenthal, T. L., & Zimmerman, B. J. *Social learning and cognition*. New York: Academic Press, 1978.

Saltz, E., Dixon, D., & Johnson, J. Training disadvantaged preschoolers on various fantasy activities: Effects on cognitive functioning and impulse control. *Child Development*, 1977, *48*, 367-380.

Saltz, E., & Johnson, J. Training for thematic-fantasy play in culturally disadvantaged children: Preliminary results. *Journal of Educational Psychology*, 1974, *66*, 623-630.

Scheffman, J. *Effects of group and individualized dramatic play on preschooler's perspective-taking concepts*. Unpublished doctoral dissertation, University of Western Ontario, London, Ontario, 1980.

Siegel, L. S., & Hodkin, B. The garden path to the understanding of cognitive development: Has Piaget led us into the poison ivy? In S. Modgil & C. Modgil (Eds.), *The taming of Piaget: Crossfires and crosscurrents*. London: National Foundation for Educational Research, in press.

Siegler, R. S. Three aspects of cognitive development. *Cognitive Psychology*, 1976, *8*, 481-520.

Siegler, R. S. *A rule-assessment approach to cognitive development*. Paper presented as part of the symposium, "New Approaches to Cognitive Development," Society for Research in Child Development, San Francisco, March, 1979.

Siegler, R. S. Developmental sequences within and between concepts. *Monographs of the Society for Research in Child Development*, 1981, in press.

Siegler, R. S., Liebert, D. E., & Liebert, R. M. Inhelder and Piaget's pendulum problem: Teaching preadolescents to act as scientists. *Developmental Psychology*, 1973, *9*, 97-101.

Siegler, R. S., & Richards, D. D. The development of time, speed, and distance concepts. *Developmental Psychology*, 1979, *15*, 288-298.

Siegler, R. S., & Vago, S. The development of a proportionality concept: Judging relative fullness. *Journal of Experimental Child Psychology*, 1978, *25*, 371-395.

Simon, H. An information processing theory of intellectual development. In W. Kessen & C. Kuhlman (Eds.), Thought in the young child. *Monographs of the Society for Research in Child Development*, 1962, *27* (2, Whole No. 83).

Smedslund, J. Apprentissage des notions de la conservation et de la transitivité du poids. *Études d' Épistémologie Génétique*, 1959, *9*, 3-13.

Smothergill, D. *Perception and conservation*. Paper presented as part of symposium "Theoretical Approaches to Conservation Acquisition," American Educational Research Association, San Francisco, April, 1979.

Strauss, S. Inducing cognitive development and learning: A review of short-term training experiments. I. The organismic developmental approach. *Cognition*, 1972, *1*, 329-357.

Theios, J., Leonard, D. W., & Brelsford, J. W. Hierarchies of learning models that permit likelihood ratio comparisons. *Journal of Experimental Psychology: General*, 1977, *106*, 213-225.

Thomas, H. Evaluating the stage learning hypothesis. *Journal of Experimental Child Psychology*, 1980, *29*, 507-518.

Tighe, T. J., & Tighe, L. S. Stimulus control in children's learning. In A. D. Pick (Ed.), *Minnesota symposium on child development* (Vol. 6). Minneapolis, Minnesota: University of Minnesota Press, 1972.

Vanden Daele, L. Qualitative models in developmental analysis. *Developmental Psychology*, 1969, *1*, 303-310.

Wohlwill, J. F. Un Essai d'apprentissage dans le domaine de la conservation du nombre. *Études d'Epistéologie Génétique*, 1959, *9*, 125-135.

Youniss, J. Classificatory schemes in relations to class inclusion before and after training. *Human Development*, 1971, *14*, 171-183.

Zimmerman, B. J., & Rosenthal, T. L. Conserving and retaining equalities and inequalities through observation and correction. *Developmental Psychology*, 1974, *10*, 260-268.

Index